**MORE THAN
350 AMAZING
COLOR PHOTOS
THROUGHOUT THE BOOK**

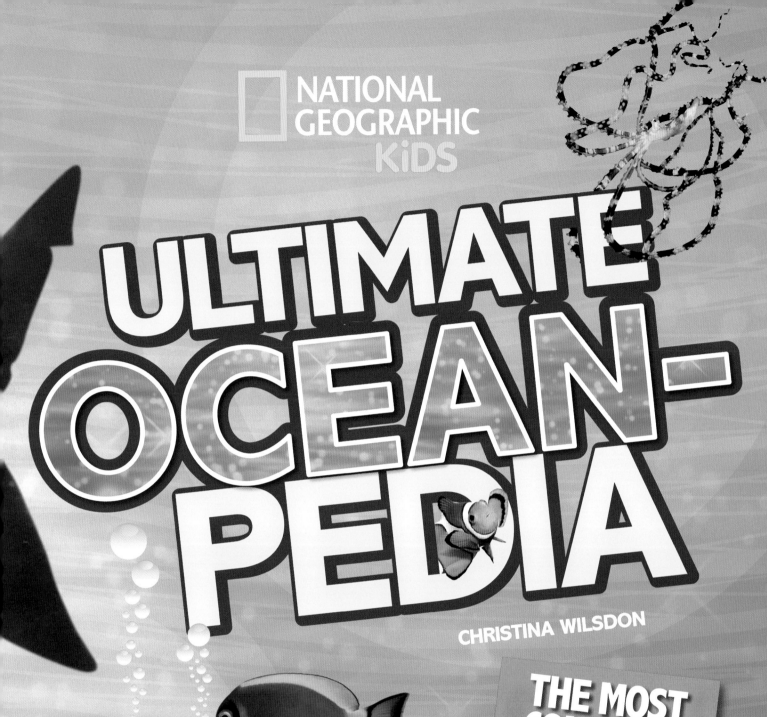

NATIONAL GEOGRAPHIC
KiDS

ULTIMATE OCEAN-PEDIA

CHRISTINA WILSDON

THE MOST COMPLETE OCEAN REFERENCE EVER

CONTENTS

INTRODUCTION

Water, water, everywhere! That's Earth, a rocky planet with an ocean that covers nearly three-fourths of its surface.

We humans are land-dwellers, with bodies adapted to breathe air and walk. We live, work, and play on land—even if we sometimes jump into water to swim, sail, or surf. But even though we feel at home on land, many creatures feel more at home in water. It's estimated that as much as 80 percent of all organisms live in the ocean. In fact, about 99 percent of all "habitable space" on Earth is in the ocean. Habitable space is where life can survive. The ocean offers habitable space from its surface to its depths and in all the water in between. The remaining one percent of habitable space is made up of the land surface where you and I live, along with everything from ants to zebras.

The ocean also produces about half the oxygen in the atmosphere—a gas that most living things, including plants, need to survive. The ocean and the atmosphere are constantly interacting. Winds blow across the water, building waves and pushing currents, cooling or warming the water, and picking up water vapor. The ocean likewise cools or warms the air—and that water vapor turns into clouds that later pour out rain or snow. Raindrops that fall on the head of a person in a desert may have started out as water vapor far from the shore!

Amazing animals and other organisms make themselves at home in, on, and around the sea. Many marine animals are familiar to us—think of whales, sharks, polar bears, penguins, and octopuses. But the ocean is also full of organisms that look like creatures dreamed up by a science-fiction writer: fish that light up, sea cucumbers that eject their guts when alarmed, and "zombie worms" that eat the bones of dead whales.

As a kid, I spent many happy hours digging in the sand and watching birds on East Coast beaches of the United States. As an adult, I've lived near the crashing waves and rocky shores of the northwestern United States. I have truly enjoyed researching oceans to write *Oceanpedia*, and I hope you enjoy diving into its pages, too.

CHRISTINA WILSDON
SCIENCE WRITER AND AUTHOR OF *ULTIMATE OCEANPEDIA*

cushion sea star

sea cucumber

Close your eyes and imagine that you are deep in the sea. It is dark and cold, and you hear the sound of whales coming from miles away.

Some of the strange and wonderful creatures you encounter will think you want to eat them; others will ponder how good you might taste. You are much larger than most of the creatures you meet, so you feel pretty safe. As you get used to being under the ocean, the deep sea begins to fill with small flashes of light. Looking like fireflies dancing in the air on a summer's evening, that light could be fish communicating with each other or using light to attract something to eat. Shrimp might flash light as a warning sign to "stay away!" or an octopus could release a trail of light as it flees a predator. It is an eerie, fascinating world.

The ocean is so vast that much of it still remains unexplored. Every year new creatures are discovered and new underwater mountains are studied. The ocean influences a vast array of things, such as the composition of the air we breathe and the temperature outside your house right now. To say that we rely on the ocean is perhaps a surprise since we don't live in it, but it's true. Without our oceans we would not be able to survive.

As an oceanographer, I find that there is little better than being on the sea—that's where I conduct research and try to unravel some of the mysteries of the ocean. My job brings me across the world and shows me again and again how beautiful Earth is, especially its ocean. The ocean can be calm and peaceful, raging and angry, crystal clear or cloudy with sediment, cold or warm, hospitable or unforgiving. Whatever the ocean's mood, it is always alive and calling to us to explore and understand it. Enjoy your exploration with this book, and I hope one day to see you out on the oceans with me!

RICK KEIL
OCEANOGRAPHER
UNIVERSITY OF WASHINGTON

spot-fin porcupinefish

DISCOVERING THE OCEAN

A harp seal's **plumpness** helps keep it warm in the **icy waters** along Canada's coast.

The pyramid **butterflyfish** lives on tropical **coral reefs** in parts of the Pacific Ocean.

Some sea creatures look like plants, but they're actually **animals** that feed on plankton!

A **nudibranch**, which is a kind of **sea slug**, creeps across a living sponge.

A **lemon shark** prowls among the roots of **mangrove trees** in tropical waters.

CHAPTER 1
OCEANS

A group of adult sperm whales swim with a newborn calf.

EARTH: WORLD OF WATER

We live on one wet, wonderful planet. It's called Earth, but if you could see Earth from outer space, you might think "Ocean" would be a better name for it! The ocean covers 71 percent of our planet's surface.

That fact shows up clearly in Earth's first complete portrait: a picture taken from space by the crew of Apollo 17 on December 7, 1972, as they traveled to the moon. The photo of a mostly blue Earth etched with swirls of white clouds became world-famous as the "Blue Marble" shot.

The ocean not only covers much of Earth, but also contains most of its water—about 97 percent of our planet's supply. Most of the remaining 3 percent of water is frozen in glaciers and icecaps, with a splash left over to fill lakes and ponds, flow in rivers and streams, fall as rain, and trickle out of sight as groundwater.

The world's ocean is actually divided into four separately named oceans. Their borders are formed mainly by the edges of big chunks of land, as well as by features of the ocean floor, such as underwater mountain ranges called ridges. These four oceans are called the Pacific, the Atlantic, the Indian, and the Arctic.

THE "SOUTHERN" OCEAN?

You'll often read that Earth has not four but five oceans. Most oceanographers describe the waters around Antarctica as a separate ocean, called the Southern or Antarctic Ocean. These waters have long been considered to be part of the Atlantic, Pacific, and Indian Oceans. Whether called an ocean or not, these waters near Antarctica are cold! In winter, sea ice forms around this frozen continent, which is mostly covered by a thick ice sheet. Almost 90 percent of Earth's ice is part of Antarctica's frozen blanket.

Bet you didn't know

The world ocean contains about 320 million cubic miles (1.34 billion cubic km) of water. That's enough water to fill about 352,670,000,000,000,000,000 gallon-size milk jugs. If you could line up those jugs, they'd stretch from the sun to the planet Neptune and back nearly six million times!

THE PACIFIC OCEAN

The Pacific Ocean is the largest ocean. It's so big that it could hold all of Earth's continents, with room to spare. It contains nearly half of Earth's ocean water.

But the Pacific isn't just the biggest ocean. It's also the deepest. The average depth of the Pacific is about 14,040 feet (4,280 m)—more than 10 times the height of New York City's Empire State Building. It's also home to the deepest place on Earth: Challenger Deep, which sits in the Mariana Trench, a canyon on the ocean floor. Challenger Deep plunges 35,827 feet (10,920 m)—a distance of almost seven miles (11 km). Earth's tallest land mountain, Mount Everest, is 29,035 feet (8,850 m) tall, but it would completely disappear beneath the waves if you could drop it into Challenger Deep. Its peak would still be 6,792 feet (2,070 m) below sea level!

The Pacific contains more than 25,000 islands. They range in size from New Guinea, which is about 309,000 square miles (800,000 sq km), to islands so small you can walk across them in just one minute. Many scattered islands are combined to form nations, such as the Marshall Islands and the Philippines. (See if you can find them on the map!)

TOTAL AREA:	69,000,000 square miles (178,800,000 sq km)
DEEPEST POINT:	35,827 feet (10,920 m), at Challenger Deep
TWO LARGEST SEAS:	Coral Sea: 1,615,500 square miles (4,184,000 sq km)
	South China Sea: 1,388,400 square miles (3,596,000 sq km)

EUROPE

ASIA

AFRICA

South China Sea

Philippines

Mariana Trench

Challenger Deep

INDIAN OCEAN

Papua New Guinea

Great Barrier Reef

AUSTRALIA

Ocean Depth

0   35,827 feet

0   10,920 meters

the deep-ocean submersible *DEEPSEA CHALLENGER*

The
Pacific Ocean
covers about
**a third of
Earth's**
surface.

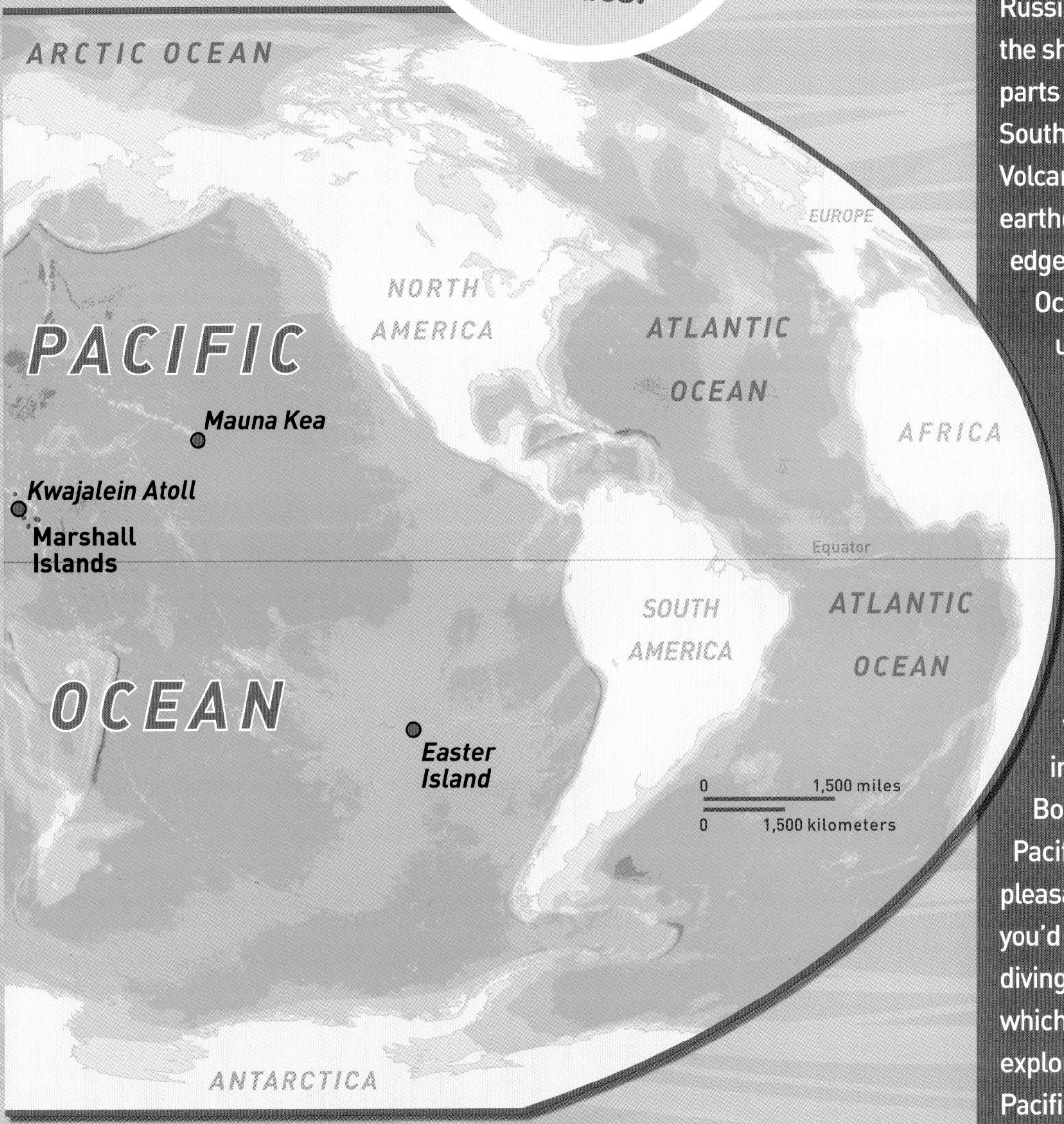

ARCTIC OCEAN

NORTH
AMERICA

EUROPE

ATLANTIC

OCEAN

AFRICA

PACIFIC

Mauna Kea

Kwajalein Atoll

**Marshall
Islands**

Equator

OCEAN

SOUTH
AMERICA

ATLANTIC

OCEAN

*Easter
Island*

0   1,500 miles
0   1,500 kilometers

ANTARCTICA

MAP OF THE PACIFIC

In the north, the Pacific bumps up against Alaska and eastern Russia. Its southern waters lap the shores of Australia and parts of Asia in the west and South America in the east. Volcanoes rumble and earthquakes rattle along its edges, where the Pacific Ocean's seafloor shoves underneath the continents. This activity inspired the nickname "Ring of Fire" for the lands surrounding the Pacific Ocean.

Temperatures vary widely across the Pacific Ocean: You would enjoy swimming in the sea around Bora Bora, an island in the South Pacific, where the water is a pleasant 80°F (26°C). But you'd need an extra-warm diving suit called a dry suit, which keeps out all water, for exploring parts of the North Pacific in winter, where sea ice forms at 28.6°F (-1.9°C).

PACIFIC OCEAN: WILD PLACES

The enormous Pacific Ocean has plenty of room for amazing places! Here are just a few of its remarkable sites.

The South China Sea is one of the world's largest seas. It covers about 1,388,400 square miles (3,596,000 sq km)—an area nearly half the size of Australia. An estimated 10 percent of all fish caught globally are pulled out of its waters. It's also a major shipping route. About half of all cargo shipped on freighters travels through the South China Sea, as well as about a third of the world's crude oil.

The Pacific Ocean boasts the world's largest coral reef. It's the **Great Barrier Reef,** which is made up of about 3,000 reefs and stretches for about 1,429 miles (2,300 km) along Australia's northeastern coast and covers an area of about 134,479 square miles (348,300 sq km). That's an area about the size of Germany. The reef is home to about 400 kinds of coral, 1,500 species of fish, and 4,000 species of mollusks.

An atoll is a ring of coral reefs and islands that circle an area of water. Among the Pacific Ocean's many atolls is the world's largest: **Kwajalein Atoll,** which is part of the Republic of the Marshall Islands. About 90 tiny islands dot the ocean around the lagoon, which covers about 655 square miles (1,722 sq km)—an area nearly half the size of the state of Rhode Island.

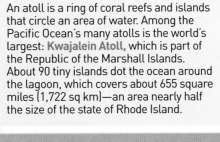

Among the many islands of the Pacific is mysterious **Easter Island,** where statues made of volcanic rock stand guard. The statues, called moai, range in height from 4 to 33 feet (1.2 to 10 m). There are nearly 900 moai. Some of them stand tall, while others have fallen, and many remain in the place where islanders dug out the rock to build them. Easter Island is known as Rapa Nui to Polynesian people. It sits about 2,300 miles (3,700 km) off the coast of Chile.

The world's tallest mountain is in the Pacific Ocean. It's **Mauna Kea,** a dormant volcano that forms part of the Big Island of Hawaii. Mauna Kea is 32,696 feet (9,966 m) high from its base on the seafloor to its stony top. More than half of Mauna Kea is underwater. On land, you only see the top 13,796 feet (4,205 m).

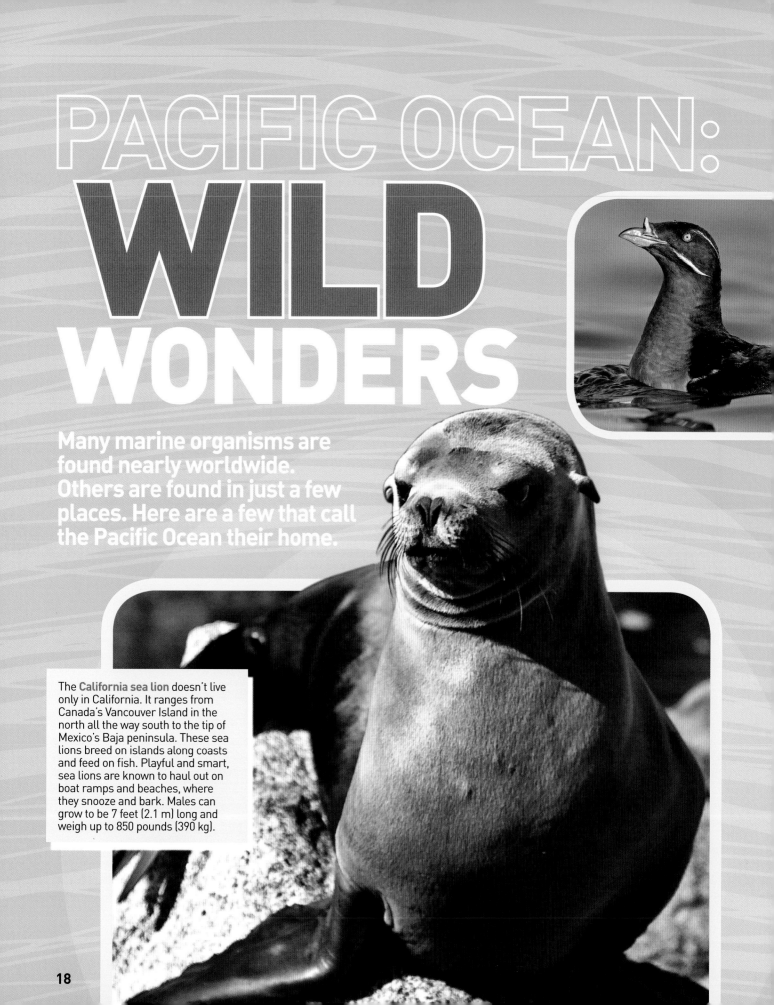

PACIFIC OCEAN: WILD WONDERS

Many marine organisms are found nearly worldwide. Others are found in just a few places. Here are a few that call the Pacific Ocean their home.

The **California sea lion** doesn't live only in California. It ranges from Canada's Vancouver Island in the north all the way south to the tip of Mexico's Baja peninsula. These sea lions breed on islands along coasts and feed on fish. Playful and smart, sea lions are known to haul out on boat ramps and beaches, where they snooze and bark. Males can grow to be 7 feet (2.1 m) long and weigh up to 850 pounds (390 kg).

The **marine iguana is a reptile** that lives on the Galápagos Islands in the eastern Pacific. It's the only lizard in the world that swims and feeds in the ocean. It lazes on rocks to warm up in sunshine before slipping into the cold water to chew seaweed off rocks.

The **rhinoceros auklet** is a chubby seabird that lives in the North Pacific. It can be found from Japan all the way across the top of the Pacific and south to California. It's about 11 inches (28 cm) long and is named for a stubby white "horn" that sticks up from the base of its beak. It nests in a burrow on shore. It eats fish and squid, which it catches by diving deep into the water. To avoid gulls that might bully it into dropping its catch, it carries food back to its young only at night.

The **Pacific white-sided dolphin** lives only in the North Pacific. It sticks to temperate waters near coasts. Temperate waters are not as cold as an icy ocean or as warm as a sea in the tropical zone, which wraps around Earth's middle at the Equator. As many as a hundred of these dolphins may swim as a group. They feed on squid and small fish. This species is about 7 to 8 feet (2.1 to 2.4 m) long. Its Atlantic "cousin" is a little bigger.

The **Japanese spider crab** lives in the western Pacific near Japan. It's also called the giant spider crab, and for a good reason: Its legs may span as much as 13 feet (3.9 m) across! It weighs in at about 40 pounds (18 kg). It's not only the world's biggest crab, but also the largest arthropod, or "jointed leg" animal—a group that includes insects and crustaceans, among others. Spider crabs feed on the seafloor at depths of about 1,000 feet (300 m) and can live up to a hundred years or more.

THE ATLANTIC OCEAN

The Atlantic Ocean is the second largest ocean and covers about 20 percent of Earth's surface. It's about half the size of the Pacific, if you don't count all the seas attached to it. (If you do, then the Atlantic is about two-thirds as big as the Pacific.)

One of the Atlantic's standout features is a massive chain of undersea mountains called the Mid-Atlantic Ridge. This ridge stretches from the edge of the Arctic all the way south to the waters of the Antarctic. It curves like a snake so that its total length is about 10,000 miles (16,000 km), making it the world's longest mountain chain. It's about four times as long as the Himalaya, the Andes, and the Rocky Mountains combined! In some places, peaks in the ridge stick out of the water to form islands, such as Iceland and the Azores.

The Atlantic Ocean also contains the world's largest island, Greenland. Icebergs that snap off Greenland's frozen landscape float in the waters of the North Atlantic. In the middle of the Atlantic, the climate's a lot warmer. Tropical islands near the Equator include the Bahamas and Caribbean Islands.

Some of the world's largest seas are part of the Atlantic, including the North Sea, famous for its oil reserves; the Mediterranean, busy with ship traffic; and the Caribbean Sea, known for its clear, warm water.

ARCTIC OCEAN

ASIA

PACIFIC OCEAN

NORTH AMERICA

Equator

PACIFIC OCEAN

AUSTRALIA

Ocean Depth

0   35,827 feet

0   10,920 meters

Cliffs of Moher, on the west coast of Ireland, face the Atlantic Ocean.

TOTAL AREA:	35,400,000 square miles (91,700,000 sq km)
DEEPEST POINT:	28,232 feet (8,605 m) in the Puerto Rico Trench
TWO LARGEST SEAS:	Caribbean Sea: 1,094,200 square miles (2,834,000 sq km)
	Mediterranean Sea: 953,300 square miles (2,469,000 sq km)

The Atlantic Ocean **grows wider** by 0.4 to 4 inches (1 to 10 cm) per year. Meanwhile, the Pacific Ocean is **shrinking** at about the same rate.

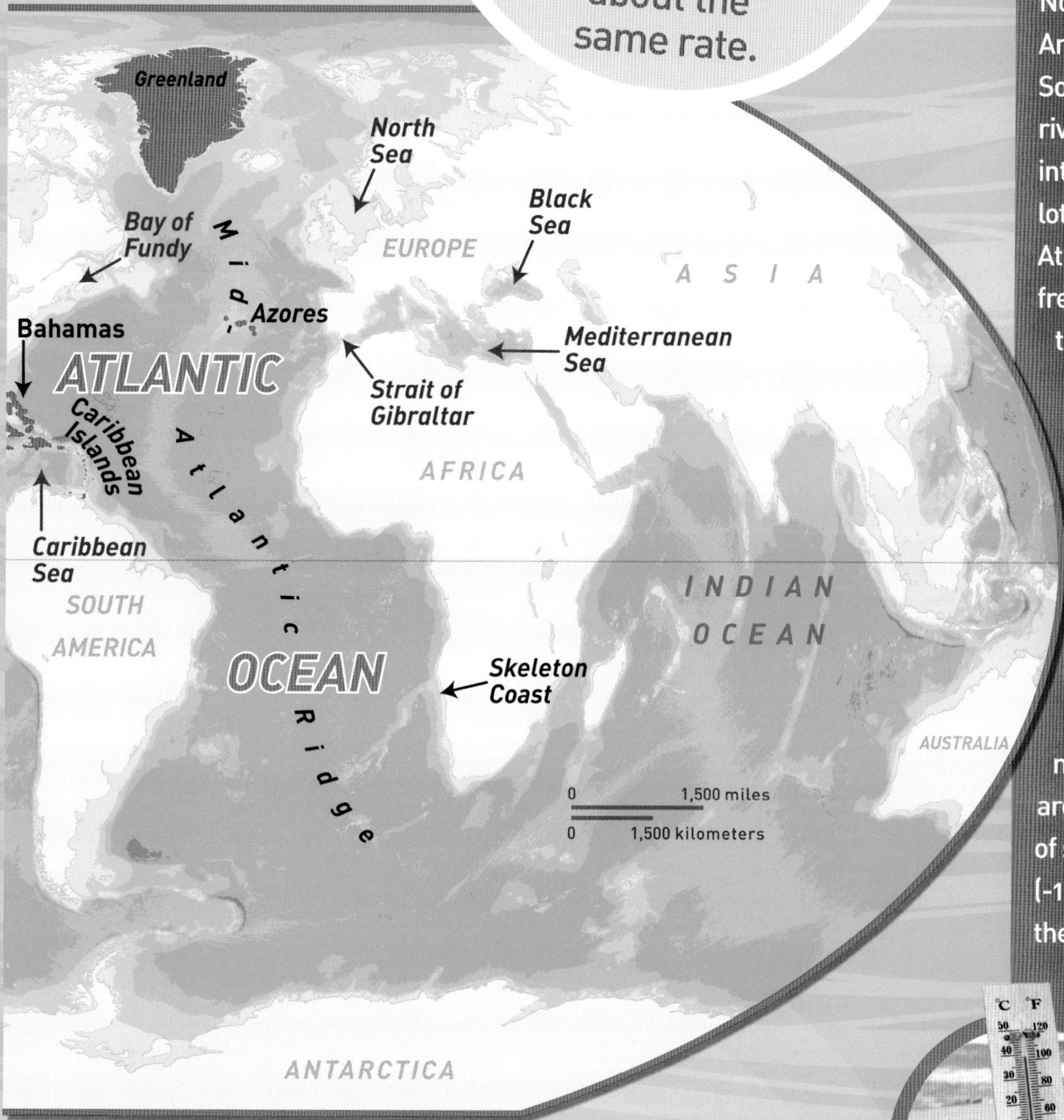

MAP OF THE ATLANTIC

The Atlantic Ocean is surrounded by four continents: North America, South America, Europe, and Africa. Some of the world's mightiest rivers run off these continents into the Atlantic, pouring in lots of freshwater. In fact, the Atlantic receives more freshwater from more rivers than any of the other oceans. Like the Pacific Ocean, the Atlantic Ocean stretches very far from north to south, so it includes warm tropical places as well as cold ones near Earth's North and South Poles. Temperatures of its surface waters in its most northern and southern areas are close to the freezing point of seawater—about 28.6°F (-1.9°C). In the sunny tropics, the water may be more than 86°F (30°C).

Greenland

North Sea

Black Sea

Bay of Fundy

EUROPE

ASIA

Mid-Atlantic Ridge

Azores

Mediterranean Sea

Bahamas

ATLANTIC

Strait of Gibraltar

Caribbean Islands

AFRICA

Atlantic Ridge

Caribbean Sea

SOUTH AMERICA

INDIAN OCEAN

OCEAN

Skeleton Coast

AUSTRALIA

0   1,500 miles

0   1,500 kilometers

ANTARCTICA

ATLANTIC OCEAN: WILD PLACES

The Atlantic Ocean contains everything from huge icebergs to volcanoes that erupt from the water. Here are just a few of this ocean's cool places.

The Skeleton Coast is eerie, no bones about it! Cold currents and dry desert air meet on the west coast of southern Africa—a meet-up that creates thick fog. In the past, many ships crashed there, and their wrecks still lie on the shore. You'll also find whale skeletons from the days of whaling.

According to legend, the island of Atlantis once existed just west of the Strait of Gibraltar. The strait is a narrow waterway that lies between Africa and Spain. It connects the Atlantic to the Mediterranean Sea. The legend claims earthquakes caused the island to sink into the ocean as a punishment for the islanders' wicked ways. The story of Atlantis may have been inspired by a volcano on a Greek island that erupted about 3,600 years ago.

Greenland, the world's biggest island, is in the North Atlantic. It's about three times the size of the U.S. state of Texas. A massive, thick ice sheet covers most of its land. Greenland's glaciers form big icebergs when pieces drop off into the ocean. One glacier, called Jakobshavn Isbrae, is thought to be the source of the iceberg that sank the *Titanic* in 1912. In recent years, it has flowed toward the ocean faster than any other glacier in Greenland. It usually moves about 100 feet (30 m) per day and has been recorded traveling as much as 150 feet (46 m) per day.

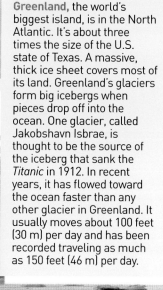

The **Black Sea** is an inland sea—it's almost completely surrounded by land. Its surface waters are only half as salty as the ocean. Underneath this surface layer is saltier water, and the two do not mix much. As a result, fish and other animals live in the sea's upper layers but can't survive below 330 to 490 feet (100 to 150 m) because the deeper layers lack oxygen. The deep waters, however, are full of hydrogen sulfide—also known as sewer gas! It's home, sweet home only for sulfur-eating microbes that don't use oxygen.

The world's highest tides roll in and out of the **Bay of Fundy** in Canada every day. The bay lies between New Brunswick and Nova Scotia. High tide can exceed 53.5 feet (16.3 m). The bay is also famous for its tidal bore—a rush of water flowing upstream quickly through a narrow channel. It may look like a wall of water 3.3 to 6.6 feet (1 to 2 m) tall rolling up the river and forcing it to change direction.

ATLANTIC OCEAN:
WILD
WONDERS

Many marine organisms are found nearly worldwide. Others are found in just a few places. Here are a few that call the Atlantic Ocean their home.

The **Atlantic wolffish** lives in cold coastal waters on both sides of the Atlantic. It's named for its fierce-looking teeth, which it uses to crunch its meals of echinoderms, mollusks, and crustaceans. Its blood contains substances that prevent freezing in its ice-cold habitat. Wolffish are endangered in the Gulf of Maine because they are accidentally caught in fishing nets by fishers who are hunting other species. The nets also damage their rocky seafloor habitat.

Neptune grass grows only in the Mediterranean Sea. It makes seeds but also spreads by sending up new shoots from stems that spread under the seabed. Neptune grass is a very important habitat for fish, mussels, crabs, anemones, and other animals, and it also provides food for green sea turtles.

The **North Atlantic right whale** has a name that tells you where it lives: in the Atlantic north of the Equator. The whale holds its mouth open as it swims forward, straining food from the water that flows through strips of a tough material that hangs from its upper jaw. This material is called baleen. The "right" in the whale's name comes from long-ago whalers who said it was the "right whale" to hunt. Whaling wiped out right whales in parts of the ocean. They are still an endangered species today, though they're now protected by law.

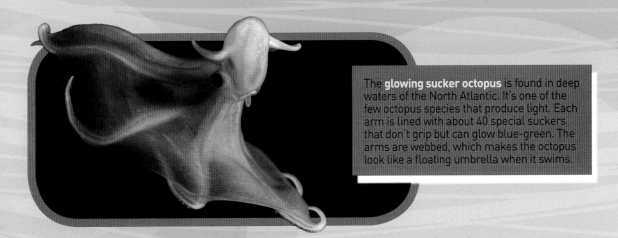

The **glowing sucker octopus** is found in deep waters of the North Atlantic. It's one of the few octopus species that produce light. Each arm is lined with about 40 special suckers that don't grip but can glow blue-green. The arms are webbed, which makes the octopus look like a floating umbrella when it swims.

The **Atlantic humpback dolphin** lives in the eastern Atlantic in the tropics. This rare dolphin feeds on fish in shallow waters along parts of Africa's west coast. Some fishers in one country, Mauritania, work with humpback dolphins to catch fish. The dolphins chase fish toward the fishers on the shore. The fishers catch some fish in nets, and the dolphins eat fish that avoid the nets.

THE INDIAN OCEAN

The Indian Ocean is the third largest ocean.

Much of it lies in the world's tropical zone. As a result, water near the surface is very warm in many places. For example, the Bay of Bengal is in the northeastern part of the Indian Ocean. Its surface water can be as warm as 82°F (28°C)—almost as toasty as a heated pool. But in southern waters near Antarctica, the Indian Ocean's surface water is a bone-chilling 30°F (–1°C).

The Indian Ocean also contains the largest amount of river sediments—materials such as sand and soil that are moved from one place to another. A big portion of this sediment is dumped into the Indian Ocean by the Ganges River, which flows across India and Bangladesh. It empties into the Bay of Bengal, where it forms the "Ganges Fan"—a carpet of sediment that's about 621 miles (1,000 km) wide, 1,864 miles (3,000 km) long, and up to 6.8 miles (11 km) thick!

The Indian Ocean's currents also behave differently from currents in other oceans. A current is the movement of water from one place to another. Currents at or near the ocean's surface are caused by winds blowing across it. Wind-driven currents in the other three oceans travel in the same direction year-round, but they switch directions twice a year in the northern Indian Ocean.

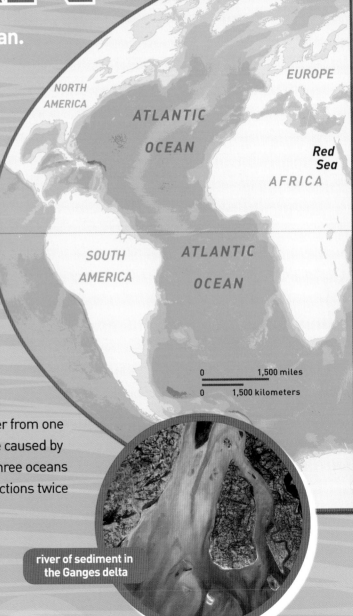

river of sediment in the Ganges delta

TOTAL AREA:	29,400,000 square miles (76,200,000 sq km)
DEEPEST POINT:	23,376 feet (7,125 m) in the Java Trench
TWO LARGEST SEAS:	Arabian Sea: 1,491,000 square miles (3,862,000 sq km)
	Bay of Bengal: 839,000 square miles (2,173,000 sq km)

26

In 2012, shark scientist Paul Clerkin studied deep-sea sharks that were accidentally caught in fishing nets in the southern Indian Ocean. He found rare species as well as a few sharks that had never been seen before!

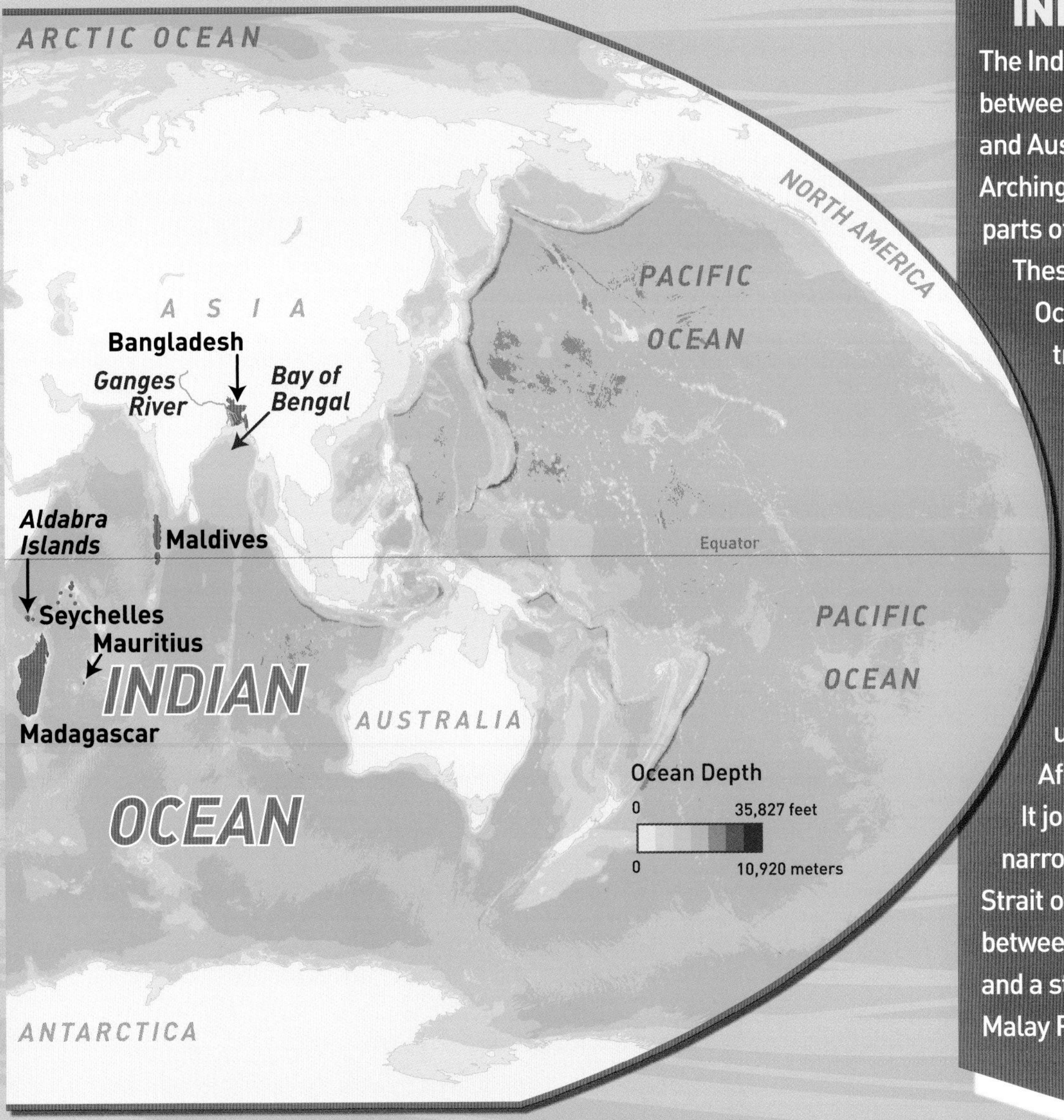

ARCTIC OCEAN

NORTH AMERICA

PACIFIC OCEAN

ASIA

Bangladesh

Ganges River

Bay of Bengal

Equator

Aldabra Islands

Maldives

PACIFIC OCEAN

Seychelles
Mauritius

INDIAN

AUSTRALIA

Madagascar

OCEAN

Ocean Depth

0	35,827 feet
0	10,920 meters

ANTARCTICA

MAP OF THE INDIAN OCEAN

The Indian Ocean sprawls between Africa's eastern coast and Australia's western coast. Arching over it to the north are parts of the continent of Asia. These lands give the Indian Ocean a roughly triangular shape. The tip of this triangle pokes above the Equator into the northern half, or hemisphere, of the globe. The rest lies south of the Equator. The Indian Ocean links up with the Atlantic at Africa's southern tip. It joins the Pacific in a narrow waterway called the Strait of Malacca, which lies between the island of Sumatra and a strip of land called the Malay Peninsula.

INDIAN OCEAN: WILD PLACES

A small continent may lie deep in the Indian Ocean!

Scientists have discovered bits of minerals on the island of Mauritius that are millions of years older than the island itself. These minerals may have come from an ancient "microcontinent" and were raised from the seafloor by volcanoes that formed the island. Here are a few other amazing sites in the Indian Ocean.

This coral reef is in the Red Sea. The **Red Sea** is a long, skinny sea attached to the Arabian Sea, which sits in the northwestern Indian Ocean. Its floor is an active "rift" zone, where the crust is pulling apart and molten rock is rising to fill the gap. As a result, the Red Sea is widening at a rate of about 0.6 inch (1.5 cm) a year (your fingernails grow nearly three times faster than that!). Deep in the sea are pools of super-salty water heated by molten rock to temperatures as high as 140°F (60°C). The Red Sea is really blue, but it sometimes turns red-brown when large amounts of algae die.

The **Maldives** is a country made up of about 1,200 islands spread across about 510 miles (820 km) of the Indian Ocean. It's famous for its beautiful white beaches and coral reefs. Visitors come to go scuba diving and see whale sharks, rays, and other animals. People who live in the Maldives work mainly in the tourism and fishing industries. The highest island here is less than 10 feet (3 m) above sea level, so a rise in sea level due to climate change (see pages 182–183) is a big concern for this nation.

The **Seychelles** are a group of about 115 islands in the western Indian Ocean. The main islands in this group are different from all other islands in the middle of an ocean because they're made of a rock called granite—the same rock that forms continents. These granite islands rise up from a plate of rock that broke off Africa and slowly moved away many millions of years ago. The smaller islands around the granite ones are coral islands.

The **Aldabra Islands** form one of the world's largest atolls (ring of raised coral reefs). The four big coral islands surround a shallow lagoon. Together they span an area about 19 miles (30.5 km) long and 8 miles (13 km) wide. They're famous as the home of the Aldabra giant tortoise, the world's second-largest tortoise. Males have shells as much as 4 feet (1.2 m) long! About 152,000 of these giant reptiles live here. Seagrass meadows grow in the lagoon, and mangrove forests surround it.

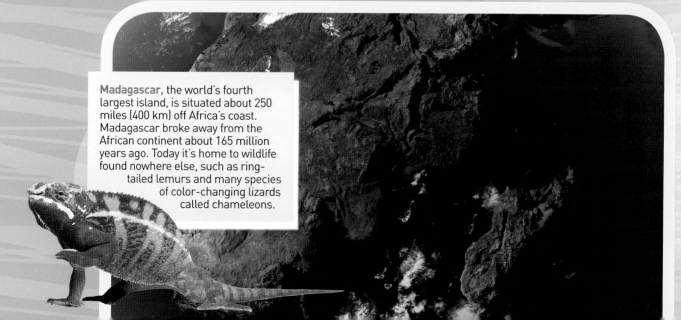

Madagascar, the world's fourth largest island, is situated about 250 miles (400 km) off Africa's coast. Madagascar broke away from the African continent about 165 million years ago. Today it's home to wildlife found nowhere else, such as ring-tailed lemurs and many species of color-changing lizards called chameleons.

INDIAN OCEAN:
WILD
WONDERS

Many marine organisms are found nearly worldwide. Others are found in just a few places. Here are a few that call the Indian Ocean their home.

The **dugong** lives in warm coastal waters of the Indian Ocean as well as part of the Pacific. It grazes on seagrass, which it gathers with its big, floppy lips. It's a mammal, so it needs to breathe air, but it can stay underwater for up to six minutes. A dugong can grow to be 10 feet (3 m) long and weigh up to 1,100 pounds (499 kg). It can eat 70 pounds (32 kg) of seagrass in one day!

The **Christmas frigatebird** nests only on Christmas Island in the eastern Indian Ocean. This big seabird is famous for attacking other seabirds in flight and stealing their fish. A male frigatebird has a big red throat pouch. To attract a female, he inflates his pouch and makes loud rattling sounds. A frigatebird can soar over the ocean for more than a week at a time.

The **masked puffer** is a fish found in the Red Sea. It lives on coral reefs, where it feeds on mollusks, corals, and other invertebrates. If threatened by a predator, it takes in water and blows up into a big ball. It also contains a deadly poison in some of its organs and its skin.

The **veined octopus** lives throughout the Indian Ocean and a few areas in the western Pacific. It is found in shallow tropical waters. This species is also called the coconut octopus because it uses old coconut shells as shelter. It will also hide from danger inside an old clamshell or by burying itself in sand or mud.

The **zebra angelfish** lives in the Indian Ocean and the Red Sea. It eats plankton. The male zebrafish has a striped body, but the female has stripes only on its tail. These fish live in small groups of one male and several females. If the male dies, a female in the group actually turns into a male and becomes leader!

THE ARCTIC OCEAN

The Arctic Ocean is the smallest ocean. It's about one-sixth the size of the Indian Ocean. In winter, most of it is covered by ice. A lot of this ice is about 6.6 feet (2 m) thick, but can be as much as 12 to 15 feet (4 to 5 m) thick in places. Snow lies on top of the ice, forming hills as wind blows it around.

Sea ice is also called pack ice. Individual pieces of pack ice are called floes. Narrow cracks open up between floes as wind and currents push them around. In summer, about half of the pack ice melts.

Pack ice is important habitat for Arctic wildlife. Walruses and seals give birth to their young on the ice. Seals slip under the ice to hunt for fish, poking their snouts up through holes when they need to take a breath. Polar bears, in turn, venture onto pack ice to hunt seals. Algae growing on the underside of the ice is eaten by shrimplike animals and other small swimmers.

Scientists and sailors have names for the different kinds of ice that form in the Arctic. "Multi-year ice" is ice that lasts for many years because it doesn't melt completely in summer. A "hummock" is a hill of broken ice. "Grease ice" is a thin, slushy film of floating ice.

As grease ice is jostled about by waves, it forms thin disks called "pancake ice." These "pancakes" bump against each other, which pushes up their edges to form rims. A sea full of pancake ice looks like a giant frozen jigsaw puzzle!

TOTAL AREA:	5,600,000 square miles (14,700,000 sq km)
DEEPEST POINT:	18,599 feet (5,669 m)
TWO LARGEST SEAS:	Norwegian Sea: 550,200 square miles (1,425,000 sq km)
	Greenland Sea: 447,100 square miles (1,158,000 sq km)

an ice arch carved by the wind in a giant iceberg in Greenland

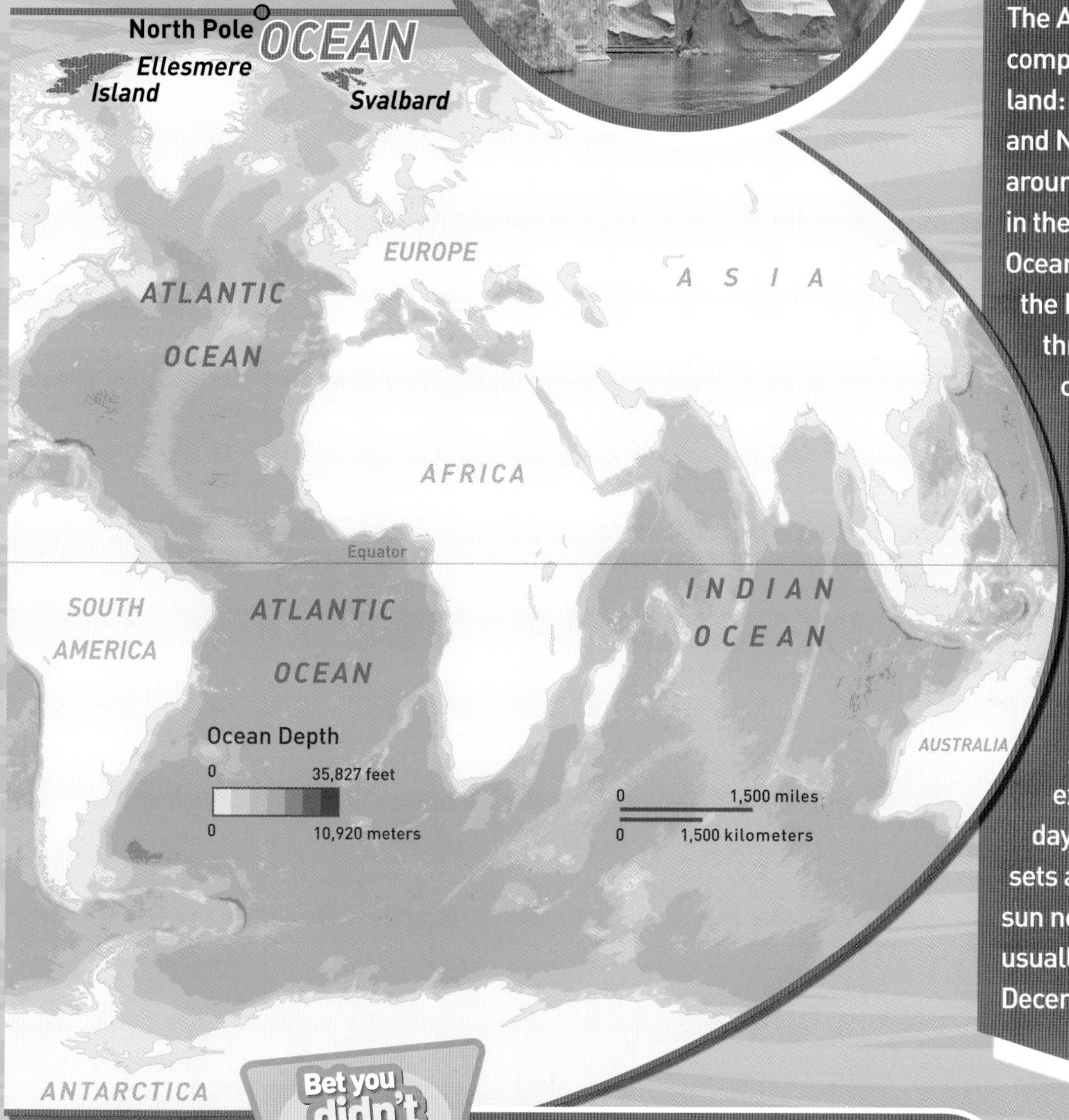

MAP OF THE ARCTIC OCEAN

The Arctic Ocean is almost completely surrounded by land: Asia, Europe, Greenland, and North America wrap around it. Yet there is no land in the middle of the Arctic Ocean itself. It is connected to the Pacific and the Atlantic through narrow waterways called straits. The Arctic Ocean shares its name with the part of the world it occupies—the Arctic, which lies above an imaginary line around Earth called the Arctic Circle. Places north of the Arctic Circle all experience at least one day when the sun never sets and one day when the sun never rises. Those days usually fall around June 21 and December 21.

North Pole
OCEAN
Ellesmere Island
Svalbard

EUROPE

ASIA

ATLANTIC OCEAN

AFRICA

Equator

SOUTH AMERICA

ATLANTIC OCEAN

INDIAN OCEAN

AUSTRALIA

Ocean Depth

| 0 | 35,827 feet |
| 0 | 10,920 meters |

| 0 | 1,500 miles |
| 0 | 1,500 kilometers |

ANTARCTICA

Bet you didn't know

In 1958, a submarine called the U.S.S. *Nautilus* traveled across the Arctic Ocean beneath the ice from Alaska to Greenland. It was the first submarine to glide beneath the North Pole.

ARCTIC OCEAN: WILD PLACES

Wherever you go in the Arctic Ocean, the water's very cold! Its average surface temperature is about 28.6°F to 30.2°F (–1.9°C to –1.0°C). Even the "warm" water flowing in from the Atlantic Ocean is only about 41°F (5.2°C)—just a few degrees above the freezing point of freshwater. But if you bundle up, here are some of the amazing places to see in the Arctic Ocean and on its shores.

Giant, shaggy horned animals called **musk oxen** live on Ellesmere Island, the most northern island in Canada. Ellesmere lies northwest of Greenland and is the world's tenth largest island. Sticking out of its glaciers is Barbeau Peak, the highest mountain east of the Rockies in North America. Around the island's edges are wide ice shelves—ledges of sea ice attached to the land. Climate change has caused some ice shelves that have hung on for more than 3,000 years to break off and float away in the ocean (see pages 182–183).

On a map, the **Chukchi Sea** sits in a sort of bowl formed by the coasts of Russia and Alaska. Many kinds of whales as well as walruses live in or migrate through this sea. About 2,000 polar bears—a tenth of the world's population—hunt for seals in this sea. Native peoples living along its coast hunt and fish for a living.

Svalbard is a group of islands that are part of Norway. They lie about 620 miles (1,000 km) from the North Pole. Svalbard was a whaling center in the past. Today, coal mining is the main industry. The islands are home to about 3,500 polar bears and about 2,500 people. Svalbard is also where you'll find the world's most northern museum, church, hospital, ATM, and city of more than a thousand people.

There's no pole at the North Pole! There isn't any land, either. The North Pole is simply the northern end of Earth's axis—the imaginary line around which Earth spins. It sits in the Arctic Ocean about 450 miles (725 km) north of Greenland. Two explorers claimed to have reached the North Pole first: Frederick A. Cook in 1908 and Robert E. Peary in 1909.

The **Bering Strait** is a narrow passage that links the Arctic Ocean to the Pacific. About 12,000 years ago, however, this place wasn't underwater! The world was in an ice age, with lots of water locked up in ice sheets. As a result, the sea level was about 300 feet (91 m) lower than today. A wide land area linked Russia with Alaska. Prehistoric horses, woolly mammoths, and other animals roamed across it, and so did humans. Today, you can see what this land looked like by visiting Bering Land Bridge National Preserve in Alaska.

ARCTIC OCEAN: WILD WONDERS

Many marine organisms are found nearly worldwide. Others are found in just a few places. Here are a few that call the Arctic Ocean their home.

The **narwhal** is a whale that lives in the Arctic Ocean near coasts. A male narwhal has two teeth in his upper jaw. One of them grows into a spiral tusk that's up to 10 feet (3 m) long! The tusk may be used by males to compete for mates. But scientists have found that it contains many nerves, so it may be a sense organ as well. Narwhals eat fish, shrimp, and squid. In winter, most of them lurk under sea ice between Canada and Greenland.

The **dovekie** nests on rocky cliffs and coasts of the Arctic Ocean. As many as 30 million dovekies gather to nest in one area of northwestern Greenland! A dovekie lays its egg in a nest of pebbles in an opening among the rocks. It feeds on plankton, crustaceans, and little fish, which it catches by diving into the water and swimming with its wings. Dovekies migrate to the open ocean in winter, but rarely travel farther south into the Atlantic than the northeastern United States.

Bathykorus bouilloni is a new species of jellyfish discovered in the Arctic Ocean. Scientists discovered this marble-size jelly in 2002. It's found at depths between 4,600 and 6,500 feet (1,400 and 2,000 m). Unlike most jellyfish, it holds its tentacles forward as it swims instead of trailing them. The tentacles carry venom for stinging prey. It's nicknamed the "Darth Vader jellyfish" because it's shaped like the helmet of this character in *Star Wars* movies.

The **Arctic cod** is found in the Arctic Ocean and its seas. It lives farther north than any other ocean fish. Like many Arctic fish, it has substances in its blood that keep it from freezing in icy Arctic waters. Arctic cod eat zooplankton and small crustaceans that feed on algae growing on the underside of sea ice. The cod, in turn, is eaten by fish, seals, seabirds, and whales. They're a favorite food of narwhals.

The **ringed seal** lives throughout the Arctic Ocean. It dives as deep as 300 feet (90 m) and can stay underwater for up to 45 minutes as it hunts for fish and crustaceans. A ringed seal uses its claws to scrape open breathing holes in sea ice so it can pop up, take a breath, and dive again. Polar bears often wait next to these holes to catch ringed seals, which are their favorite food.

SALTY WATER

Lick your lips after a splash in the ocean, and you'll taste how salty seawater is. About 96.5 percent of seawater is actually water. The rest is made up of dissolved substances. Most of these substances are salts of different kinds. The most plentiful kind of salt is the same that you pour out of a saltshaker at the table: sodium chloride.

The saltiness of water is called salinity. It is measured by figuring out how much salt is dissolved in a sample of water. The result tells you how many "parts" of salt there are in one thousand "parts" of water. Freshwater, for example, contains very little salt—less than one "part" of salt per a thousand "parts" of water. The saltiest ocean water, however, contains 35 "parts" of salt mixed in with a thousand "parts" of water.

This salt washed into the ocean from the land over the course of billions of years—and all that salt has added up to make a salty ocean. Today, rivers still pick up salts and other minerals from rocks and soil and deliver them to the ocean. Salt is also added by undersea volcanoes and bubbling fountains called hydrothermal vents. The ocean doesn't keep getting massively saltier every year, though, because some of the salt turns into clumps of rock in its deepest parts.

On average, salt makes up about 2.5 percent of the ocean's water. So if the ocean is 2.5 percent salt and 96.5 percent water, what makes up the remaining 1 percent? Answer: substances, such as nitrogen and phosphorus, and gases absorbed from the atmosphere, such as oxygen and carbon dioxide.

TRY THIS!

The ocean's water looks like it's all the same when you view it from shore. But it actually varies widely in salinity from place to place and even from top to bottom. That's because water with lots of salt dissolved in it is denser, or heavier, than the same amount of water with less salt in it. The large amount of salt dissolved in seawater, for example, makes it denser than freshwater. A cup of seawater weighs more than an equal amount of freshwater at the same temperature.

You can check out how salinity and density work right in your kitchen. Fill a measuring cup to the half-cup (.12 L) level with water. Add two tablespoons (30 ml) of salt and stir. Add a little food coloring too. Next, fill a clear drinking glass about halfway with water. Then add the prepared salt water to the freshwater, slowly, drop by drop. The dense "seawater" will sink to the bottom of the less dense, less salty freshwater.

If you could take **all the salt** out of the ocean and spread it evenly on Earth's land, it would form a layer about as tall as a **40-story building!**

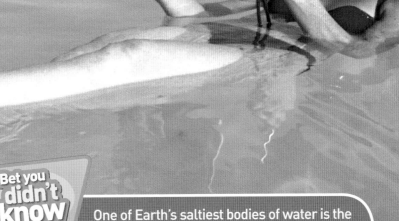

Bet you didn't know

One of Earth's saltiest bodies of water is the Dead Sea (which is actually a lake). The Dead Sea lies between Israel and Jordan. It loses more water to the air by evaporation than it gets from rainfall, so its water is about 10 times saltier than seawater! This salinity makes the water so dense, people float easily on its surface and simply cannot sink in it.

SEA LEVELS:
THE OCEAN'S
LAYERS

What do you see when you look at the sea? Maybe it's smooth as glass on a calm, sunny day. Maybe it's pounding the shore with foamy waves on a windy winter day. It might look turquoise blue if you're on a tropical island, or dark gray if you're in the Arctic.

Slip below the surface, and you'll find that the ocean is much more than a very deep basin of water. Just as your surroundings change on land as you move farther north or south—or up a mountainside—so, too, do the surroundings change as you move into deeper waters. The deeper the water, the darker and colder it gets. The pressure grows, too, because of the weight of all that water pressing down from above.

Oceanographers divide the ocean into five different zones based on depth, light, and other features.

- The sunlit zone, which reaches to a maximum depth of about 660 feet (200 m)
- The murky twilight zone, which ranges from the sunlit zone down to about 3,250 feet (1,000 m)
- The dark midnight zone, which drops from the twilight zone down to about 13,100 feet (4,000 m)
- The abyssal zone, just as dark as the midnight zone and extending to 19,700 feet (6,000 m) deep
- The hadal zone, which plunges down to the bottom of the ocean's deepest trench at 35,827 feet (10,920 m). ("Hadal" comes from Hades, the name of a dark underworld in ancient Greek myths.)

Different organisms in the different zones are adapted to the conditions in their zone—even such extremes as crushing pressure and near-freezing cold.

TRUE BLUE

Water is a colorless liquid—so why does the ocean look blue? The dark blue of the ocean comes from the way light is absorbed by water. Sunlight is made up of all the colors of light, called the spectrum: red, orange, yellow, green, blue, indigo, and violet. Water absorbs the colors at the red end of the spectrum quickly. That leaves the bluish colors to be scattered and reflected back to your eyes.

This basic blue is affected by what's floating in the water. It might look bright green or vivid blue-green if seaweed and other algae—especially microscopic kinds—are blooming in the water. Particles of dirt suspended in the water make water look brown. Bubbles on the surface of a wind-tossed ocean reflect sunlight, making water whitish. If it's cloudy or raining, the ocean tends to look greenish gray.

Bet you didn't know

Many people call the ocean "the sea." But to an oceanographer, a sea is a body of water that's smaller than the ocean, but connected to it. A sea is located at the edge of an ocean, where water and land meet, and is also enclosed or partly enclosed by land.

sunlit zone

murky twilight zone

dark midnight zone

abyssal zone

hadal zone

THE SUNLIT ZONE

From angelfish to zebra moray eel, the sunlit zone is a place of abundant life. This zone occupies the top 660 feet (200 m) of the ocean. Here, sunlight brightens the water. This sunny zone is also known as the photic zone. "Photic" means "of or relating to light."

The uppermost part of this zone gets enough sunlight for plants to grow. Microscopic algae called phytoplankton float on or near the surface. Long strands of algae, called seaweed, swish back and forth in the water.

Like plants on land, the algae use the sun's energy to turn water and carbon dioxide into food. This process is called photosynthesis. ("Photo" means "light," and "synthesis" means "putting together.") Photosynthesis can only happen in sunlight, so that's why you'll find live plants and plantlike organisms only in the sunlit zone.

Parts of the sunlit zone close to shore contain a wide variety of life. Here, rivers and streams empty into the sea. They carry substances washed from land, such as nitrogen and phosphorus, which are nutrients that help seaweeds and phytoplankton grow. Likewise, waves stir up nutrients from the shallow seafloor and circulate them, too.

Across the ocean, the sunlit zone functions as a feeding ground for many sea animals. One-celled organisms called zooplankton float in the water feeding on the phytoplankton. Fish eat the zooplankton and each other. Jellyfish drift and are gobbled up by sea turtles. Giant whale sharks lumber through the water with their mouths open, filtering meals of plankton and fish from the water.

WARMER WATERS

The sunlit zone is typically warmer than the zones below it. Just how much warmer depends on the location and season. In the Persian Gulf, for example, water at the surface can be as warm as 97°F (36°C)—that's almost as warm as a hot tub. The Persian Gulf is surrounded by desert lands in a very hot climate. Up near the North Pole, however, surface water may be a bone-chilling 28.6°F (-1.9°C). That's the freezing point of salt water. (Freshwater freezes at a higher temperature of 32°F [0°C].)

Sunlight heats the topmost layer of the ocean. Waves mix the water and distribute the heat further in the sunlit zone. Heat is also carried by the surface waters as they flow through the ocean from warm regions on Earth to cooler ones.

Bet you didn't know Sea skaters are among the few insects that live at sea. A few species live hundreds of miles from the nearest shore. They are able to walk on the ocean's surface, where they eat tiny bits of food and lay eggs on floating objects, such as feathers.

THE TWILIGHT ZONE

Next stop: the twilight zone. Here, light barely penetrates the water. During the day, there's just enough light for a diver to see while swimming in the upper parts of this zone. There isn't much color beyond blue and some green because all the other colors of light have been absorbed. The water is also much colder. And with all the weight of the water above pressing down, the pressure is much greater, too. No plants or algae grow here because there's not enough light for photosynthesis.

Some animals in this zone wait for food to drift down from above. Other animals swim to the sunlit zone to eat. Small fish called bristlemouths, for example, spend the day in the twilight zone. At night, they swim up to the sunlit zone to feed near the surface, without fear of being eaten by seabirds. But predators lurk in the twilight zone, too. Many of them, such as the sharp-toothed lancetfish, wait for prey to come close before seizing it.

Many animals in the twilight zone have adapted to their murky world by evolving their own lights! Hatchetfish, for example, have light-producing organs called photophores on their undersides. The glow of their lights helps them blend in with the dim light coming from above and hides them from predators below. Hatchetfish have also evolved eyes that point up to help search for prey above them. Another species, the barreleye fish, even has a transparent head to make peering upward easier!

IT'S GETTING COLDER

In many parts of the ocean, the temperature in the twilight zone drops steadily from surface temperatures down to a chilly 46 to 50°F (8 to 10°C). This sharp drop is called the thermocline. The thermocline separates surface waters from deeper, colder water. Above the thermocline, surface water varies in temperature worldwide, from warm, sunny regions to cooler areas closer to the poles. Below the thermocline, temperatures drop more slowly to nearly freezing.

The thermocline isn't a fixed boundary, however. Storms, waves, and seasonal changes can roil the waters and mix up the layers. The thermocline tends to be stronger the closer you are to the Equator. At the poles, there is no thermocline. That's because the water is cold enough at the surface for ice to form, so there is hardly any temperature difference between the surface and the depths.

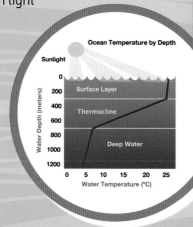

Ocean Temperature by Depth

Sunlight

Surface Layer

Thermocline

Deep Water

Water Depth (meters): 0, 200, 400, 600, 800, 1000, 1200

Water Temperature (°C): 0, 5, 10, 15, 20, 25

The blobfish is a gooey, blobby fish with a **droopy face!** It doesn't need powerful swimming muscles because it simply hangs out in the twilight zone, waiting for food to swim by.

a school of southern pygmy squid at night in the Pacific Ocean

THE MIDNIGHT ZONE

No sunlight reaches the midnight zone. Here, the only light that flickers comes from the bodies of fish, squid, jellyfish, and other creatures that make a "living light" called bioluminescence.

The midnight zone plunges from about 3,250 feet (1,000 m) to a depth of 13,100 feet (4,000 m). It's not only pitch dark, it's also extremely cold: The temperature hovers around 39°F (4°C), just a few degrees above the freezing point of freshwater.

The pressure is also intense. Scientific instruments have recorded pressure of more than 5,850 pounds per square inch (411 kg/sq cm). That amount of concentrated pressure is like having a hippopotamus stand on your thumb! Midnight-zone animals, however, are adapted to life under high pressure. Jellyfish, for example, consist mainly of water, which can't be squashed the way air can.

Animals in the midnight zone are faced not only with these intense conditions—they also face a lack of food. There just isn't much to eat here. Many animals depend on food that drifts down from the surface, such as dead plankton and dead fish. A dead whale sinking to the midnight zone is like a Thanksgiving feast!

Other midnight-zone animals use light to help them catch food. An anglerfish, for example, has a long lure on its head that bobs above its huge mouth. The end of the lure is filled with glowing bacteria. Prey attracted to the glow are grabbed in the anglerfish's toothy jaws and quickly gulped down into its big, stretchy stomach.

LIGHTS, ACTION!

The Atolla jellyfish uses light to holler for help! The jellyfish is normally red—a color that looks black in deep water, because there is no red light this far down to reflect from objects. But if a predator attacks it, the jellyfish turns into a whirl of flashing blue lights. If it's the jellyfish's lucky day, its display will attract a bigger predator that will eat the animal attacking it.

This deep-sea anglerfish attracts prey with a glowing lure on its head, as well as a flowing, glowing beard! Only females have lures. The tiny males do not.

INTO THE ABYSS

Beyond the midnight zone is yet another region of darkness: the abyssal zone. This deep, dark world begins at a depth of 13,100 feet (4,000 m) and plunges down to 19,700 feet (6,000 m).

It's hard to imagine anything could survive here. Yet the ocean floor is dotted with living things. Poking up from the muddy ooze are sea lilies and sea pens—animals that look like flowers, feathers, and fireworks. Fat sea cucumbers trudge across the mud. Crablike animals called sea spiders tiptoe on spindly legs in search of sea anemones and sponges to eat.

Like a lot of animals in the midnight zone, many creatures of the abyss depend on food trickling down from upper layers. This downward drift of dead sea creatures and other bits and pieces is called "marine snow." Sea lilies and sea pens filter marine snow from water. Sea cucumbers slurp it out of the sludgy seafloor.

For a long time, oceanographers assumed that most deep-sea life survived on marine snow. Then, in 1977, scientists made an amazing discovery. Instead of finding a barren desert, scientists discovered a whole new world of life that didn't depend on sunlight for energy. They found cracks in the seafloor that spewed jets of hot water. Around these hydrothermal vents were species of clams, crabs, sea slugs, mussels, shrimp, and worms that nobody had ever seen before.

Colonies of bacteria live inside giant tube worms, mussels, and clams, making food for them. Octopuses eat the clams and mussels as well as shrimp and crabs.

GOING DOWN

We can't go scuba diving in the ocean's depths. The pressure of water is simply too great. The world record for deepest dive, set in 2014, is just 1,090 feet 4.5 inches (332.35 m)—a big dive for humans, but a small drop in the ocean.

Using specially designed vehicles, however, people have managed to reach the deepest parts of the ocean. The vehicle that enabled scientists to visit hydrothermal vents in 1977 is a submersible called *Alvin. Alvin* started bringing scientists deep in the ocean in 1964, and it was the first one to carry passengers. *Alvin* can dive to 14,760 feet (4,500 m), and engineers are upgrading it so it can dive even deeper.

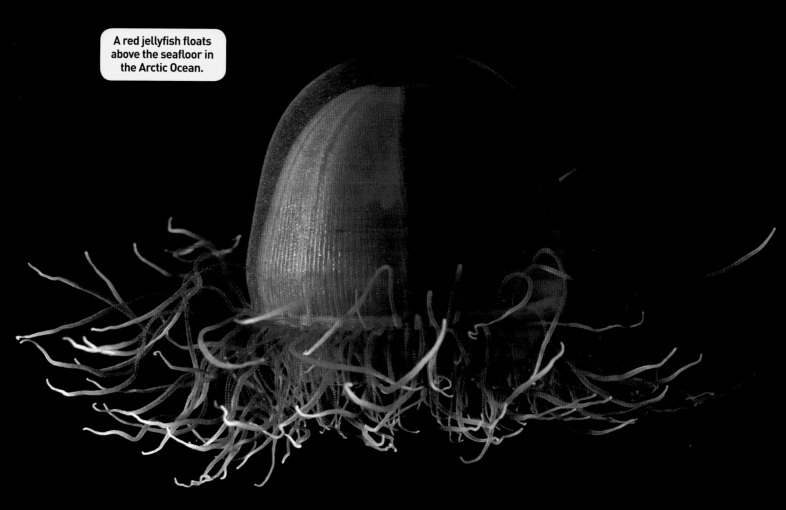

A red jellyfish floats above the seafloor in the Arctic Ocean.

Bet you didn't know The sea pig is a plump, blobby animal found nearly worldwide deep in the ocean. It eats mud and digests the tiny organisms living in it. It measures about 4 to 6 inches (10 to 15 cm) long. Sometimes little deep-sea snails burrow into a sea pig's skin and live there—and even eat the sea pig's body.

DEEP-SEA LIFE

The deep-sea world is a harsh environment.

The pressure is about 100 times greater than the air pressure you feel on land. The water is freezing cold and pitch-dark, and food is scarce. But as eerie as this world is, it's home, sweet home for many animals that are adapted to living here. Some creatures have large, sensitive eyes to gather what little light there is. Many animals are bioluminescent. A variety of animals, such as squid, have rubbery bodies without air spaces in them, which helps them cope with heavy pressure. No air spaces means no squashing!

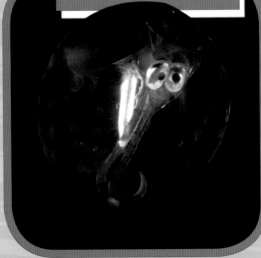

The **googly-eyed squid** lives at depths of 1,000 to 1,500 feet (305 to 450 m). Its transparent body helps conceal it from goblin sharks, whales, and other predators. But if it's attacked, the squid has another trick: It puffs up its body with water, so that it suddenly turns into a giant water balloon! This trick startles a predator for a split second, which gives the squid a chance to escape.

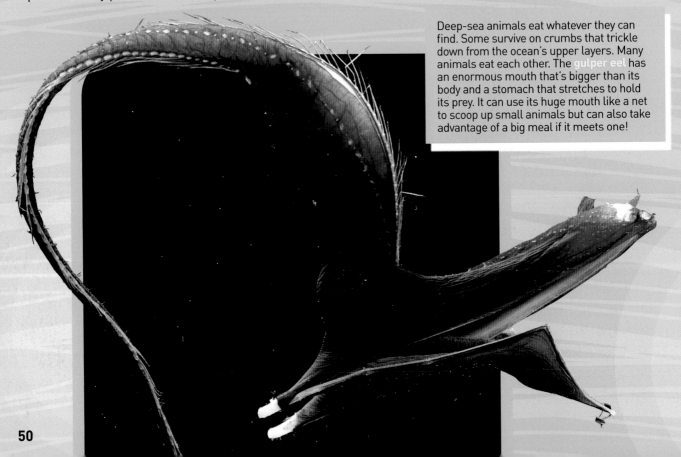

Deep-sea animals eat whatever they can find. Some survive on crumbs that trickle down from the ocean's upper layers. Many animals eat each other. The **gulper eel** has an enormous mouth that's bigger than its body and a stomach that stretches to hold its prey. It can use its huge mouth like a net to scoop up small animals but can also take advantage of a big meal if it meets one!

Spit-tooie! Some **deep-sea shrimp** scare off predators with a burst of glowing goo, as seen in this enhanced photo. This lit-up liquid is produced in the shrimp's body and comes out of its mouth. The cloud surprises a predator, which may stop its attack long enough for the shrimp to make a quick getaway.

The **giant flashlight fish** has pockets under its eyes filled with billions of bacteria that produce light. It can turn the pocket so the light doesn't show, or turn it so that the light can be seen. The fish flashes the light quickly to scare away predators. It can also control its "blinks" to communicate with other flashlight fish or lure prey. The bacteria are "paid" for their work by getting a safe home.

Bioluminescent deep-sea animals usually glow blue or blue-green. That's because blue and green light travels farther in water than other colors. Red light, however, doesn't travel far at all. Since they don't use red light, many deep-sea animals have lost the ability to see it—which means they can't see the sneaky **stoplight loosejaw** when it turns on its red "headlights." This fish can communicate secretly with other loosejaws, and the little bit of extra light helps it find prey, too.

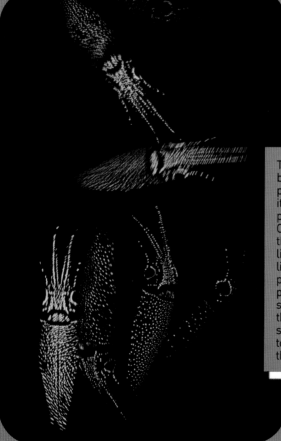

The little **firefly squid's** body is dotted with photophores. Some of its arms are tipped with photophores, too. Chemical reactions in these organs produce light. The firefly squid lights up to scare predators and attract prey. In Japan, certain seashores are lined with the blue glow of firefly squid that have migrated to the surface during their mating season.

CHAPTER 2

OCEAN LIFE

Fish and other marine animals live in a tropical coral reef.

A SEA OF WONDER

Corals that look like brains.

Crabs that decorate their bodies with seaweed and sponges. Fish that tie themselves in knots, and sharks as long as buses. These strange creatures are among many thousands of organisms that have evolved fascinating and often weird adaptations to survive in different ocean habitats—warm ones, cold ones, sunlit ones, pitch-dark ones. Some animals are even adapted to live in places where the water pressure is so great, it would feel as if you were trying to carry 50 jumbo jets on your back! Here are just a few of the ocean's many living wonders.

Antarctic icefish live in the bitter-cold but oxygen-rich waters around Antarctica. An icefish's body makes substances that prevent ice crystals from forming in its blood. The icefish also has clear blood instead of red blood like all other animals with bones. Red blood cells carry oxygen and make blood thicker. In icefish, oxygen simply dissolves in its watery blood like sugar in tea. Scientists are studying the icefish to see if thin, clear blood helps it survive in cold water—or if the lack of red blood cells is an evolutionary mistake that the icefish somehow managed to survive.

The leafy seadragon slurps up zooplankton and other tiny organisms with its tube-like snout. Its frilly fins and leafy flaps help it blend in with seaweed and seagrass. Eggs laid by a female seadragon are stuck to a special patch of skin on the male's tail until they hatch. Seadragons live along Australia's southern coast.

The **Halmahera epaulette shark** lives on reefs near Indonesia in the western Pacific Ocean. It uses its fins as legs to walk on the seafloor as it hunts for shrimp and other small prey. It's one of nine known species of walking shark.

The **red slate pencil urchin** is found in tropical waters of the Indian Ocean and parts of the Pacific Ocean. Its "pencils" are spines that are up to 4.7 inches (12 cm) long. The spines protect the urchin from predators as it feeds on algae growing on rocks and coral reefs.

Most jellyfish swim with their tentacles hanging down. Not the **upside-down jellyfish!** It lies on the seafloor so its tentacles, which are filled with photosynthesizing algae, get lots of sunlight. The jellyfish provides the algae with a home and gets some of its nutrition from food made by the algae. Upside-down jellyfish live in tropical waters of the western Atlantic Ocean and the Pacific Ocean.

These tiny shells, seen next to the eye of a needle, were made by single-celled organisms called **foraminifera** ("forams" for short). Forams of different species are found nearly everywhere in the ocean. Each species can be identified by its shell. The shells of dead forams make up a large part of the squishy mud on the seafloor.

FOOD WEBS

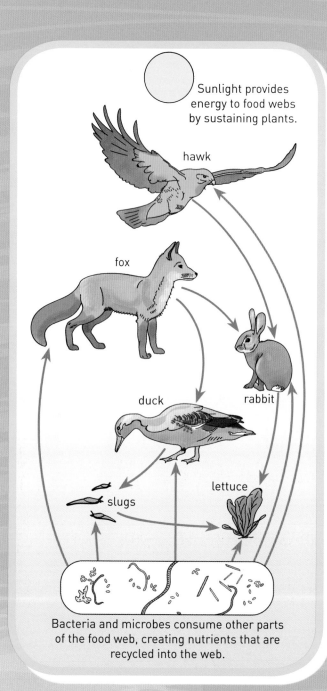

Sunlight provides energy to food webs by sustaining plants.

hawk

fox

duck

rabbit

slugs

lettuce

Bacteria and microbes consume other parts of the food web, creating nutrients that are recycled into the web.

Munch, chomp, gulp, slurp! Finding food and avoiding being eaten are major jobs for creatures in the ocean, just as they are on land. Some of these creatures are predators that hunt and eat other animals. The animals they hunt are called prey. Some creatures eat only plants and plantlike organisms. And some living things are primary producers—organisms that make food using energy from sunlight or chemicals.

On land, for example, a lettuce plant is a primary producer. It uses energy from sunlight to turn water and carbon dioxide into food. Its leaves grow larger. One day, a rabbit eats the leaves. The energy and nutrients in the lettuce become part of the rabbit. Later, a hawk catches and eats the rabbit. The energy and nutrients in the rabbit become part of the hawk.

All together, the lettuce, rabbit, and hawk form a series of links called a food chain. Add slugs that eat lettuce, a duck that eats slugs, and a fox that eats rabbits and ducks, and you've got a food web—a lot of food chains linked together. Food webs also include bacteria and other microscopic organisms that break down dead organisms and waste material, turning them into chemicals that will be used as nutrients by other living things.

In the same way, ocean organisms are joined together in food webs. The producers in the ocean are organisms that use energy from sunlight or chemicals to make food, such as seagrass and seaweed. Animals large and small eat the producers, and many of them become meals for predators.

Here is an example of some of the organisms that make up an ocean food web.

SHARK

STINGRAY

SEA TURTLE

CRAB

SEA STAR

JELLYFISH

SHRIMP

MUSSELS

ZOOPLANKTON

PHYTOPLANKTON

SUN

FLOATING FEAST
PHYTOPLANKTON

The base of the ocean's food web floats on its surface! That's where you'll find phytoplankton. "Phyto" means "plantlike" and "plankton" means "drifting." Phytoplankton turn sunlight into food by photosynthesis, just as plants do on land.

Phytoplankton includes "microalgae"—one-celled algae that are related to the many-celled algae called seaweed. You can sometimes see microalgae without a microscope because a crowd of microalgae can turn seawater green.

Phytoplankton also includes bacteria. One special group of bacteria is called cyanobacteria. (They're also called blue-green algae, even though they're not algae!) Cyanobacteria are thought to be one of the oldest living things on Earth. They are credited with totally changing Earth's atmosphere 2.4 billion years ago by adding oxygen to it through the process of photosynthesis.

Phytoplankton float near the surface because they depend on sunlight, though they can be found up to 980 feet (300 m) deep in very clear water. In parts of the world that have warm and cold seasons, phytoplankton increase greatly in springtime because the days grow longer and bring more sunlight. Phytoplankton are eaten by other tiny organisms, called zooplankton (pages 62–63).

DIATOMS

The ocean's phytoplankton includes lots of microscopic algae called diatoms. A diatom uses a chemical compound in the water called silica to make a glasslike, boxy shell. Each species has its own shape and pattern of shell. They look like miniature works of art when viewed through a microscope. Old diatom shells sink to the seafloor, where they may clump together over millions of years to form a soft rock called diatomaceous earth.

You can find diatomaceous earth in garden stores, too! It's collected, ground into powder, and used to make products for controlling garden pests such as slugs and snails. Diatomaceous earth is also used to make filters, cat litter, toothpaste, dynamite, and other products.

Phytoplankton reproduce quickly, or "bloom," when they get lots of nutrients and sunlight.

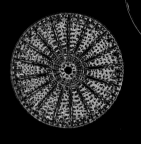

Phytoplankton produce about **half** of the **oxygen** in the atmosphere.

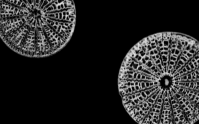

Fireworks in a night sky? Nope.
These are tiny diatoms floating in water
as viewed through a microscope!

SEA OF SEAWEED

Have you ever stepped on squishy, slippery seaweed while splashing in the waves? Seaweeds are a many-celled form of algae. Scientists often refer to them as "macroalgae" ("macro" means "large").

Like plants and phytoplankton, seaweeds are producers. They use photosynthesis to make food.

Green seaweeds are bright green thanks to chlorophyll, the pigment that captures the energy in sunlight. These seaweeds grow in shallow water, in estuaries, and on rocky shores.

Brown seaweeds also contain chlorophyll, but it's hidden by brown pigments that can absorb different colors of light (such as more blue light) than green seaweeds. Some species of brown seaweed grow very large and form huge underwater forests (pages 226–227).

Red seaweeds have red and blue pigments in addition to green and brown ones. They're even more sensitive to blue light than brown seaweed, so they can grow in even deeper water. Thanks to their pigments, they come in brilliant colors, such as scarlet, pink, and purple.

The extra pigments are adaptations for coping with dim light. Different seaweeds boast other adaptations, such as rubbery stalks that help them survive in rough waves, or slimy coverings that protect against drying out.

SEAWEED FEED

Seaweeds provide oxygen, carbon dioxide, and shelter for many marine species. They're eaten by many fish, sea snails, crabs, and other marine animals. Since ancient times, they have also been used as fertilizer and animal food by farmers living near seashores.

Seaweed is also eaten by people. It's long been an important food in Asia and is grown widely there on seaweed farms. Many of the foods you buy at the grocery store also contain seaweed. Seaweed extracts are used to make foods thicker, smoother, or jellylike. You can find seaweed in a variety of foods including ice cream, chocolate milk, cookies, salad dressing, chicken nuggets, and onion rings. If the ingredients list says "alginate," "agar," or "carrageenan," that's seaweed!

The **kelp crab** lives in forests of kelp and other seaweeds. It feeds on **seaweed,** too. Its body gets its color from the seaweed it eats, which helps camouflage it.

This greenish grower is actually a brown seaweed that lives along shores in areas of the Pacific Ocean.

A hungry
blue whale
may eat about
40 million krill
in just one day!

A young manta ray opens
its mouth wide to feed as it
swoops through a cloud of
zooplankton.

ZILLIONS OF ZOOPLANKTON

"Zoo" means "animal," and that's just what zooplankton are: the animals found in ocean plankton. Many zooplankton spend their entire lives drifting in the water. Others live as drifters only when they're young.

Some zooplankton are microscopic, one-celled creatures, such as tiny shelled animals called radiolaria and foraminifera.

Other zooplankton are very small but can be seen without a microscope. These larger organisms include tiny "cousins" of shrimp and lobsters called copepods. Many copepods are so small that they can swim through the eye of a needle! Copepods have 10 legs and are not strong swimmers, but they can jet quickly by slapping their antennae against their bodies.

Zooplankton also includes small species of shrimp, marine worms, jellyfish, jellylike animals called salps, and snail-like creatures called pteropods. The tiny, floating eggs and young of oysters, crabs, lobsters, sea stars, many species of fish, and plenty of other animals are also part of the zooplankton.

The smallest zooplankton feed on phytoplankton. Bigger zooplankton eat other zooplankton, or both zooplankton and phytoplankton. Big zooplankton, in turn, are eaten by larger animals ranging from fish to the largest animal ever, the blue whale. Krill, for example, are shrimplike zooplankton that are just 2 inches (5 cm) long—but they're the main food of humongous blue whales.

ON THE MOVE

Zooplankton travel up and down in many parts of the ocean every day. They swim down in the water when the sun's shining, which puts them out of reach of seabirds feeding on the ocean's surface. They're also out of sight of fish and other sea creatures that hunt using their eyesight. When night comes, zooplankton travel back up to the surface and feed in the safety of darkness. The distance of this daily migration ranges from 1,312 to 3,280 feet (400 to 1,000 m) up and down, depending on the species. That's an extremely long journey for a tiny creature. If you migrated like this, you would travel 500 miles (800 km) in one direction and then travel back again the same distance—every day! But this behavior doesn't totally protect zooplankton from predators. Some predators migrate up and down, too—and there are also plenty of deep-swimming hunters to catch them.

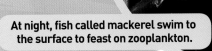

At night, fish called mackerel swim to the surface to feast on zooplankton.

GOOEY JELLYFISH

A jellyfish isn't a fish at all. It's a gooey animal that has no blood or heart. It doesn't have a brain, either. Instead, a jellyfish has a net of nerves that can sense light, touch, and chemicals. It has a single opening in its body for taking in food and expelling waste.

Most species of jellyfish have stinging tentacles for defense and for killing prey. Jellyfish don't attack people on purpose, but swimmers sometimes get stung by accidentally brushing up against the tentacles. Most jellyfish look like bells or little spaceships drifting in the water. This is the adult form of the jellyfish and is called the medusa. A jellyfish spends its early days as a polyp (a tubelike animal with one opening) that is attached to a surface. It becomes a medusa as it grows. A medusa floats with the currents and can also pump its body to move through the water.

Jellyfish range in size from tiny blobs about 0.4 inch (1 cm) wide to the biggest species, the lion's mane jellyfish, which can grow tentacles more than 100 feet (30.5 m) long! (see pages 66–67).

Jellyfish are related to animals called hydrozoa (which are often called jellyfish, too). Some hydrozoa live as individual polyps, but other species form colonies of polyps that drift like jellyfish. Amazingly, different polyps take on different jobs, like ants in an ant colony. Some adapt to capture food; others specialize in reproducing or digesting. One famous colonial hydrozoan that looks like a jellyfish is the man-o'-war, which can trail highly venomous tentacles up to 160 feet (50 m) long!

COMB COUSINS

Comb jellies are blobby like jellyfish, but they're not closely related. They look like oval balloons lined with zippers. These "zippers" are the combs—rows of bristles that beat to move the comb jelly through water. A comb jelly has eight of these combs.

The bristles, called cilia, reflect light in a way that turns them into rainbows of color. Many comb jellies also contain chemicals that allow them to flash blue and green colors. Most comb jellies have sticky tentacles for catching prey, but they don't have stingers like jellyfish do.

About **95 percent** of a jellyfish's body is made of **water.**

These young purple-striped jellies will develop stripes as they grow. This species lives along the coast of California.

LION'S MANE JELLYFISH

The lion's mane jellyfish is named for the shaggy tentacles that dangle from its round body. It has hundreds of these tentacles, which can grow to be more than 100 feet (30.5 m) long. Each tentacle contains stinging cells called nematocysts, which work like miniature harpoons.

The lion's mane jellyfish can't hear, and it can't see—it can only sense light and dark. But it has a sense of smell, taste, and touch. It catches prey by spreading its tentacles to form a net. The nematocysts sting any prey touched by the tentacles. Special tentacles called "oral arms" drag prey to its mouth, which is located on its underside. ("Oral" means "mouth.")

This venomous, giant jellyfish is gobbled up by predators such as leatherback sea turtles and fish. Some small fish even hang out among the jellyfish's tentacles! Young butterfish, for example, find safety from predators by swimming among the tentacles. Not that the jellyfish gets much thanks—butterfish often munch on its bell!

This big jellyfish starts life as a tiny larva. After hatching from its egg, the larva quickly settles on a surface such as the seafloor. There it grows into a polyp, which looks a little like a flower. It then produces new jellyfish by copying, or "cloning," itself. The copies pile up, so that the polyp looks a bit like a stack of dishes! The top "dish" breaks free to swim away and grow into a bell-shaped medusa.

FAMILY:	Cyaneidae
OTHER COMMON NAMES:	sea blubber, hair jellyfish
SCIENTIFIC NAME:	*Cyanea capillata*
SIZE:	Up to 8 feet (2.4 m) wide, not including tentacles
FOOD:	zooplankton, small fish, shrimp and other small crustaceans, comb jellies, other jellyfish
HABITAT:	open ocean
RANGE:	cold waters of the Arctic Ocean, North Atlantic Ocean, North Pacific Ocean from Alaska to Washington State, Baltic Sea; sometimes found as far south as the Gulf of Mexico in the Atlantic Ocean

Small silver fish hang out among the tentacles of a lion's mane jelly. Predators won't bother them there.

The largest lion's mane jellyfish on record had tentacles that measured **120 feet** (36.5 meters) long.

The common kingslayer is a box jellyfish no bigger than your thumb—but its **venom can kill** a human.

A swarm of box jellyfish swim close to shore.

BOX JELLYFISH

The box jellyfish contains one of the world's most deadly venoms. A touch from one of its tentacles is enough to kill a person. Fortunately, scientists have developed antivenom—a medicine that works against the jellyfish venom—which is life-saving if it's quickly injected into the victim of a sting.

The box jellyfish's sting isn't meant for humans, of course. Its actual purpose is for stunning and killing prey. The powerful venom is contained in nematocysts on the jellyfish's tentacles. A box jellyfish has up to 15 tentacles on each corner of its box-shaped bell. Each tentacle contains about 5,000 nematocysts.

Many jellyfish are mainly drifters, but the box jellyfish and its relatives are able to swim by pulsing their bells very strongly. They can even swim over, under, and around obstacles—and they can do this quickly! The box jellyfish can move as fast as 4.5 miles (7.2 km) an hour—faster than most people can walk.

Box jellyfish also have eyes—in fact, they have 24 of them! A box jellyfish has 4 sides, and there are 6 eyes clumped together on each side. In each clump, one eye is always looking upward. Scientists think these eyes let the jellyfish look out of the water to see mangrove trees. Why would a jellyfish need to see mangrove trees? Because the crustaceans they eat are often found hanging out on the trees' roots underwater.

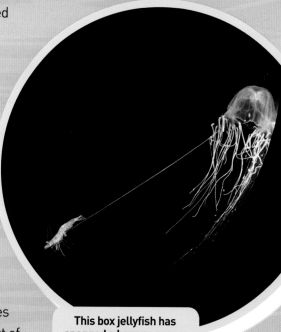

This box jellyfish has snagged a banana prawn with its tentacles. It will reel the catch to its mouth to eat it.

FAMILY:	Cyaneidae
OTHER COMMON NAMES:	sea wasp, marine stinger
SCIENTIFIC NAME:	*Chironex fleckeri*
SIZE:	up to 9.8 feet (3 m)
FOOD:	small fish, shrimp and other ocean crustaceans
HABITAT:	shallow coastal ocean waters; found in among mangroves and in freshwater rivers during breeding season and polyp stage
RANGE:	parts of Indian Ocean and Pacific Ocean around Australia and Southeast Asia

COLORFUL CORAL

Corals are small, soft-bodied animals. Like young jellyfish, they're tube-shaped polyps, with an opening for taking in food and getting rid of waste on one end. The most famous corals are stony corals. Stony corals build reefs in shallow, warm seas, where sunlight fills the water and the temperature doesn't drop below 64°F (18°C).

A reef has very humble beginnings. Its growth starts when polyps stick to a rock or other sturdy spot on the seabed. There the polyps grow, forming strong limestone cups around themselves. The reef enlarges as polyps grow new polyps on their bodies in a process called budding. The new polyps build their own limey skeletons, which add up over time to create a colony. Several colonies link up to form a reef. When polyps die, their skeletons remain. Living polyps build on top of them. Coral reefs grow very slowly, from 0.2 to 4 inches (0.5 to 10 cm) per year.

Coral reefs are colorful thanks to the algae that live inside polyps. A polyp gives the algae a place to live and supplies it with carbon dioxide and nutrients in the form of waste products. The algae make food by photosynthesis and share it with the polyp. A polyp gets about 90 percent of its algae's food!

Coral polyps are predators, too. They catch prey, such as plankton and fish, with their sticky tentacles and shoot it with nematocysts.

Two other main groups of corals are soft corals and deep-sea corals. Soft corals contain tough, flexible materials. But they don't have limestone skeletons and don't build reefs. Deep-sea corals live in cold, dark water at depths of up to 19,685 feet (6,000 m). They must catch all their own food.

A bleached coral looks bony.

COLORLESS CORAL

Coral polyps are sensitive to changes in water temperature, light levels, and salinity. Too much light, or water that's too warm, can cause polyps to eject their colorful algae. This causes the reef to turn white because the polyps lose their color without algae, leaving the limestone material as all that's visible. This process is called bleaching. Without algae, the polyps will also weaken and die.

Coral reefs can often recover from a bout of bleaching. But scientists are concerned that climate change will cause severe cases of bleaching by making seawater warmer and more acidic due to carbon dioxide building up in it.

Some **coral reefs** alive today got their start more than 50 million years ago!

Colorful soft corals and leather corals grow on a reef in Indonesia.

LIFE ON A CORAL REEF

Coral reefs are rainbow-colored gardens of life in the ocean! They cover less than one percent of the seafloor, yet about one-quarter of ocean species depend on them for food and shelter. Here are just a few of the many thousands of species that live on different coral reefs around the world.

Bargibant's pygmy seahorse lives on coral reefs in parts of the Pacific and Indian Oceans. It clings to a relative of coral known as a gorgonian or sea fan. This tiny seahorse is just over an inch (2.7 cm) long. Its colorful, bumpy skin camouflages it so well that it went undiscovered for many years.

Cleaner shrimp operate "cleaning stations" on coral reefs. A shrimp dances with a special movement to attract passing fish. If a fish stops, the shrimp climbs onto it and eats any tiny pests on the fish's body. The fish gets rid of harmful parasites, and the shrimp gets a meal. Some species of fish, called cleaner wrasses, clean other fish, too.

The **elephant ear sponge** grows on reefs near Florida and the Bahamas and in the Caribbean Sea. It's not elephant-size, but it can grow to be 6 feet (1.8 m) wide. It doesn't always look like an elephant's ear—it can also grow to look like a lump or a mat. Like other sponges, it filters bacteria and other food from seawater.

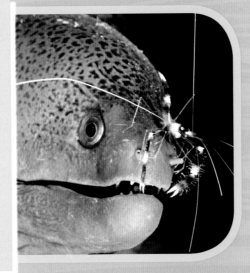

An anemone has stinging cells in its tentacles for killing prey, but **orange clownfish** live safely among them. Their bodies form a coat of mucus that shields them from stings. The clownfish hides from predators by ducking into the anemone, where it's protected by the tentacles. In return, the clownfish protects the anemone by chasing off polyp-eating predators such as butterflyfish.

The **golden wentletrap** is a yellow sea snail that lives on orange cup coral. Its bright color is a perfect camouflage in this setting. The snail eats cup coral and also lays its eggs on it. Orange cup coral doesn't contain any algae to make food, so it has to catch everything it eats. At night, it sticks out its tentacles to filter plankton from the water.

Staghorn corals look like deer antlers sticking out of a reef. But these "antlers" can be 6.6 feet (2 m) tall! A staghorn coral's branches can grow as much as 8 inches (20 cm) in one year. It lives in warm waters in parts of the western Atlantic Ocean. This species is suffering from harm caused by diseases, bleaching, and other problems. Efforts are being made to grow staghorn corals in labs and then "plant" them in the ocean.

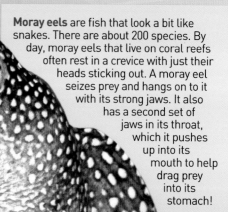

Moray eels are fish that look a bit like snakes. There are about 200 species. By day, moray eels that live on coral reefs often rest in a crevice with just their heads sticking out. A moray eel seizes prey and hangs on to it with its strong jaws. It also has a second set of jaws in its throat, which it pushes up into its mouth to help drag prey into its stomach!

A **Christmas tree worm's** two "trees" are actually frilly organs sticking out of its back. The worm uses them to take in oxygen from seawater and catch phytoplankton to eat. The rest of its body is safely hidden in a burrow that it has dug in the coral. If startled by a predator, the worm quickly yanks in its "trees" and disappears into its burrow.

The crown-of-thorns starfish lives in the Indian and Pacific Oceans. A big crown-of-thorns can have as many as 21 arms and measure up to 27.6 inches (70 cm) across. Venomous spines cover its body. This species feeds on coral polyps and can damage coral reefs when the crown-of-thorns population grows too large.

73

SPONGY SPONGES

Tubes, barrels, fans, vases, ropes, balls, mats, bushes, branches—sponges look like almost everything except animals! But they are animals—a fact we've known since the mid-1700s. Before that, people thought sponges were plants. You can't really blame them. Sponges can't move, and they don't have any true tissues or organs!

A sponge is made up of cells clumped on a skeleton. This skeleton is made of fibers called spongin or hard spikes called spicules. Some species' skeletons include both materials.

A typical sponge's outside is dotted with little openings called pores. Water flows into the sponge through the pores and out one or more larger openings, which are on the top or sides depending on the species. The sponge filters tiny particles of food from the flowing water. Cells in the channels that run through the sponge keep the water moving by waving tiny, whiplike structures. A few recently discovered deep-sea sponges, however, catch small prey with tiny hooks on their branches.

Animals that eat sponges include snails, chitons, and some kinds of sea slugs and fish. Marine worms, brittle stars, and other animals live in and on sponges. Decorator crabs stick sponges on their shells as camouflage. Many sponges contain algae that make food for them.

SPONGES IN YOUR HOUSE

That bright yellow sponge sitting by the kitchen sink isn't from the ocean. It's made in a factory out of plant fibers mixed with man-made materials. But some sponges used by people are natural sponges that were raised in coastal "sponge farms." The sponges are collected and then squeezed, washed, and dried until there are no more living cells left on the spongy skeletons.

bath sponge

The **huge** barrel sponge lives on reefs in and around the Caribbean Sea. It can grow to be 6 feet (1.8 m) wide and live for more than **2,000 years.**

A SPLENDOR OF SPONGES

Sponges are found at all depths in all oceans. They range in size from sponges less than 0.4 inch (1 cm) wide to ones that are bigger than an adult human. There are more than 5,000 known species of sponges, and more are being discovered as researchers explore deep-sea coral reefs.

"Encrusting" sponges are sponges that grow in sheets over other objects. They exist in a rainbow of colors. The bright color often signals that the sponge is poisonous and warns animals not to eat it. However, many sea slugs eat sponges and often recycle the poison into their own body cells to use as protection from predators, too!

The **branching vase sponge** usually looks like a bunch of tube-shaped vases. But tubes can also grow together to form a fanlike shape. This sponge is found in parts of the western Atlantic Ocean along coasts. There it grows on coral reefs and shallow seafloors where the rock bottom is only thinly covered with sand. Brittle stars often live in it.

Stovepipe sponges are another kind of tube-shaped sponge. They can grow up to 59 inches (150 cm) long. As many as 22 tubes may join together and share a thick base. Stovepipe sponges are pink or purple. They grow in deeper water than many coral reef sponges because their tubes are fragile and can break off in places where waves are active.

The **harp sponge** lives in water as deep as 11,500 feet (3,500 m). There it clings to the seafloor with its rootlike base. Unlike most other sponges, it feeds by catching prey instead of filtering water. Its rows of branches are lined with tiny hooks. When prey is caught, the sponge slowly seals it in a thin envelope of sponge cells and starts digesting it.

The **Pacific marine sponge** lives on reefs along the coasts of Papua New Guinea, the Solomon Islands, Vanuatu, and northern Australia. Its yellow or orange rubbery tubes look like a clump of pool noodles. Scientists are studying chemicals made by this sponge for their use as a cancer treatment.

Suberites domuncula is known as a "hermit crab sponge" because it often lives on snail shells being used by hermit crabs. Hermit crabs protect their soft bodies by wearing shells left behind by dead snails. The sponge grows until it completely covers the shell, and the crab may leave the shell and live in part of the sponge instead.

The **Venus's flower basket** is a sponge with a glassy skeleton. A web of tissue covers this skeleton. The sponge lives on rocky seafloors in the western Pacific in the Philippines. A pair of shrimp—one male, one female—often live inside this funnel-shaped sponge. Their behavior has made the Venus's flower basket a symbol of love in Japan.

The **fire sponge** got its name because touching it can cause a painful, burning rash. The chemical is meant to stop predators, but some kinds of fish, sea stars, and sea turtles can safely eat it. Fire sponges grow on rocks and among mangrove roots and seagrass meadows in parts of the western Atlantic from Florida south to Brazil.

MOLLUSKS

Do you look for shells on beaches? Shells are made by animals called mollusks. There are more than 90,000 species of mollusk. This large group includes everything from little snails in gardens to squid as long as trucks! As different as they are, all mollusks have a few things in common: They all have soft bodies made up of a head, a foot, and a bundle of guts.

Gastropods are mollusks that usually have a single shell, which is often spiral-shaped. Sea snails, such as whelks and limpets, are gastropods. So are sea slugs and nudibranchs, which lack shells. All gastropods have a rough "tongue" called a radula for feeding. Some species eat algae while others eat bivalves, worms, or fish.

Bivalves are mollusks with hinged shells. Each half of the two-part shell is called a valve. Clams, scallops, oysters, and mussels are all bivalves. Many kinds of clams spend their lives buried in mud or sand. They stretch their necklike siphons to the surface to get rid of waste and take in water so they can filter food from it. A clam uses its foot to pull itself deeper into the ground. Mussels and oysters don't burrow—they attach themselves to rocks and other sturdy spots. Scallops lie on the seafloor and can also "clap" their valves to jet through the water.

Chitons are mollusks with eight hard plates on their backs. They cling tightly to rocks while scraping algae off them.

Cephalopods are mollusks with jaws and limbs. These include octopuses, cuttlefish, and squid. Octopuses have eight arms lined with suckers. Cuttlefish and squid have eight arms, as well as two tentacles with suckers at the tip. These animals have an amazing ability to change the color and texture of their skin to communicate and to camouflage themselves.

MYSTERIOUS MOLLUSK

The chambered nautilus is a cephalopod with a shell. It's named after the "chambers," or compartments, inside the shell. Its soft body is tucked into the biggest chamber. Air in the other chambers helps the nautilus float.

More than 90 tentacles dangle from its shell. The tentacles don't have suckers. Instead, they have grooves and bumps that help grip crabs, fish, and other prey.

Nautiluses existed more than 400 million years ago—long before dinosaurs appeared on the scene! They have hardly changed in all that time.

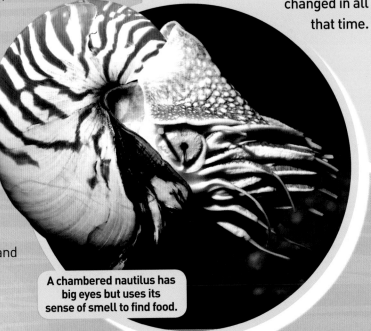

A chambered nautilus has big eyes but uses its sense of smell to find food.

The giant squid is the world's **longest** invertebrate (animal without a backbone). The largest giant squid ever measured was **59 feet** (18 m) long.

A giant octopus prowls the seafloor in the Sea of Japan off the Russian coast.

GIANT CLAM

The giant clam is well named—it's the world's biggest bivalve! It can grow to weigh more than 440 pounds (200 kg). A clam this size needs lots of food. Up to 90 percent of its diet consists of food produced by algae living in its flesh, which make food by photosynthesis. Without its algae, the clam would die.

Like other mollusks, the giant clam's body is made up mainly of muscle and organs surrounded by tissue. This tissue is called the mantle. The mantle not only contains the organs but also stretches out to form body parts, such as the big, colorful "lips" that stick out of the giant clam's shell. The mantle also produces the materials that form the shell.

A full-grown giant clam may look as if it's puckering up to give a big kiss, but its mantle is actually so large, it can't shut its shell completely. It wouldn't want to, anyway—the algae in the mantle need sunlight to make food. The algae live just under the mantle's surface. The mantle, which ranges in color from yellow-green to blue and purple, is lined with clear patches called windows. The windows help focus sunlight onto the algae.

People have harvested giant clams for food for a long time. Illegal hunting, however, removed too many giant clams from the wild. As a result, it has become rare and could become endangered. Scientists are raising giant clams in captivity to plant on coral reefs. People in the Philippines also grow the big bivalves in "clam farms" for use as food, which may help reduce how many wild clams are harvested.

Clams and oysters cover irritating particles such as sand with layers of smooth material produced by the mantle. The result: a pearl! A giant clam produced the largest known pearl, which weighs 14 pounds (6.4 kg).

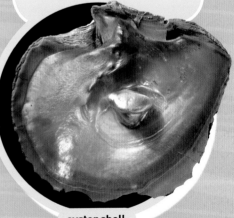

oyster shell with pearl

FAMILY:	Tridacnidae
OTHER COMMON NAMES:	Taklobo (Philippines)
SCIENTIFIC NAME:	*Tridacna gigas*
SIZE:	up to 4 feet (1.2 m) wide
FOOD:	plankton and other food filtered from seawater; food made by algae
HABITAT:	coral reefs, shallow lagoons
RANGE:	tropical Indian Ocean and Pacific Ocean, Red Sea

A giant clam in the Red Sea opens wide to let sunlight shine on its mantle.

MIMIC OCTOPUS

Octopuses are masters of disguise. They can change their skin color and even their texture to blend in with their surroundings. But the mimic octopus uses a different trick. It can change both its color and its behavior so that it looks like a poisonous fish or a venomous reptile!

If it sees a predator, the mimic octopus might clamp its arms together and zoom forward. As it swims, its body and arms ripple gently. This behavior makes it look like the banded sole, a flat-bodied fish that has poisonous flesh. The octopus can also choose to look like a predator itself. It changes its pattern to black-and-white stripes and flings its arms wide. This pose makes it look like a lionfish, which has spiky, venomous fins.

The mimic octopus can even imitate a venomous banded sea snake. It does this by hiding its body and six of its eight arms inside a burrow in the seafloor. It stretches the other two arms out of the burrow and wiggles them so they look like the two ends of a long snake.

Scientists discovered the mimic octopus in 1998. Some think this species also mimics other animals, such as a jellyfish and the mantis shrimp (pages 88–89). In 2011, researchers noticed a fish that seems to mimic the mimic octopus! It's called the harlequin jawfish and was observed swimming among a mimic octopus's arms, looking like nothing more than an extra arm.

Bet you didn't know

The wunderpus is a striped octopus that looks much like a mimic octopus. It's found in some of the same places as the mimic octopus, too. However, they can easily be told apart by their behavior: The wunderpus hunts in the evening and at dawn, unlike the mimic octopus, which hunts during the day.

wunderpus

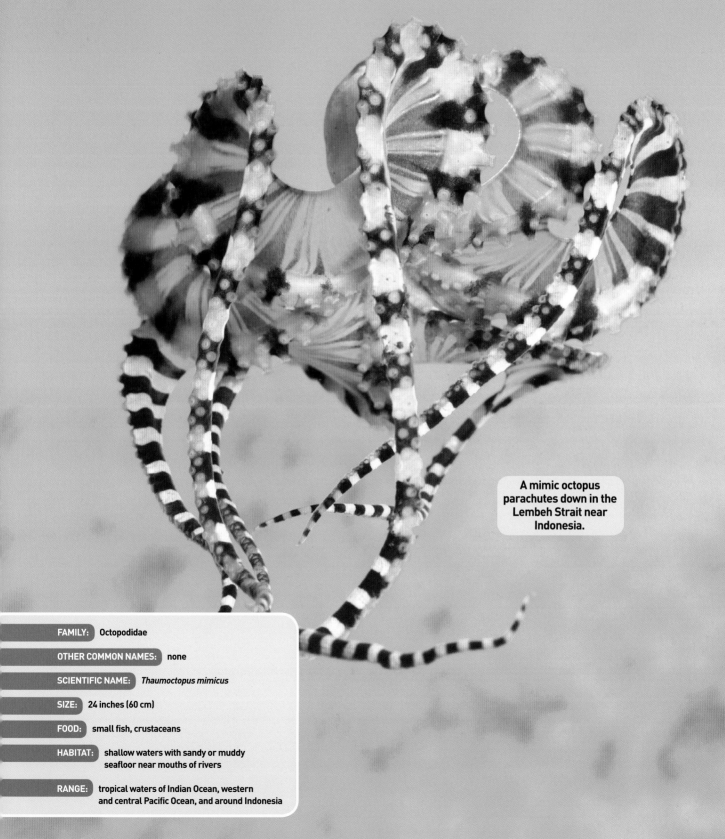

A mimic octopus parachutes down in the Lembeh Strait near Indonesia.

FAMILY: Octopodidae

OTHER COMMON NAMES: none

SCIENTIFIC NAME: *Thaumoctopus mimicus*

SIZE: 24 inches (60 cm)

FOOD: small fish, crustaceans

HABITAT: shallow waters with sandy or muddy seafloor near mouths of rivers

RANGE: tropical waters of Indian Ocean, western and central Pacific Ocean, and around Indonesia

83

HUMBOLDT SQUID

The squid captures its prey with its two long tentacles, which shoot out quickly and grab victims with their hooked tips. The prey is dragged toward the squid's mouth by its eight arms, which are lined with hundreds of suckers surrounded by small, toothlike hooks. Finally, it's sliced and diced by the squid's sharp beak.

A Humboldt squid starts life as a tiny egg clumped with a million or more other eggs in a jellylike blob that floats in the ocean. Scientists estimate that an egg mass contains from 600,000 to 2 million eggs, and that a female squid produces up to 20 of these masses in her life. Seabirds and other predators eat many of the eggs. The ones that hatch produce little squid that are only about .04 inch (1 mm) long. By the time a Humboldt squid is grown up, it will weigh about 110 pounds (50 kg), making it a fine meal for predators such as sperm whales, sharks, big fish, and fur seals.

A Humboldt squid's skin can change color from gray-white to orange to deep purple-red. On underwater cameras, the color changes look as if they ripple along the length of the squid's body. Scientists think the squid change colors to communicate with each other, but they don't know yet what the squid's messages are.

Humboldt squid have expanded where they live in recent years. They were once found mainly in tropical waters, but they now show up as far north as Alaska. Scientists are researching to find out if this range change is a result of warmer waters caused by El Niño events (pages 176–177).

A SQUID'S LIFE

The Humboldt squid lives a short and fierce life. This big squid, which can be larger than a person, lives only about one year—possibly two. During that time, it eats just about anything it can catch, including big fish such as salmon and hake. A hungry squid will eat smaller or injured squid, including squid caught on a fishing line. It sometimes even eats other Humboldt squid!

Scientists estimate that more than **10 million** Humboldt squid live in an area of just 25 square miles (65 sq km) in the Gulf of California.

A Humboldt squid zooms through the waters of the Sea of Cortez in the Gulf of California in Mexico.

FAMILY: Ommastrephidae

OTHER COMMON NAMES: jumbo squid, jumbo flying squid, red devil

SCIENTIFIC NAME: *Dosidicus gigas*

SIZE: up to 8.2 feet (2.5 m)

FOOD: zooplankton, fish, crustaceans, other squid

HABITAT: open ocean

RANGE: eastern Pacific Ocean from Alaska south to Chile, Gulf of California

ROUGH, TOUGH CRUSTACEANS

Crustaceans are animals as crusty as their name sounds! They have hard outer skeletons (called exoskeletons) and jointed legs. They're part of the large group of animals called arthropods, which also includes insects and spiders. Marine crustaceans include shrimp, crabs, barnacles, lobsters, and krill. They range in size from tiny water fleas to Japanese spider crabs with legs that span 13 feet (4 m).

Many marine crustaceans start life as small larvae that either drift as zooplankton or live on the seafloor. A larva changes into a miniature version of an adult. Its exoskeleton can't stretch to make room for its growing body, so the small crustacean will shed its exoskeleton and form a new one in order to grow bigger. A king crab, for example, may molt about 20 times over the course of its life.

Crustaceans live everywhere in the ocean and have adapted to feeding on a wide variety of foods. Little water fleas have fluffy "oars" to help them paddle as they feed on zooplankton. Crabs pinch enemies with their claws and also use them to pick up bits of dead animals to eat. Lobsters' strong claws crush and tear apart fish and other prey. Sea spiders' long legs help them tiptoe across the seafloor as they feed on prey, using their snoutlike mouths to pierce invertebrates and slurp their insides. Barnacles glue themselves upside down to rocks and then stick out their legs to grab plankton to eat!

Crustaceans, in turn, are eaten by many animals of both land and sea. They're a popular human food, too.

CRAFTY CRABS!

The abdomen (hind end) of a hermit crab is soft and unprotected. So the hermit crab uses old shells as armor. Some species of hermit crab put anemones on their shells for extra protection. The anemones sting predators and are "paid" by getting scraps from the crabs' meals (crabs are messy eaters!). When a crab needs a new, bigger shell, it removes the anemones from the old shell and sticks them on the new one.

Pompom crabs also use stinging anemones for self-defense. The crab holds an anemones in each claw. Hooks on the claws help the crab hang on to the anemones, which look like a cheerleader's pompoms when the crab waves them. These crabs are also called boxer crabs because they jab the anemones at other crabs and look as if they're boxing.

The Japanese spider crab can live up to **100 years.**

A spotted cleaner shrimp hangs out on an anemone as it waits for fish to stop by for a cleanup.

87

PEACOCK MANTIS SHRIMP

The peacock mantis shrimp hides in a burrow, watching carefully with its big eyes for prey. It kills by punching at snails, crabs, and other animals with special hammerlike claws that move as fast as 75 feet per second (23 m/sec)—a speed 50 times faster than a blink of your eye. This punch is so fast, it causes water to turn into vapor with a pop, a flash of light, and some heat, which adds to its force. A mantis shrimp can even punch through the glass of an aquarium tank!

The mantis shrimp's claws are so hard, they can be used 50,000 times without breaking. By the time they're worn out, the mantis shrimp will have molted and grown a new exoskeleton—equipped with brand-new claws for hammering. These claws are being studied by researchers who design new man-made materials for possible use in airplanes, armor, and sports helmets.

A peacock mantis shrimp is very protective of its burrows. It may use its clubs to pummel a trespasser, including another mantis shrimp. It usually aims for the trespassing mantis shrimp's tail—but that tail is thick and heavy, which protects it from the punch.

The male peacock mantis shrimp has brighter colors than the female. After mating and egg laying, a female mantis shrimp carries her bundle of eggs in her front legs. She guards them in her burrow and keeps them clean. She doesn't feed while caring for the eggs. The larvae that hatch will drift up, up, and away to the surface to live as plankton for a few weeks before returning to the seafloor to start their own exciting lives.

Bet you didn't know

A mantis shrimp's eyes are able to detect ultraviolet light, which is invisible to humans. Each eye is on a stalk and can be swiveled around independent of the other eye.

A peacock mantis shrimp stands guard at its burrow in the Andaman Sea off Thailand.

FAMILY: Odontodactylidae

OTHER COMMON NAMES: painted mantis shrimp, clown mantis shrimp

SCIENTIFIC NAME: *Odontodactylus scyllarus*

SIZE: 1.2 to 7 inches (3 to 18 cm)

FOOD: mollusks, crabs

HABITAT: near coral reefs on sandy, gravelly, or shell-littered seafloor

RANGE: warm waters in the Indian and Pacific Oceans

GIANT HERMIT CRAB

The giant hermit crab, like smaller species of hermits, must protect its soft abdomen inside a discarded snail shell. By the time it's an adult, it needs a really big shell, like that of the queen conch. This big shell can measure 6 to 12 inches (15 to 31 cm) in length.

The giant hermit crab uses its claws to poke through sand and mud for small bits of food. The right claw is usually bigger than the left. It's also the dominant claw, which means the crab is right-handed—or rather, right-clawed! A male giant hermit crab's right claw is extra big. Scientists think males may use their claws to battle other males over territory and mates.

After mating, a female giant hermit crab carries her eggs on her abdomen. The larvae that hatch spend from one to nearly three months floating in the plankton before turning into mini-giants in need of a snail shell.

Giant hermit crabs often share their borrowed homes with a tiny crustacean called the porcelain crab. This little crab tucks itself inside the hermit's shell, where it can feed on scraps from the big crab's meals. As many as 11 porcelain crabs may lodge in one shell! One or two zebra flatworms may also move in.

Bet you didn't know

Giant hermit crabs that are desperate for a new shell have been known to battle other crabs to get one. Sometimes they even kill live snails for their shells.

FAMILY:	Diogenidae
OTHER COMMON NAMES:	giant red hermit crab
SCIENTIFIC NAME:	*Petrochirus diogenes*
SIZE:	up to 7.8 inches (20 cm), including legs and claws
FOOD:	invertebrates, seaweed
HABITAT:	seagrass meadows, sandy seafloor near reefs, rocky shorelines, muddy seafloor around mangroves
RANGE:	Gulf of Mexico, Caribbean Sea, coastal waters from North Carolina to southern Florida in North America, coastal waters south to Brazil in South America

A giant hermit crab has hooks on its back legs that help it hold on to its adopted shell.

YETI CRAB

Imagine being able to grow snacks on your arms! That's what yeti crabs do. These crabs are crustacean sensations that live around deep-sea hydrothermal vents in the ocean.

The species of yeti crab shown here is so new to science, it hasn't gotten an official scientific name yet! But researchers have found that the fuzzy bristles on its body are covered with bacteria. These bacteria use energy and chemicals spewed out by hot-water vents to make food for themselves. The yeti crab, in turn, gets food by nibbling the bacteria off its bristles.

The first yeti crabs were discovered in March 2005. That's when a team of scientists in the submersible *Alvin* explored the seafloor about 900 miles (1,500 km) south of Easter Island in the South Pacific Ocean. There they found hairy white crabs at a depth of 7,540 feet (2,300 m). They were able to catch one using a "slurp gun," which sucks up specimens like a vacuum cleaner, and bring it back to the lab for further study.

Researchers found that the strange crabs were unlike any other kind of crab. They were so different, scientists had to create a group, called a "family," for them. They learned that the bristles covering the crabs' legs and claws were used for "farming" bacteria. Another species of yeti crab with shaggy claws has also been found in the Pacific near Costa Rica in South America.

The crab shown here was one of two species of yeti crabs with fuzzy bellies that were discovered in the Atlantic Ocean near Antarctica. Scientists think that these crabs' ancient ancestors lived along mid-ocean ridges in the Pacific. Over time, ocean currents helped the species spread to hydrothermal vents between the tip of South America and the continent of Antarctica.

Bet you didn't know

Kiwa tyleri is the other fuzz-bellied yeti crab scientists found in the South Atlantic Ocean. It lives on an ocean ridge around vents spewing water that's hotter than 700°F (370°C). *K. tyleri* crabs crowd around the vents so thickly, scientists have counted more than 700 crabs piled up in a space no bigger than a bathtub! The crabs cluster around vents because the vents are a warm spot in an otherwise freezing-cold ocean. The crabs' bacteria "farms" also need the chemicals in the warm water to make food.

FAMILY:	Kiwaidae
OTHER COMMON NAMES:	Hoff yeti crab
SCIENTIFIC NAME:	*Kiwa sp. tyleri*
SIZE:	1.4 to 1.5 inches (3.6 to 3.7 cm)
FOOD:	bacteria, possibly other hydrothermal species
HABITAT:	deep-sea hydrothermal vents
RANGE:	Indian Ocean

The yeti crab is named after the Yeti, which is a mythical **"abominable snowman"** said to live in the Himalaya mountains of Asia.

ECHINODERMS

Echinoderms are animals with a skeleton of tough plates locked together and covered by hard skin that often has prickles. Their circular-shaped bodies are symmetrical, with arms or other appendages that extend outward from the center. You can easily see this in sea stars, but even a sausage-shaped sea cucumber shows the pattern if you look at it from one end.

Crinoids are echinoderms with cuplike bodies and five or more arms. Some crinoids are called sea lilies because they look like flowers on stalks attached to the seafloor. Other crinoids called feather stars do not have stalks and can use their fluffy limbs for swimming. Both sea lilies and feather stars feed on small particles of food in the water.

Sea cucumbers use tentacles around their mouths to eat plankton and slurp up particles from the seafloor. If threatened by a predator, some species eject their guts to scare it away! They grow new guts later. Other species spit out sticky white threads that tangle up predators.

Brittle stars have longer, thinner, more flexible arms than sea stars. Unlike sea stars, they have muscles for moving these arms, so they can move much faster. Common brittle stars lie on the seafloor with their arms linked together, so currents don't wash them away. To feed, each star holds up an arm or two to catch plankton.

Sea urchins and sand dollars have tube feet, like sea stars. Sea urchins are spiny and round, with sharp teeth for feeding on algae. A sand dollar is like a squashed sea urchin. It feeds on algae and tiny animals in sand and mud. This animal is called the slate pencil urchin.

Sea stars have a central disk surrounded by arms—usually five, but some species have more. Each arm is lined with tube feet that work like suction cups. A sea star can clamp its arms around a clam's shell and slowly force the clam to open just a bit. Then the sea star turns its stomach inside out and pushes it into the shell, where it digests its meal.

Echinoderms do **not** have **brains.**

SUNFLOWER STAR

The sunflower star is the world's largest sea star. It also has the most arms—up to 24 of them! It doesn't start off with all those arms, however. It starts life as a tiny larva floating in seawater, eating phytoplankton. After about 10 weeks, it drifts to the seafloor and becomes a five-armed sea star. Then it begins to grow more arms. First, it grows a single arm so that it has a total of six. Then arms begin growing in pairs until the sea star has up to two dozen.

Like other sea stars, a sunflower star can grow a new arm to replace one that is lost. Sea stars can also deliberately drop arms to escape a predator. The lost arm can grow into an entirely new sea star if a bit of the original body is attached to it.

A sunflower star moves pretty quickly—for a sea star. It wriggles after prey at speeds up to 40 inches (1 m) per minute. If a predators such as a big fish attacks a sunflower star, it gives off chemicals that warn other sea stars in the area.

Bet you didn't know

Most sea stars look a lot like stars—even if they don't have as many arms as a sunflower star. But some sea stars look more like bats, cushions, and even cookies! The granulated sea star, for example, has plump arms that make it look like a rubber glove filled with water. Its funny shape has earned it another common name: doughboy star.

FAMILY: Asteriidae

OTHER COMMON NAMES: sunflower sea star

SCIENTIFIC NAME: *Pycnopodia helianthoides*

SIZE: up to 39 inches (1 m) wide

FOOD: fish, crabs, barnacles, chitons, mussels, clams, sea snails, sea cucumbers, sea urchins, sand dollars, other sea stars

HABITAT: muddy, sandy, gravelly, or rocky coastal areas in the intertidal and subtidal zone

RANGE: Pacific Ocean coastal waters from the Aleutian Islands of Alaska south to San Diego, California

A sunflower star has about **15,000 tube feet** on the underside of its body and arms.

LEOPARD SEA CUCUMBER

If you visit a shallow seafloor and see a polka-dotted sausage the size of a loaf of bread, it's likely to be the leopard sea cucumber. This echinoderm has leathery, spotted skin that covers an endoskeleton (skeleton inside the body) made up of small, hard plates. The plates are linked by tough connective material. The animal's underside is lined with rows of tiny tentacles called tube feet, which are used for walking.

The sea cucumber feeds by slowly trudging along the seafloor, picking up grains of sand with tentacles that surround its mouth. Each grain is covered with a thin layer of bacteria and other microscopic organisms. This material, as well as bits of algae and other particles in sand and mud, keeps the sea cucumber well fed as it vacuums up the seafloor. The sand and anything else that can't be digested is pooped out as waste.

If a predator attacks the leopard sea cucumber, it has a nasty surprise for it. Sticky white threads suddenly burst out of its hind end! These threads are called Cuvierian tubules. They contain substances that are poisonous to fish and also irritate skin. Predators can also get tangled in the stretchy, sticky tubules.

But a small, slender fish called the pearlfish is not bothered by this defense. The pearlfish is so at home with the sea cucumber, it lives in the sea cucumber's body! A pearlfish actually swims right into the sea cucumber's hind end to shelter there. It may even eat some of the sea cucumber's guts while inside. Fortunately, a sea cucumber can regrow its organs.

Bet you didn't know

A tiny shrimp called the emperor shrimp sometimes hangs out on leopard sea cucumbers. It's thought to eat parasites it finds on a cucumber's skin. Emperor shrimp also buddy up with other species of sea cucumbers, as well as sea slugs.

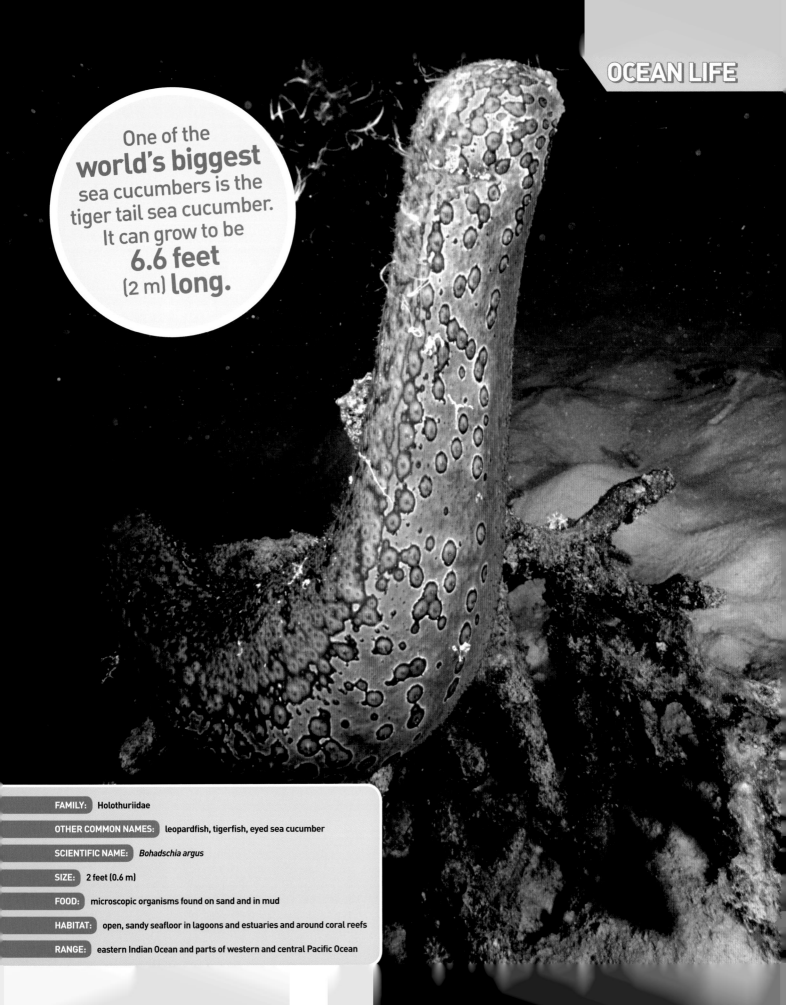

One of the **world's biggest** sea cucumbers is the tiger tail sea cucumber. It can grow to be **6.6 feet** (2 m) **long.**

FAMILY:	Holothuriidae
OTHER COMMON NAMES:	leopardfish, tigerfish, eyed sea cucumber
SCIENTIFIC NAME:	*Bohadschia argus*
SIZE:	2 feet (0.6 m)
FOOD:	microscopic organisms found on sand and in mud
HABITAT:	open, sandy seafloor in lagoons and estuaries and around coral reefs
RANGE:	eastern Indian Ocean and parts of western and central Pacific Ocean

SEA SQUIRTS

Meet your distant cousin, the sea squirt! Never mind that it looks like a rubbery bag with two spouts. It belongs to the same group, or phylum, that you do: the Chordata.

Most animals in Chordata are vertebrates—animals with backbones. Sea squirts, however, are invertebrates like octopuses or clams—no backbones! So how did they end up in Chordata? The answer is found in the young, or larval, form of the sea squirt.

A sea squirt larva's body contains a stiff rod called a notochord. It also has a nerve cord. These body parts are like the ones found in the bodies of vertebrates as they grow and change inside an egg, like a bird, or inside the mother's body, like a human. In a vertebrate, however, these structures disappear into the backbone and spinal cord. In a sea squirt, they just disappear.

When a sea squirt larva is ready to become an adult, its body absorbs its tail, notochord, and nerve cord. This happens very quickly, in just a few hours—or even just a few minutes or seconds—depending on the species. Most species of sea squirts attach themselves to rocks and other hard surfaces and then stay there the rest of their lives. Some species mesh together to form colonies.

A sea squirt eats by pulling water into its baggy body through one of its two siphons. The water flows through a basketlike filter, sticky with mucus, which traps food particles. The waste is squirted out from the other siphon.

Sea squirts belong to a group of animals known as tunicates. This word refers to the tough covering, or "tunic," on a sea squirt's body.

BIG SQUIRT

Imagine going for a dive and meeting a glowing, blue-green tube longer than a pickup truck snaking through the water! You've just encountered a pyrosome, a name that means "fire body."

A pyrosome is a colony of tunicates. It's made up of hundreds or thousands of tiny squirtlike individuals, called zooids, contained in a jellylike tunic. They're all copies, or clones, of each other because the whole colony starts with one zooid that reproduces itself. Each zooid takes in water, filters out food, and then ejects the water into the hollow center of the tube. Their combined squirting moves the colony through the water.

A pyrosome drifts in the waters off Pico Island in the Azores.

The two siphons of a sea squirt are easily seen on these blue squirts.

FISH

You and a tuna fish have something important in common: You're both vertebrates—animals with backbones. Fish make up more than half of all vertebrate species. More than 30,000 species of fish have been described by scientists—and about 150 new species of ocean fish are discovered each year!

Fish are adapted for life underwater, with fins for swimming and the ability to absorb oxygen from water. Most fish breathe through slits, called gills, that are located on the sides of their head. Water enters the fish's mouth and then flows across blood-rich, thin sheets in the gills. These sheets take in oxygen from the water, in much the same way as your lungs absorb oxygen from air. Some fish can also gulp air and absorb oxygen through areas in their throats or digestive organs, and a few species have evolved special organs for air breathing.

A ray is a fish that looks like a bat! It swims by flapping its winglike fins. The largest species is the giant manta ray, which can measure up to 26 feet (8 m) wide. This huge fish is harmless, however—unless you're plankton! It uses the fins on its head to sweep plankton into its mouth.

Colorful **angelfish** species live on coral reefs in tropical parts of the Atlantic Ocean, Indian Ocean, and Pacific Ocean. They eat algae and small invertebrates, such as shrimp. All angelfish have a sharp spine on the bottom edge of each gill cover, which helps protect them from predators. The young of many species have different colors and patterns than adults.

The **shortfin mako** is a shark found around the world in all but the coldest ocean waters. It can grow to be 12.5 feet (3.8 m) and weigh up to 1,260 pounds (570 kg). It can hit speeds up to 22 miles (35 km) per hour, making it the fastest shark species. It feeds on other speedy fish, such as tuna and swordfish, and also eats squid—as well as other sharks!

Groupers are fish with big mouths and stout bodies. They live in warm waters of the Pacific, Atlantic, and Indian Oceans. Many species hunt fish and crustaceans on coral reefs. Groupers range in size from a species that is barely as long as your finger to the giant goliath grouper, which can be 8.2 feet (2.5 m) long.

Many species of small fish in the wide-open ocean find safety in numbers by swimming together in schools. A predator can find it hard to pick out individual prey. Sometimes, fish will even form a huge "bait ball" when they panic, with every fish trying to hide in the middle. Some predators, however, simply charge into the bait ball and gobble up fish right and left.

BONY FISH

"Bony fish" form the biggest group of fish.

These fish all have skeletons made out of bone. They make up more than 96 percent of all living species of fish. About two-thirds of bony fish live in the ocean for most or all of their lives (some species migrate up and down rivers of freshwater).

Bony fish have very flexible fins. They can twist, spread, and fold their fins to stop short, turn sharply, and even swim backward. They have the same senses of sight, hearing, touch, taste, and smell that you do. Fish also have a row of sense organs running down their sides. They help a fish detect predators and prey and also help schools of fish swim together.

Long, venomous spines form part of the fin on top of a lionfish's body. The lionfish also flares long fins from its sides to force prey into a corner, where it can be easily caught. Lionfish are normally found only in parts of the Indian and Pacific oceans, but they now also live in the Atlantic in the Caribbean and along the coast of Florida and other states. These fish don't have any natural predators in the Atlantic, and their appetite for small fish and other prey is posing a threat to coral reefs and other habitats. Scientists are keeping a close watch on how this "invasive species" is affecting sea life.

Sockeye salmon start life in a lake, stream, or river. They spend from one to three years in this freshwater habitat. Then they migrate downriver to the Pacific Ocean. A few years later, sockeyes migrate back to where they hatched to mate and lay eggs. They change color from silver to red and green as they travel upstream. After mating, the adults die.

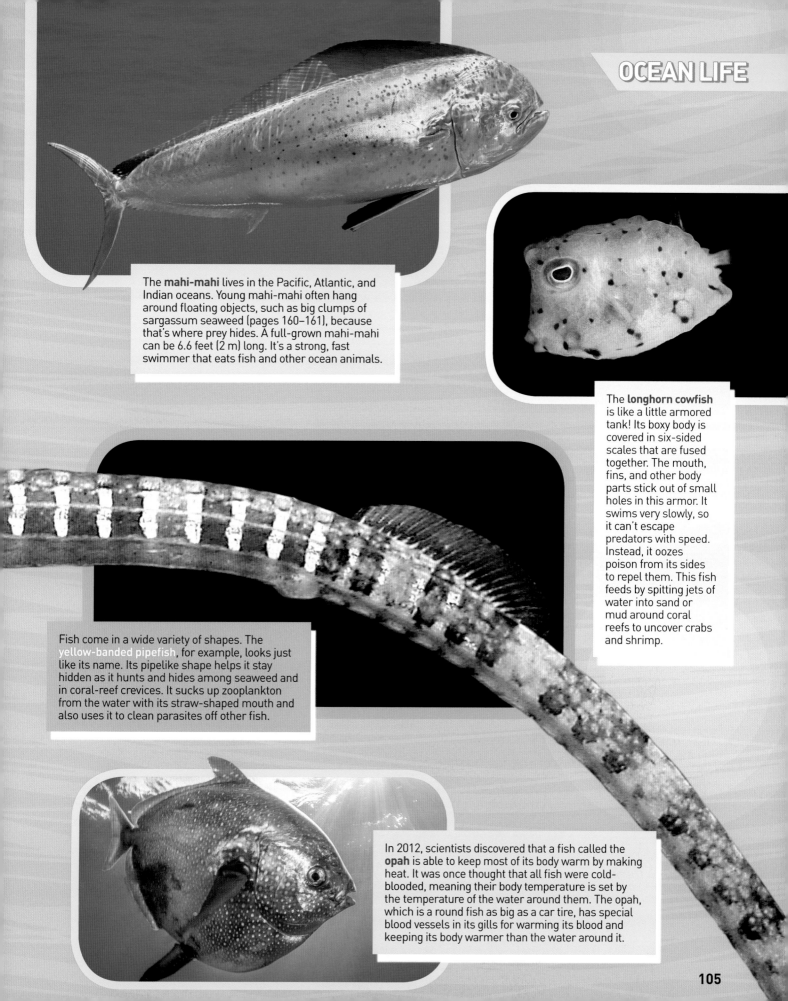

The **mahi-mahi** lives in the Pacific, Atlantic, and Indian oceans. Young mahi-mahi often hang around floating objects, such as big clumps of sargassum seaweed (pages 160–161), because that's where prey hides. A full-grown mahi-mahi can be 6.6 feet (2 m) long. It's a strong, fast swimmer that eats fish and other ocean animals.

The **longhorn cowfish** is like a little armored tank! Its boxy body is covered in six-sided scales that are fused together. The mouth, fins, and other body parts stick out of small holes in this armor. It swims very slowly, so it can't escape predators with speed. Instead, it oozes poison from its sides to repel them. This fish feeds by spitting jets of water into sand or mud around coral reefs to uncover crabs and shrimp.

Fish come in a wide variety of shapes. The **yellow-banded pipefish**, for example, looks just like its name. Its pipelike shape helps it stay hidden as it hunts and hides among seaweed and in coral-reef crevices. It sucks up zooplankton from the water with its straw-shaped mouth and also uses it to clean parasites off other fish.

In 2012, scientists discovered that a fish called the **opah** is able to keep most of its body warm by making heat. It was once thought that all fish were cold-blooded, meaning their body temperature is set by the temperature of the water around them. The opah, which is a round fish as big as a car tire, has special blood vessels in its gills for warming its blood and keeping its body warmer than the water around it.

SAILFISH

The sailfish is the fastest fish in the sea! It can zip at speeds up to 68 miles an hour (110 km/h). A sailfish might hit this speed when it leaps out of the water, or when it rushes to attack its prey.

Most of the time, however, a sailfish cruises along at a lower speed. Sailfish often swim near the surface of the water, and sometimes their sails even stick out of the water. The sail, as you might guess, gives this species its name. The sail is actually its first back, or dorsal, fin. This fish can fold down its sail when it wants to move fast.

To catch prey, a group of sailfish cooperates to herd a large school of small fish. They flare their sails to startle their prey. Then, again and again, sailfish take turns darting into the school and slashing back and forth with their swordlike bills. This action injures a number of fish, making them easier to catch and eat.

The sailfish's hunting ability is helped by special muscles under its brain that produce heat. This heat warms its brain and eyes and helps the sailfish see better as it hunts in deep, cold water.

Scientists once thought there were two species of sailfish—one in the Atlantic Ocean, the other in the Pacific and Indian Oceans. Today, they're considered to be the same species.

Bet you didn't know

A sailfish is usually blue and silver, but it often changes colors as it hunts. It may turn black, develop stripes, or sport blue, silver, and orange dots. Scientists aren't sure why.

FAMILY:	Istiophoridae
OTHER COMMON NAMES:	Indo-Pacific sailfish, Atlantic sailfish
SCIENTIFIC NAME:	*Istiophorus platypterus*
SIZE:	up to 11 feet (3.4 m)
FOOD:	octopuses, squid, and fish such as tunas, mackerels, sardines, and anchovies
HABITAT:	coastal and island waters as well as open ocean
RANGE:	Atlantic, Pacific, and Indian Oceans

Sardines form a bait ball as they flee from a hungry pair of sailfish.

A porcupinefish can **inflate** its body to about **three times** its normal size.

SPOT-FIN PORCUPINEFISH

Most of the time, a spot-fin porcupinefish looks sort of cuddly. It has big eyes, a polka-dotted body, and a wide mouth that looks as if it's smiling a little. But a frightened porcupinefish turns into a huge ball of prickles!

If threatened by a predator (or a curious diver), the porcupinefish quickly swallows a lot of water. The water inflates a stretchy, stomach-like sac, which bulges into other parts of the porcupinefish's insides and inflates its elastic skin. Its tail and fins disappear as they're surrounded by the blown-up body. This action makes the spines, which normally lay flat on its body, stick out in all directions. These spines can be up to 2 inches (5 cm) long. A predator may decide to find prey that's smaller and less painful to swallow.

A porcupinefish's own meals aren't easy to eat. It feeds mainly on animals with strong shells and exoskeletons, such as sea snails and sea urchins. But that's not a problem for the porcupinefish. It has strong jaw muscles and teeth that are fused together to form a powerful beak for crunching.

Porcupinefish are solitary animals. They would rather not be noticed than be forced to puff up. Their spotted pattern helps camouflage them. They hide by day and emerge at night to feed.

Bet you didn't know

Porcupinefish are related to pufferfish, which also inflate their bodies but don't have long spines. Some species of porcupinefish and pufferfish contain a deadly poison in their skin and some of their organs. A single fish contains enough poison to kill 30 people.

FAMILY:	Diodontidae
OTHER COMMON NAMES:	black-spotted porcupinefish, giant porcupinefish
SCIENTIFIC NAME:	*Diodon hystrix*
SIZE:	15.8 to 35.8 inches (40 to 91 cm)
FOOD:	crustaceans, mollusks, marine worms, echinoderms
HABITAT:	near shores in lagoons, on reefs, under ledges, in caves, around seamounts and shipwrecks
RANGE:	warm coastal and island waters of Atlantic Ocean and Pacific Ocean; western Indian Ocean; Mediterranean Sea; Red Sea

GREENTHROAT PARROTFISH

Crunch! Chomp! Crunch! Some divers report that they hear parrotfish before they see them. That's because parrotfish graze on algae that grows on coral, and their teeth make noise as they scrape on the coral and bite off small chunks. This gritty meal doesn't hurt a parrotfish's mouth. Its hard, sharp teeth are fused together so that they form a strong beak, like a parrot's. The parrotfish also has rows of teeth in its throat that grind the meal once it's swallowed.

What goes in must come out—and what comes out of parrotfish includes sand made out of coral! The beautiful white coral beaches so popular with tourists are made up largely of coral sand pooped out by parrotfish. Some big species of parrotfish produce as much as 840 pounds (381 kg) of sand a year.

The oddity of the parrotfish doesn't stop there. Many parrotfish species also make their own sleeping bags at night—out of mucus! The mucus comes from glands near the gills. It takes less than an hour for the fish to ooze a snooze bag. Scientists haven't pinned down the reason for the bag. It may protect the fish from predators or blood-sucking parasites.

Parrotfish are also famous for their beautiful colors—another feature they share with parrots in addition to their beaks. The greenthroat parrotfish is named after the colorful male of this species. Female greenthroat parrotfish aren't green—they're dark brown with white spots.

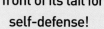

Bet you didn't know

The blue tang lives on coral reefs in parts of the Indian and Pacific Oceans. Like the parrotfish, it eats algae. It has tiny, sharp teeth for nibbling algae out of nooks and crannies. The blue tang is both blue and yellow when it's young. It becomes totally blue when it's full grown. It's also called the common surgeon because it has two scalpel-sharp spines in front of its tail for self-defense!

FAMILY:	Scaridae
OTHER COMMON NAMES:	Singapore parrotfish, green-face parrotfish, blue-faced parrotfish, dusky parrotfish
SCIENTIFIC NAME:	*Scarus prasiognathos*
SIZE:	up to 27.5 inches (70 cm)
FOOD:	algae
HABITAT:	coral reefs
RANGE:	tropical waters of Indian Ocean and western Pacific Ocean

A parrotfish doesn't have a stomach. Its **throat and intestines** do a fine job of **digesting** its food without one.

A greenthroat parrotfish nibbles on algae.

SHARKS, RAYS, AND SKATES

Sharks, rays, skates, and little-known fish called chimaeras form a group called the "cartilaginous fish." These fish don't have bony skeletons. Instead, their skeletons are made of a tough, flexible material called cartilage—the same material that forms your nose and ears.

Most sharks are shaped like torpedoes, which helps them zoom quickly through the water. Rays and skates, however, have flat bodies and "fly" underwater by flapping wide, winglike fins. Chimaeras are big-eyed fish with large fins and slender tails. A shark's skin is covered with toothlike points called dermal denticles that make it rough, like sandpaper. Many skates and rays have rows of thorny denticles on their backs.

Cookiecutter sharks range from 16.5 to 22 inches (42 to 56 cm) in length. But they prey on larger fish, seals, and even whales. These little sharks use their suction-cup lips to attach themselves to their prey's body. Then they spin around so their sharp teeth carve out a round lump of flesh to eat.

The **jawless fish** make up the third, and smallest, group of fish. This group includes lampreys and hagfish. Like sharks, they have cartilage skeletons. Unlike sharks, they don't have jaws. Instead, lampreys cling to prey with suction-cup mouths and use their rasping teeth to drill a hole through its skin. A hagfish has a rough, tongue-like structure for catching marine worms and tearing flesh from fish—usually dead or dying ones.

Chimaeras are distant relatives of sharks, rays, and skates. They have beaklike mouths with teeth for crushing the shells and exoskeletons of prey they find in the seafloor. Chimaeras also have a spine at the base of a fin on the back, which is venomous in some species. The spotted ratfish is a chimaera that's common in parts of the eastern Pacific Ocean.

A **great hammerhead shark's** eyes sit at either end of its wide head. This arrangement gives the shark excellent vision for hunting fish, squid, and other prey. Like other sharks, the hammerhead can also sense the weak electrical field that surrounds living things. That's how it finds stingrays hidden in the sand!

A **skate**, like a ray, has a flattened body. Its tail, however, is thicker, and it doesn't have venomous spines. But it does have thornlike spikes on its back and tail. The common skate, which lives in the northern Atlantic Ocean and nearby seas, is the largest species. It measures up to 8.2 feet (2.5 m) in length.

The **thresher shark** measures up to 24.9 feet (7.6 m) long. About half that length is made up of the long upper part of its tail. The shark uses its tail to herd schools of fish. It then strikes at the fish with its tail to stun them before grabbing and eating them.

Stingrays have flattened bodies and long tails, with eyes on top of the body and a mouth on the underside. They typically have one or more sharp, venomous spines on the tail, which they use for self-defense. The yellow stingray lives in warm coastal waters of the western Atlantic Ocean, where it hunts for shrimp, clams, crabs, worms, and fish on the sandy seafloor.

GREAT WHITE SHARK

The great white shark is the lion of the seas.

It is a powerful predator that swims as fast as 25 miles an hour (40 km/h) and may even zip in short bursts up to 35 miles an hour (56 km/h)—that's about as fast as a racehorse runs. It can smell a single drop of blood drifting in 26 gallons (100 L) of water. And it can sniff out a tiny bit of blood in the water from a distance of 3 miles (5 km)! Like other fish, it also has a sensitive "lateral line" running down each side of its body that can pick up faint vibrations in the water, which helps it sense the movement of prey.

A great white shark's mouth is a huge cave filled with razor-sharp teeth—dozens of them. It has about 300 teeth lined up in several rows. About 50 of these teeth are in use. The rest are folded back and lie in wait for their turn. If the shark loses a tooth, a replacement tooth moves into place from behind. New teeth are produced continually, so a great white shark may grow many thousands of teeth over the course of its long life (this species can live for 70 years or more).

Even though it can gobble up a whole seal at once, the great white is actually pretty picky about what it eats. It uses its teeth to test unfamiliar objects to see if they're edible. The teeth move in the jaw as the shark applies pressure, so it can feel the object just as you might use your hands to squeeze a fruit to see if it's ripe.

But a shark's "gentle" nibble can be dangerous to a fragile human. Most shark "attacks" on swimmers are the result of sharks being curious or simply mistaking people for their natural prey. Sharks don't target people as food because we're just too bony. A shark would rather eat a plump sea lion!

Bet you didn't know

A great white shark can bite off 44 pounds (20 kg) of fat and flesh from the body of a dead whale with just one snap and a shake of its head. So turning a seal into "fast food" comes very naturally to this predator!

A great white shark's **mouth** can be 4.3 feet (1.3 m) wide.

FAMILY: Lamnidae

OTHER COMMON NAMES: white shark, white death, maneater

SCIENTIFIC NAME: *Carcharodon carcharias*

SIZE: 13.1 to 23 feet (4 to 7 m)

FOOD: seals, sea lions, elephant seals, dolphins, fish, sea turtles, seabirds, squid, crustaceans, remains of dead whales

HABITAT: tropical to cold (not freezing) ocean waters, often near coasts

RANGE: Atlantic, Pacific, and Indian Oceans

WHALE SHARK

The biggest fish in the world is also the ocean's gentle giant. The whale shark can grow to be almost as long as a typical 18-wheeler truck. It can weigh up to 37 tons (34,000 kg)—more than four times as much as a male African elephant! A whale shark's mouth is big, too. It's up to 5 feet (1.5 m) across—you could just about fit a bicycle into it. Inside this mouth, about 300 rows of little teeth sit in each jaw. But the whale shark doesn't use them for eating fish. Instead, it filters plankton from seawater.

A whale shark feeds by swimming with its huge mouth wide open to let water flow into its mouth and through its gills. Inside the gills are netlike pads called gill rakers, which filter out plankton. The filters in the gill rakers are so fine, they can trap prey that is just 0.04 inch (1 mm) in size. A whale shark can also suck water into its mouth to filter it. When the shark shuts its mouth, water is forced out of the gills and the filtered food is swallowed.

Like other big sharks, the whale shark has few predators when it's an adult. Some whale sharks have scars that show where a killer whale or another shark may have bitten them. The biggest threats to whale sharks are people. In some countries, they are hunted for food and leather. But other places, such as India and the Philippines, have protected this species by banning fishing for whale sharks.

Bet you didn't know

A whale is a mammal and usually has one young at a time. A whale shark, however, may give birth to as many as 300 pups in one litter! Many of them are probably eaten by predators. Pups that survive grow quickly and can live to be 100 years old or more.

FAMILY:	Rhincodontidae
OTHER COMMON NAMES:	basking shark
SCIENTIFIC NAME:	*Rhincodon typus*
SIZE:	up to 65.6 feet (20 m)
FOOD:	zooplankton, phytoplankton, small fish and squid
HABITAT:	coastal waters, lagoons
RANGE:	tropical and warm waters of Atlantic, Pacific, and Indian Oceans and their seas, except for Mediterranean Sea

The whale shark has the **thickest skin** of any animal. Skin on its back can be up to 4 inches (10 cm) thick.

A whale shark swims near Australia's coast. Some of the fish swimming near it eat parasites off the shark's skin.

FAMILY: Mobulidae

OTHER COMMON NAMES: giant mobula ray, devil fish, Mediterranean devil ray

SCIENTIFIC NAME: *Mobula mobular*

SIZE: up to 17 feet (5.2 m) wide

FOOD: plankton, small shrimplike crustaceans, small fish

HABITAT: deep water over continental shelves along coasts

RANGE: northeastern Atlantic Ocean and Mediterranean Sea

GIANT DEVIL RAY

Like the whale shark (pages 116–117), the giant devil ray is a filter feeder. It uses the two paddle-shaped flaps on the front of its head to wave plankton toward its mouth as it swims. The water is strained by sheets of tissue in the gills. Also like the whale shark, its jaws contain many rows of very small teeth.

Rays sometimes leap out of the water and seem to fly through the air. Devil rays and other species of rays have been observed zooming out of the ocean and then landing back in the water with a huge splash. Munk's devil rays, for example, can leap more than 6.6 feet (2 m) high. Scientists think the behavior may be part of a display for attracting a mate, as it's often performed when rays are gathering in large numbers. But it might just be a way a ray can play!

This big ray has few predators, and historically hasn't been heavily hunted by humans in most places where it lives. But today it's an endangered species. One of the biggest threats to its survival is being accidentally caught in nets set for other kinds of fish. Some of these nets are used illegally in parts of its range. People are working to do a better job of enforcing laws meant to protect rays. In the Middle East, for example, scientists who study devil rays are educating fishers in the region about how rare the rays are and why there are laws to protect them.

A smoothtail mobula leaps in the Gulf of California.

SEA TURTLES

Sea turtles are reptiles that are adapted for a life at sea. Their front legs have evolved into huge flippers for swimming, and their hind legs into paddles for steering. Like land turtles, the world's seven species of sea turtles have shells, but they can't pull their heads, tails, and limbs into them like land turtles can. Unlike land turtles, sea turtles live in salt water, and salt builds up in their bodies. They get rid of this extra salt by shedding salty tears from their eyes.

Most sea turtle species are listed by the International Union for Conservation of Nature (IUCN) as being in danger of extinction. Threats to sea turtles include getting accidentally caught in fishing nets, loss of habitat, and being used as food. Fortunately, many people worldwide are working to help sea turtles. In the United States, for example, shrimp-fishing boats are required to use special nets, which stop sea turtles from getting caught.

Green turtles hang around coral reefs and eelgrass meadows in tropical waters and also swims in the open ocean. They eat jellyfish, crustaceans, and other prey when they're young. Adults eat mainly seagrass and algae.

Olive ridley turtles are closely related to the Kemp's ridley. Like their "cousins," female olive ridleys are famous for climbing ashore by the thousands to nest at the same time on a beach. These huge group nestings are called *arribadas*, which is a Spanish word meaning "arrival by sea."

The **loggerhead turtle** (see pages 122–123) swims in all but the coldest waters in the ocean. It's named for its large head, which has powerful jaws for crunching the shells of big sea snails and clams and the hard exoskeletons of crabs and lobsters.

The **hawksbill turtle** is named for its hooked snout. It feeds mainly on sponges but also eats sea cucumbers, sea squirts, sea anemones, crabs, sea stars, sea urchins, and sea snails. Hawksbills live in coral reefs and lagoons and along coasts in tropical and warm waters.

The **leatherback turtle** swims far and wide in the open ocean and returns to coasts to nest on shore. It is the world's biggest turtle (see pages 124–125) and also dives deeper than any other turtle—as much as 4,200 feet (1,280 m).

The **Kemp's ridley turtle** lives in the Caribbean Sea and the Gulf of Mexico. It sometimes journeys north along the East Coast of North America, too. Most females of this species lay their eggs on just one beach in Mexico. The beach is protected by law—people are not allowed to gather turtle eggs or turtles for food. Nests are further protected by enclosing the area to keep out predators.

The **flatback turtle** has the smallest range of all sea turtles. It lives only in shallow waters around New Guinea and northern Australia. Young flatbacks feed on plankton at the water's surface. Adults eat sea squirts, sea cucumbers, fish, and other animals.

LOGGERHEAD TURTLE

The loggerhead is the second largest sea turtle.

It can weigh about 250 pounds (113 kg)—more than a newborn baby elephant. But it starts life as a hatchling that's just 1.6 inches (4 cm) long and weighs only about 0.7 ounce (20 g)—less than a slice of bread!

A female loggerhead doesn't start laying eggs until she's about 35 years old. Loggerheads gather in coastal waters to mate, and then each female swims back to the beach where she hatched long ago to lay her eggs. Just how she finds her way there is still a bit of a mystery. Scientists think the turtles can sense Earth's magnetic field and use it as a guide.

When the female loggerhead finds her beach, she goes ashore, picks a spot, and digs a hole with her hind legs. She lays up to 120 eggs, covers them with sand, and returns to the ocean. She'll do this a few more times over the next several weeks before heading back to spend two or three years at sea.

About 60 days later, the eggs hatch. The baby turtles wait until night to crawl out of their sandy nest. They immediately rush down the beach to the ocean, with the glow of moonlight on the water as their guide. Predators such as ghost crabs catch and eat many baby turtles on the beach. More predators await in the ocean. Scientists estimate that in general, only about one in a thousand sea-turtle hatchlings live to adulthood.

The survivors will spend from 7 to 12 years drifting in the ocean, tucked among seaweed and feeding on tiny animals and growing. Then they'll return to coastal waters until they're 20 to 30 years old and ready to mate.

Bet you didn't know

Like other sea turtles, loggerheads are threatened by capture in fishing nets, habitat loss, and by being collected for food. Lights on shore can also confuse hatchlings and make them move away from the sea instead of toward it. In many beach communities, people help turtle hatchlings by dimming their lights and planning buildings so that their lights don't shine toward the beach.

FAMILY:	Cheloniidae
OTHER COMMON NAME:	loggerhead
SCIENTIFIC NAME:	*Caretta caretta*
SIZE:	up to 7 feet (2.1 m)
FOOD:	crustaceans, mollusks, fish
HABITAT:	bays, lagoons, salt marshes, estuaries, coral reefs, coastal waters, open sea
RANGE:	Mediterranean Sea and warm waters of the Atlantic, Pacific, and Indian Oceans

Female loggerheads in the Pacific Ocean **migrate** about **7,500 miles** (12,000 km) from Mexico's coast to **lay eggs** on beaches in Japan.

A loggerhead grazes on seagrass in warm Atlantic waters.

A female leatherback swims in a
marine-protected area around
Kei Kecil Island in Indonesia.

LEATHERBACK TURTLE

The leatherback is named for its shell. Other sea turtles have hard shells, but the leatherback's shell is made up of small, bony plates covered by tough, leathery skin. But "humongous turtle" would be a good name, too, because the leatherback is huge! At up to 8 feet (2.4 m) long, it's longer than the mattress on a bed. It can weigh about 1,300 pounds (600 kg).

A leatherback's big body is padded with a thick layer of fat, which helps keep it warm. The fat also holds in the heat produced by muscles as the leatherback swims. As a result, leatherbacks can swim in colder waters than other sea turtles. They've been known to swim as far north as Canada and Alaska. Full-size adult leatherbacks have been found in seawater as cold as 32°F (0°C).

But when it's time to lay eggs, leatherbacks head for warm places. Female leatherbacks, like other sea turtles, return to the beaches where they hatched to lay their eggs. This journey is long for any leatherback, but it's especially long for leatherbacks in the Pacific Ocean. There, females that feed near coasts in the eastern North Pacific travel more than 3,700 miles (6,000 km) to nesting grounds in the western Pacific. After laying a few batches of eggs, the females swim back to feeding grounds in the sea. They make this journey every two to three years.

Bet you didn't know

The biggest leatherback on record was a male that washed ashore on a beach in Wales in Europe in 1988. It weighed about 2,020 pounds (916 kg) and measured 8.5 feet (2.6 m) long.

FAMILY:	Dermochelyidae
OTHER COMMON NAMES:	luth, trunkback, coffin-back, leathery turtle, trunk turtle
SCIENTIFIC NAME:	*Dermochelys coriacea*
SIZE:	4 to 8 feet (1.2 to 2.4 m)
FOOD:	jellyfish, salps, pyrosomes, octopuses, crustaceans, fish
HABITAT:	coastal and open ocean
RANGE:	Atlantic, Pacific, and Indian Oceans

Amazingly, a leatherback gets most of its energy from a diet mainly of jellyfish. Its jaws have sharp edges, and its mouth and throat are lined with spines that point backward, making the leatherback a swimming jellyfish trap. It can eat its weight in jellyfish every day!

125

WHALES, DOLPHINS, AND PORPOISES

What do humans have in common

with whales, dolphins, and porpoises? We are all mammals—warm-blooded, air-breathing animals, with females that make milk for their young. Unlike humans and other land mammals, however, these marine mammals are totally adapted for a life at sea. They never come onto land. They even give birth in the ocean.

Whales, dolphins, and porpoises are called cetaceans (a name that comes from a Latin word for "whale"). Cetaceans lack hind legs and have flippers for front legs. Their tails are flattened sideways to form a pair of flukes for swimming. Their bodies are wrapped in a layer of fat called blubber. Scientists divide cetaceans into two main groups: toothed whales, which have teeth in their jaws for catching prey, and baleen whales, which have tough strips called baleen hanging from their upper jaws for filtering small fish and zooplankton from seawater.

The blue whale is the largest animal in the world. The biggest blue whale ever measured was 110 feet (33.6 m) long and weighed almost 200 tons (180,000 kg)! Baleen strips in its upper jaw filter krill from seawater—up to 4 tons (3,629 kg) a day. It swims in all the oceans.

The **beluga** is a toothed whale that lives in the Arctic Ocean and nearby waters. Thick blubber helps keep it warm. It measures from 13 to 16 feet (3.9 to 5 m). A beluga uses its teeth to catch and hold fish and other prey, which it swallows whole. Belugas chirp, squeak, and whistle to each other so loudly, they're also known as "sea canaries"!

Spinner dolphins are named for their spectacular leaps. They spring out of the water and spin as many as seven times before splashing down. They've been observed making as many as 14 leaps in a row! The spinning may be a form of communication. Spinner dolphins live in tropical and nearby warm waters in the Atlantic, Indian, and Pacific Oceans.

The sperm whale is the largest toothed whale. Males can be up to 60 feet (18 m) long. A sperm whale's boxy head makes up one-third of its total length. Its teeth are located in its lower jaw and fit into notches in its upper jaw. Sperm whales can dive more than 6,500 feet (1,981 m). They feed mainly on squid, including giant squid.

Dall's porpoises live in the North Pacific Ocean. They prefer cold waters, where they feed on fish, squid, and other prey. These powerful, fast swimmers like to ride on waves that form at the front, or bow, of a ship, an activity known as "bow-riding." Sometimes they even "snout ride" by catching a wave at the front of a big blue or humpback whale (see pages 128–129).

HUMPBACK WHALE

Humpback whales are acrobats and singing sensations!

They're famous for leaping out of the ocean and splashing back in with a crash—an activity called breaching. They also perform tail lobbing, which involves smacking the surface of the water with their tail. Why? Scientists aren't sure. Maybe they're playing, communicating, or just trying to get rid of skin parasites.

Scientists also aren't 100 percent sure why humpbacks sing. A humpback's song is made up of groans, whistles, and eerie, violin-like sounds. Males sing the songs, and all the males in the same area sing the same song. The song also changes from year to year. These songs can be heard underwater up to 20 miles (32 km) away. It's possible the song is used for finding mates.

It takes a lot of food to fuel a whale. A humpback whale eats up to 1.5 tons (1,361 kg) of food each day. It feeds by opening its mouth and taking in a huge amount of water. Its throat is striped with folds so it can stretch to hold it all. Then the whale forces the water out of its mouth. The baleen strips hanging from its upper jaw filter out krill and other small food. Humpbacks often hunt in groups, using an amazing behavior called bubble netting. The whales swim and sometimes make sounds as they round up fish. Meanwhile, one whale dives underwater and then swims upward in a spiral, blowing bubbles. The bubbles form a sort of wall around the fish. Finally, the whales dive and then swoop upward with their mouths open to gobble up the trapped fish.

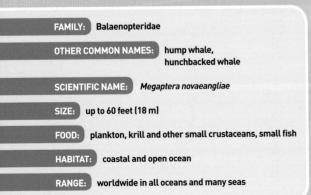

FAMILY:	Balaenopteridae
OTHER COMMON NAMES:	hump whale, hunchbacked whale
SCIENTIFIC NAME:	*Megaptera novaeangliae*
SIZE:	up to 60 feet (18 m)
FOOD:	plankton, krill and other small crustaceans, small fish
HABITAT:	coastal and open ocean
RANGE:	worldwide in all oceans and many seas

A humpback mother and calf swim close together.

et you idn't now The pattern of color on a humpback's tail can be used to identify it because no humpbacks' tails are exactly alike. These markings are very useful for scientists studying whales.

A male orca's dorsal fin—the one that sticks up from its back—can be up to **6 feet** (1.8 m) high.

FAMILY: Delphinidae

OTHER COMMON NAMES: killer whale, grampus, blackfish

SCIENTIFIC NAME: *Orcinus orca*

SIZE: up to 33 feet (10 m)

FOOD: fish (including sharks), squid, porpoises, dolphins, small whales, whale calves, seals, sea lions, sea turtles, seabirds

HABITAT: near shore and open ocean

RANGE: worldwide in all oceans, most abundant in North Atlantic and North Pacific and near Antarctica

ORCA

Orcas are the largest species of dolphin. They're also known as "the wolves of the sea." Like wolves, they travel in groups, communicate with each other, and work together to catch prey. They use different methods depending on what they're hunting.

For example, orcas hunting fish team up to herd the fish into a closely packed bunch. Then they slap at the fish with their tails to stun them before devouring them. Orcas that hunt whales go after a young or weak individual. Then they chase and bite it to wear it out. In the Arctic, orcas even work together to tip seals off ice floes and to trap smaller whales against shorelines.

Female orcas are the leaders in orca groups. A group of orcas may be made up of a few females and their calves, plus one or more males, or just one female and all her young of different ages.

Scientists who study orcas have found that different groups of them often have different behaviors. On the West Coast of the United States, there are even orcas sharing the same waters that eat completely different foods. For example, there are "resident" orcas, which tend to stay in certain areas and eat certain kinds of fish. Other orcas that occasionally visit these areas are called "transient" orcas. ("Transient" means "not long-lasting.") These orcas eat seals and other marine mammals. Farther out at sea are "offshore" orcas, which specialize in eating sharks.

Orca groups don't just have different favorite foods. They may also play differently. Orcas also seem to make calls that are special to just a few groups in an area.

Bet you didn't know

Orcas don't have predators, but they are threatened by pollution. Toxic chemicals build up in their body fat when they eat fish from polluted waters. People are working to stop toxic chemicals from entering waterways, which will help protect the health of orcas and other ocean animals—and people, too.

Noise is also a kind of pollution that's harming orcas and other whales. Orcas use sound to communicate and to find their prey. Loud sounds created by ships make it hard for orcas to hear underwater. Researchers have found that the noise is less if ships travel a little slower in places where orcas swim.

A pod of Southern Resident orcas swim near British Columbia, Canada.

131

BOTTLENOSE DOLPHIN

A bottlenose dolphin always looks as if it's smiling because its jaws are curved. Inside those jaws, however, are up to 104 sharp teeth. These teeth are used for grabbing fish and other prey, which are then swallowed whole.

Like toothed whales, bottlenose dolphins use sound to help find their food. A dolphin moves air through passages in its head to make clicking sounds. On the dolphin's head is a fatty bump, called the melon, which focuses the sound waves ahead of the dolphin in the water—like a headlamp that uses sound instead of light. The sound waves bounce off prey in the water and return to the dolphin in the form of echoes. Then the dolphin uses this information to follow and catch the prey. This process is called echolocation. A dolphin can also find its way in darkness underwater using echolocation.

Bottlenose dolphins also use sounds to communicate with other dolphins. Each dolphin even has a special sound, called a "signature whistle," that identifies it in a group. A dolphin group can be as small as two males that hang out together. It can also be made up of dozens of females with their calves. Dolphins will work together to protect an injured companion from predators, and there are also many stories of dolphins protecting human swimmers.

Bottlenose dolphins are famous for being smart and playful. They learn quickly and surprise scientists with their curiosity and how they use their brains. For example, in Shark Bay, Australia, some female dolphins carry sponges in their mouths when they search for prey on sandy or rocky seafloors. Scientists think the sponge protects a dolphin's snout from scrapes, just as pads protect a skateboarder's knees and elbows.

Bet you didn't know

A dolphin calf is born in the water. It drinks milk underwater, too. A calf nurses until it's about 18 months old. It stays with its mother for about three years.

FAMILY:	Delphinidae
OTHER COMMON NAMES:	bottlenosed dolphin, common bottlenose dolphin
SCIENTIFIC NAME:	*Tursiops truncatus*
SIZE:	6.6 to 13.1 feet (2 to 4 m)
FOOD:	fish, squid, crustaceans
HABITAT:	near coasts, in estuaries, bays, and lagoons, and in open ocean
RANGE:	tropical and warm waters of the Atlantic, Pacific, and Indian Oceans

A bottlenose dolphin can **leap** up to 16.4 feet (5 m) out of the water.

SEALS, SEA LIONS, AND WALRUSES

Seals, sea lions, and walruses are "pinnipeds"—animals that are "fin-footed." Their front legs have evolved into flippers for steering, and their hind legs into flippers for swimming. Sea lions, fur seals, and walruses can rotate their hind flippers forward so they can walk on land. Harbor seals and other "true seals" can't— they can only hitch along on their bellies. A true seal also lacks outer ear flaps—it just has earholes. Sea lions, fur seals, and walruses do have ear flaps. All pinnipeds haul themselves onto land to rest and give birth. Pinnipeds may look awkward on land, but they're sleek swimmers in the water. A thick layer of blubber stores energy, helps them float, and also keeps them warm.

Cape fur seals live at Africa's southern tip. Australian fur seals inhabit Australia's southernmost point. But they're nearly identical and belong to the same species. Scientists think some Cape fur seals swam and drifted across the Indian Ocean to Australia about 12,000 years ago. They survived in their new home and became the Australian fur seals' ancestors.

The **southern elephant seal** lives in cold Antarctic waters. This species is named for the male's giant nose, which looks a bit like a trunk. He inflates his nose to make the sound of his bellowing louder when he roars to warn other males away from his patch of beach and the females on it. Southern elephant seals are the biggest pinnipeds. Males can be up to 19.6 feet (6 m) long and weigh up to 8,818 pounds (4,000 kg).

Harp seals live in the North Atlantic Ocean and nearby parts of the Arctic Ocean. Harp seal pups have fluffy white coats, which keeps them warm and also camouflages them. A harp seal pup has no blubber at birth but quickly grows fat drinking its mother's milk. It starts shedding its white coat when it's about two weeks old.

California sea lions live along the coast of North America from British Columbia in Canada south to Baja California in Mexico. They often gather on docks and buoys, as well as rocks and beaches, to rest. In the water, they zip along at speeds up to 25 miles an hour (40 km/h).

Steller sea lions live near coasts in the North Pacific Ocean. They're big pinnipeds— males can be up to 11 feet (3.4 m) long and weigh nearly 2,500 pounds (1,134 kg). They often lie on rocky shores or large rocks when they're not swimming in search of food. Their prey includes fish as well as some smaller pinnipeds.

Ribbon seals live in the North Pacific Ocean and its seas, as well as neighboring parts of the Arctic Ocean. They give birth far from shore on pack ice (see pages 32–33). This species is named for its pale ribbon markings, which are very visible on males because the rest of their fur is black or dark brown. Females have paler-colored fur.

A walrus keeps warm in cold northern seas thanks to a **layer of blubber** that can be more than 3.9 inches (10 cm) thick.

PACIFIC WALRUS

No other pinniped has tusks like a walrus. But these big teeth aren't used for eating. Instead, the walrus puts its tusks to work chipping open a breathing hole in an ice floe when it's underwater. A walrus also digs its tusks into the top of an ice floe to get a grip when it hauls its heavy body out of the water. Male walruses use tusks to fight with other males for mates.

The walrus's bristly mustache contains as many as 700 sensitive whiskers. A walrus uses them to feel for food, such as a clam, on the seafloor. When it finds its prey, it squirts a big mouthful of water to clear away sand and mud. Then it grips the clam with its lips and rough gums. It slurps on the clam so strongly that the shell opens. The clam's body is quickly swallowed and the shell spat out. A hungry walrus can eat about 4,000 clams in just one day!

Pacific walruses gather to spend winter on pack ice in the Bering Sea. In spring, they spread out to other parts of their range. During this time, female walruses give birth to their calves. A female walrus, called a cow, cares for her calf for about three years.

A walrus may look grayish white when it climbs out of the sea. That's because blood vessels in its skin shrink in cold water to reduce the flow of blood to the skin. This reaction helps stop the blood from getting chilled. Once the walrus is out of the water, blood flows freely back into the skin and turns it pink-brown again. Walruses often gather by the hundreds or even thousands to lie on a shore and warm up.

Bet you didn't know

The Pacific walrus is related to Atlantic walruses, which live in the Atlantic Ocean along coasts in parts of Canada, Greenland, Scandinavia, and Russia's Kara Sea. They are all protected by law from overhunting.

FAMILY: Odobenidae

OTHER COMMON NAMES: aivik (Inuit), aivuk (Yu'pik), amak (Aleut)

SCIENTIFIC NAME: *Odobenus rosmarus divergens*

SIZE: 7.25 to 11.5 feet (2.2 to 3.5 m)

FOOD: clams, sea snails, sea cucumbers, marine worms, crabs, amphipods, shrimp, tunicates, fish, occasionally small seals

HABITAT: coastal waters, pack ice

RANGE: northern seas around Russia and Alaska, including the Bering Sea in the North Pacific Ocean and the Chukchi Sea in the Arctic Ocean

WEDDELL SEAL

The Weddell seal lives in a world of ice. Adult seals hunt under the ice and chew holes in it for breathing. They also use holes in the ice for entering and exiting the water. A seal saws ice by shaking its head back and forth with its teeth pressed against the sides of the hole. Large, forward-pointing teeth help it do this job.

Keeping these holes open is very important—without them, the seals would be stuck on the frozen surface without any way to get into the water. And even though Antarctic seawater is deadly cold for a human, a Weddell seal may enter it to stay warm! That's because the water under the ice can't get colder than the freezing point of seawater, which is 28.8°F (–1.8°C). That's cold—but it's toasty warm compared to temperatures above the ice in winter, which can drop well below –4°F (–20°C) … brrr!

A thick layer of blubber keeps a Weddell seal warm as it swims below sea ice. The seal also finds its food here. It can see very well in the dim light and is good at sneaking up on fish.

Orcas and leopard seals eat Weddell seals, but they don't have any land-based predators such as bears to worry about. That's why Weddell seals hanging out near a hole in the ice seldom bother to jump into the water if people walk up to them.

Bet you didn't know

The crabeater seal also lives in Antarctica. Despite its name, it doesn't eat crabs: it feeds on krill! Each tooth is covered with little bumps to make the seal's mouth work like a filter. The seal sucks in a mouthful of water and then strains it through its teeth to collect krill, which it swallows.

FAMILY:	Phocidae
OTHER COMMON NAMES:	none
SCIENTIFIC NAME:	*Leptonychotes weddellii*
SIZE:	8.2 to 11.5 feet (2.5 to 3.5 m)
FOOD:	icefish and other fish; squid; crustaceans
HABITAT:	coastal waters and fast ice (ice that is attached or "holding fast" to shore)
RANGE:	Antarctica and surrounding islands, including South Georgia and the South Sandwich Islands

A Weddell seal can **dive** more than 1,970 feet (600 m) deep and stay underwater for about **an hour.**

POLAR BEAR

The polar bear is the biggest predator on land—but these big, white bears are most at home on the sea ice of the Arctic Ocean.

A polar bear has many adaptations for surviving in ice, snow, and cold ocean water. Its wide paws have rough soles, which help it grip ice and snow. Its toes are slightly webbed, which helps it paddle in water. A thick layer of fat keeps it warm. So does its thick coat. Its white fur, which helps it blend in with snow, is actually made up of colorless hairs. Light is scattered by these clear, hollow hairs in a way that makes the bear look white.

These mighty predators start life as tiny, helpless cubs that are about the size of a guinea pig. They're born in a den dug by their mother in the snow. The family remains in the den all winter. By spring, the cubs are ready to leave the den with their mother. They'll stay with her until they're about two and a half years old.

Females with newborns are the only polar bears that spend winter in a den. The rest of the bears are traveling on the sea ice in search of seals to eat. A polar bear needs lots of energy to keep warm and stay healthy in the harsh world of the Arctic. It can eat up to 100 pounds (45 kg) of seal blubber in one meal! A polar bear often hunts by waiting next to a seal's breathing hole in the ice. It might wait for hours or even days. When an unsuspecting seal pokes up its head, the bear grabs it. Bears also stalk seals on ice.

In summer, when much of the sea ice melts, polar bears must move closer to shore. It's hard to hunt seals without sea ice, so bears often go hungry for months. They eat whatever they can find, from bird eggs to berries.

Bet you didn't know

Polar bears are especially threatened by climate change (see pages 182–183): In a warmer Arctic, sea ice will melt earlier in spring and form later in fall, and bears will go longer without eating and find it harder to get the food they need. Efforts to stop global climate change will help not only people but also polar bears.

FAMILY:	Ursidae
OTHER COMMON NAMES:	sea bear, ice bear, white bear, nanook (Inuit)
SCIENTIFIC NAME:	*Ursus maritimus*
SIZE:	up to 8 feet (2.5 m)
FOOD:	seals, carrion, fish, seabirds
HABITAT:	sea ice, also on coasts and islands
RANGE:	circumpolar Arctic in Canada, the United States (Alaska), Greenland, Russia, Norway

This cub and its mother live in Manitoba, Canada, which is home to nearly a thousand polar bears.

A polar bear can smell a dead animal from a distance of 3 miles (5 km). It will **follow its nose** to find and feast on the meal.

141

The tough outer covering of enamel on a sea otter's teeth is more than twice as strong as yours, so they don't get chipped easily by the otter's shellfish diet.

Bet you didn't know

A sea otter needs to eat up to 30 percent of its body weight every day in order to get the energy it needs to stay warm. For a big male otter, that means eating about 25 pounds (11.3 kg) of food!

SEA OTTER

Sea otters are often seen floating on their backs in the water, sometimes with kelp wrapped around their bodies to keep them anchored in place when they sleep.

When they're not floating, sea otters are often diving for food. They're among the few animals that use tools. A sea otter often carries a stone underwater to use as a hammer to bash clams off rocks. It uses its webbed front paws, as well as pockets of loose skin under its arms, to carry the stone and its prey back to the surface. There the otter floats on its back, puts the rock on its chest, and bangs the clams against the rock to smash them open.

A sea otter is covered in the thickest fur of any mammal. There are from 850,000 to a million hairs packed into just one square inch (6.5 sq cm) of its skin. (A typical person has only about 100,000 hairs on his or her entire head!) This thick fur keeps water out and also traps a layer of air around the otter's body. The trapped air works as insulation that helps keep its body warm and dry while it swims in cold water. An otter depends on its fur for survival because it doesn't have a layer of blubber to keep it warm.

A female sea otter spends a lot of time grooming her pup. The pup's fur traps so much air, it can't even dive—it pops up to the surface like a cork! Its mother carries it on her chest as she floats on her back. When she needs to dive for food, she may leave her pup nestled among kelp to stop it from floating away. A pup begins diving when it's about two months old and is independent by the time it's a year old.

Bet you didn't know

Today, sea otters are protected by laws. They're still threatened by oil spills, pollution, and disease, but thanks to conservation efforts, their population is now estimated to be from 106,000 to about 125,000. Most of these sea otters live in Alaskan waters.

FAMILY: Mustelidae

OTHER COMMON NAMES: none

SCIENTIFIC NAME: *Enhydra lutris*

SIZE: 3.5 to 4.3 feet (1.1 to 1.3 m)

FOOD: crabs, sea snails, sea urchins, clams, mussels, other invertebrates

HABITAT: kelp forests, rocky coastlines, shallow coastal waters

RANGE: North Pacific Ocean along coasts of Japan, Russia, United States (Alaska, Washington, Oregon, California), and Canada (British Columbia)

SEABIRDS

Soaring, swimming, diving, and skimming, seabirds make the most of all the food the ocean offers. There are about 10,000 species of birds, and about 350 of them make up this group of birds specially adapted for a life at sea.

Seabirds vary a lot in size, shape, and way of life, but they all have a few traits in common. All seabirds, for example, have salt glands in their heads that remove excess salt from their blood. This salt comes from the salt water the birds swallow as they eat seafood. The excess salt drains out of a bird's nostrils or tubes on the bill, depending on the species. Seabirds also have webbed feet. And all seabirds must come ashore to lay eggs and raise chicks. Many species gather in huge colonies to nest.

A **brown pelican** dives into the sea from high in the air to catch fish. It scoops up its prey and a lot of water with its pouched bill, which can hold three times more than its stomach can. It squeezes out the water before swallowing the fish. Brown pelicans are found in warm, shallow waters along coasts in the Atlantic Ocean, Pacific Ocean, and Gulf of Mexico.

The **tufted puffin** is a crow-size seabird found in the North Pacific. It nests on shorelines in burrows it digs with its bill and feet. A puffin can carry 10 to 20 fish in its beak at one time as it brings food back to its nest to feed its chicks. Tufted puffins lose their plumes in summer after the breeding season ends, and their bills lose their bright colors.

A **Leach's storm-petrel** can use its sense of smell to find food on the ocean's surface. It feeds by hovering over the water and picking small crustaceans out of the ocean. This species is usually found far from shore, scattered across the Atlantic and Pacific Oceans. It comes ashore only during nesting season.

Both male and female **blue-footed boobies** have blue feet, but the male shows his off with a special high-stepping dance during mating season to attract a female. These seabirds plunge from the air into the water to catch fish. They live in the Galápagos Islands and along the west coast of Central and South America.

The **arctic tern** makes the longest migration of any bird. It flies a loop-de-loop from its Arctic breeding grounds to its Antarctic winter feeding grounds every year. In total, the trip measures about 44,000 miles (71,000 km)!

The **Cape gannet** lives along the coast of southern Africa in parts of the Atlantic and Indian Oceans. It breeds on just six islands. A male and female gannet mate for life. Their nest is a mound made by scraping up a heap of dried bird droppings, bits of plants, old bones, and feathers.

The **red-billed gull** lives in New Zealand. It nests in huge colonies made up of many birds on cliffs and shores. It feeds on krill, small fish, crustaceans, mollusks, worms, and insects. Like most gulls worldwide, it also happily feeds on food scraps it finds in trash.

LAYSAN ALBATROSS

Like all albatrosses, a Laysan albatross has superlong, narrow wings. Its wingspan—the distance from tip to tip—is 6.6 feet (1.8 m), which is longer than most humans' arm spans. This kind of wing is perfect for soaring long distances with hardly a flap—and that's just what the albatross does.

Flapping uses lots of energy, but an albatross must save energy when it's flying for hundreds of miles across the ocean to find food. It doesn't even use much energy to hold its wings out straight, thanks to special structures in the wings that prop them up.

To keep soaring without flapping, the albatross takes advantage of winds. From high in the air, it glides quickly down toward the water, then turns and glides back up—a bit like a kid on a bike zooming downhill and racing up the next one without pedaling. As it swoops up, the bird flies into faster winds, which slow it down but also lift it up high so it can glide quickly downhill again. In this way, the bird zigzags across the ocean. An albatross can travel like this for hundreds of miles a day.

Laysan albatrosses spend time on land only when they're nesting. A pair of birds usually has just one chick, and the parents take turns watching over it while the other one flies off to find food. The albatross that's gone hunting may be gone for days. A bird with a nest on a Hawaiian Island may travel 1,600 miles (2,575 km) away from its nest to feed in cold northern waters. When it returns, it throws up, or regurgitates, a partly digested meal for its chick to eat.

Bet you didn't know

A Laysan albatross called Wisdom is known to have laid eggs even at the age of 64! Scientists estimate that she may have raised up to 35 chicks and flown more than 3 million miles (4,828,000 km) in her long life.

FAMILY:	Diomedeidae
OTHER COMMON NAMES:	gooney, gooney bird
SCIENTIFIC NAME:	*Phoebastria immutabilis*
SIZE:	32 inches (81 cm)
FOOD:	squid, crustaceans, fish, fish eggs, floating carrion
HABITAT:	open ocean
RANGE:	North Pacific Ocean from the tropics to the Bering Sea

PENGUINS

Penguins are seabirds adapted so completely to life at sea, they've lost the ability to fly. In the ocean, however, a penguin "flies" through the water as it flaps its flipperlike wings while using its webbed feet to steer. Its body stores lots of fat to help keep it warm, and its feathers form a thick, waterproof coat. Penguins have more densely packed feathers than any other bird—up to 100 feathers per square inch (6.5 sq cm).

Even the penguin's black-and-white "tuxedo" is an adaptation for survival. Being dark on top helps a penguin blend in with the dark sea around it when viewed from above. More important, its white belly helps it blend in with the light color of the sky when viewed from below—and "below" is where penguin predators lurk, such as leopard seals and killer whales.

There are 18 species of penguins. All of them live in Earth's Southern Hemisphere, except for a small number of Galápagos penguins that live on islands just north of the Equator.

Macaroni penguins nest on islands in the South Atlantic Ocean and Indian Ocean. The male and female take turns warming their egg. After it hatches, the male guards the chick. The female's job is to hunt for krill, fish, and squid. The macaroni penguin's name has nothing to do with noodles! "Macaroni" was a term that used to describe a person who wore a hat with bright feathers. The penguins' orange head plumes reminded early English explorers of that style, and that's how they got their name.

Adélie penguins spend winter on ice along the coast of Antarctica and nearby islands. They leap into the water to feed on krill. In spring, they troop to places on shore that are free of ice. There they build nests of pebbles and stones. Each female typically lays two eggs, and both parents care for the chicks.

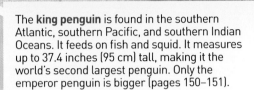

The **king penguin** is found in the southern Atlantic, southern Pacific, and southern Indian Oceans. It feeds on fish and squid. It measures up to 37.4 inches (95 cm) tall, making it the world's second largest penguin. Only the emperor penguin is bigger (pages 150–151).

The Galápagos penguin lives only on the Galápagos Islands in the Pacific Ocean. It lives farther north than any other penguin species— in the tropical zone! But cold currents in the ocean around the islands supply the food and cool water penguins need.

The **little blue penguin** is the world's smallest penguin. It grows up to 18 inches (45 cm) tall. It is found on Australia's southern coast and in New Zealand. By day, it swims and hunts for fish at sea. In the evening, little blue penguins scramble ashore and travel in groups to the area where they'll spend the night.

The **southern rockhopper penguin** lives on islands with rocky shores in the South Atlantic, South Pacific, and Indian Oceans. They are a bit smaller than northern rockhopper penguins and have shorter head plumes. As you might guess, rockhoppers hop, rather than walk, from rock to rock.

Yellow-eyed penguins live on the southern coast of New Zealand's South Island and other islands nearby. Unlike most other penguins, they don't nest in colonies. Each pair seeks a nesting spot far from other penguins in a forest.

A pair of emperor penguins huddle with their chick in Antarctica. The chick sits on a parent's feet to stay warm.

EMPEROR PENGUIN

It's winter in Antarctica. The sun barely rises during the day.
Blizzards sweep across the land, with winds as fast as 200 miles an hour (322 km/h). The temperature is bitterly cold. For emperor penguins, it's the right time to lay eggs.

Emperor penguins spend much of the year in icy waters around Antarctica and nearby islands, hunting for fish. But when winter arrives, the penguins gather on the ice sheets attached to shore. They waddle in a single-file line as they head for their rookeries—the places where they will nest and raise their chicks. The rookeries are in places where the ice will stay frozen solid until the chicks are old enough to take care of themselves. For some penguins, that journey is as much as 70 miles (113 km) away from the ocean.

At the rookery, emperor penguins pair up. A female penguin lays a single egg. There's no nest, so the egg is placed on the male penguin's feet, tucked into a warm pocket formed by his belly. Then the female leaves. She heads back to the ocean to feed. She stays away for about two months while the male keeps the egg warm.

While the females are gone, the males huddle together to keep warm. They take turns being on the colder outside of the huddle and in the warmer center. During this time, they don't eat—they live off their body fat. The females return as the eggs are hatching. They regurgitate food for the chick and take over the job of keeping the chick warm while the males head off to sea to feed. The parent birds keep taking turns until the chicks are old enough to huddle together with each other for warmth. By summer they are old enough to swim and fish on their own.

Emperors are the **biggest penguin** species. They're also the **deepest divers.** They've been known to dive as deep as 1,850 feet (565 m).

FAMILY: Spheniscidae

OTHER COMMON NAMES: none

SCIENTIFIC NAME: *Aptenodytes forsteri*

SIZE: 45.3 inches (115 cm)

FOOD: fish, squid, krill

HABITAT: coastal waters, fast ice (ice that is attached or "holding fast" to shore)

RANGE: Antarctica and nearby islands

CHAPTER 3

OCEAN IN MOTION

a huge wave at sunset, in Oahu, Hawaii, U.S.A.

WAVES

Do you like to splash in the ocean? Jump in the waves? Run in the surf as it slides up and down the shore, then stand still as water runs back out to sea, dragging sand with it and burying your feet?

The waves that make a beach visit so much fun are produced by wind blowing across the ocean's surface. The wind drags and pushes the water and makes it rise and fall in one place. This action produces the hump of rising water that you picture when you think "wave."

The water in a wave, however, doesn't travel across the ocean. The actual wave is the energy that the wind transfers to the water. It's this wave energy that travels across the water, not the water itself. You can demonstrate this process by lashing a jump rope so that a series of waves travel down its length. The jump rope itself doesn't go anywhere—the only thing moving is the energy making it ripple.

As a wave approaches land, the motion of the energy inside it bumps up against the seafloor. The bottom of the wave drags due to friction against the seafloor and it starts to slow down, just as a ball slows down as it rolls across a flat surface. This makes the wave become taller and slower. The water at the top thins out until finally the wave curls over and falls due to gravity—the same force that makes a ball come back after you toss it in the air. It's as if the wave were tripping over its own feet and landing *splat* on the beach.

Calm breezes make the ocean rise and fall in gentle swells. Boats, seabirds, and kids on inflated water toys bob lazily up and down. Strong winds produce waves that form sharp peaks. The biggest waves are created by winds that rush for long distances across the ocean without anything, such as an island, to block their way.

LIFT AND DRIFT

So if a wave is energy on the go, how do waves carry you ashore when you swim at a beach?

You drift ashore not because of the waves, but because of a current. A current is a movement of water from one place to another. The current is created when waves approach the shore at an angle and break on land. The waves release their energy as they break. Some of that energy shoves water into motion alongside the beach and creates a current that travels alongside the shore. This current is called a longshore current. It often carries sand and other material with it. If you're in the water, that material includes you! The longshore current not only nudges you ashore, but it also makes you drift slowly down the beach, away from the spot where you left your towel.

Bet you didn't know

"Pipeline" is the name of a powerful wave that crashes down on a beach on the Hawaiian Island of Oahu. It arches up to 9 feet (3 m) tall but can also reach heights of 20 feet (6 m). As the wave curls over, it forms a huge tube. Only the best surfers are able to shoot through this tube without wiping out.

CURRENTS AND GYRES

Surface currents flow like rivers for many hundreds of miles across the ocean's surface. As they flow, they carry warm water from tropical places to the North and South Poles, and cold water from the poles to the tropics.

Surface currents are driven by strong winds that blow steadily and drag the water at the ocean's surface. This is actual water on the move—not just energy, as in a wave.

But a surface current doesn't follow exactly the same path as the wind. It moves away from the wind at an angle because Earth spins from west to east like a giant top. However, Earth is wider across its middle than at its top or bottom. So it has to spin faster at the Equator than at its poles because it takes the middle longer to spin in a complete circle in one day. This difference in spinning speed makes strong winds veer to one side as they blow—and it also makes currents veer away from the winds that drag them. Scientists call this veering away "the Coriolis effect."

The Coriolis effect makes winds and currents veer to the right in the Northern Hemisphere—the part of Earth north of the Equator. In the Southern Hemisphere, they veer to the left. As the currents follow their curved paths through the ocean, they form huge loops called gyres. Gyres in the Northern Hemisphere swirl in a clockwise direction. Gyres in the Southern Hemisphere swirl in a counterclockwise direction.

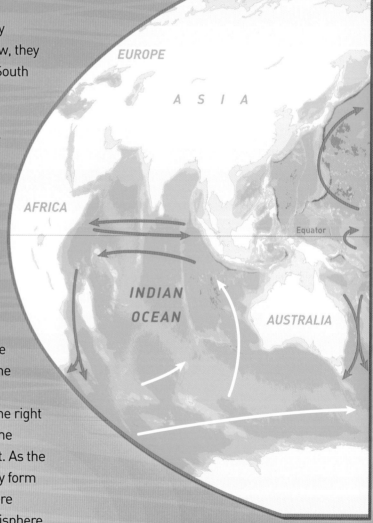

EUROPE

ASIA

AFRICA

Equator

INDIAN OCEAN

AUSTRALIA

Bet you didn't know

The biggest gyres are made up of many currents that join together and form a loop around an entire ocean. These big gyres carry heat from Earth's sun-drenched tropical waters to its cold polar regions, and cold water away from Earth's poles.

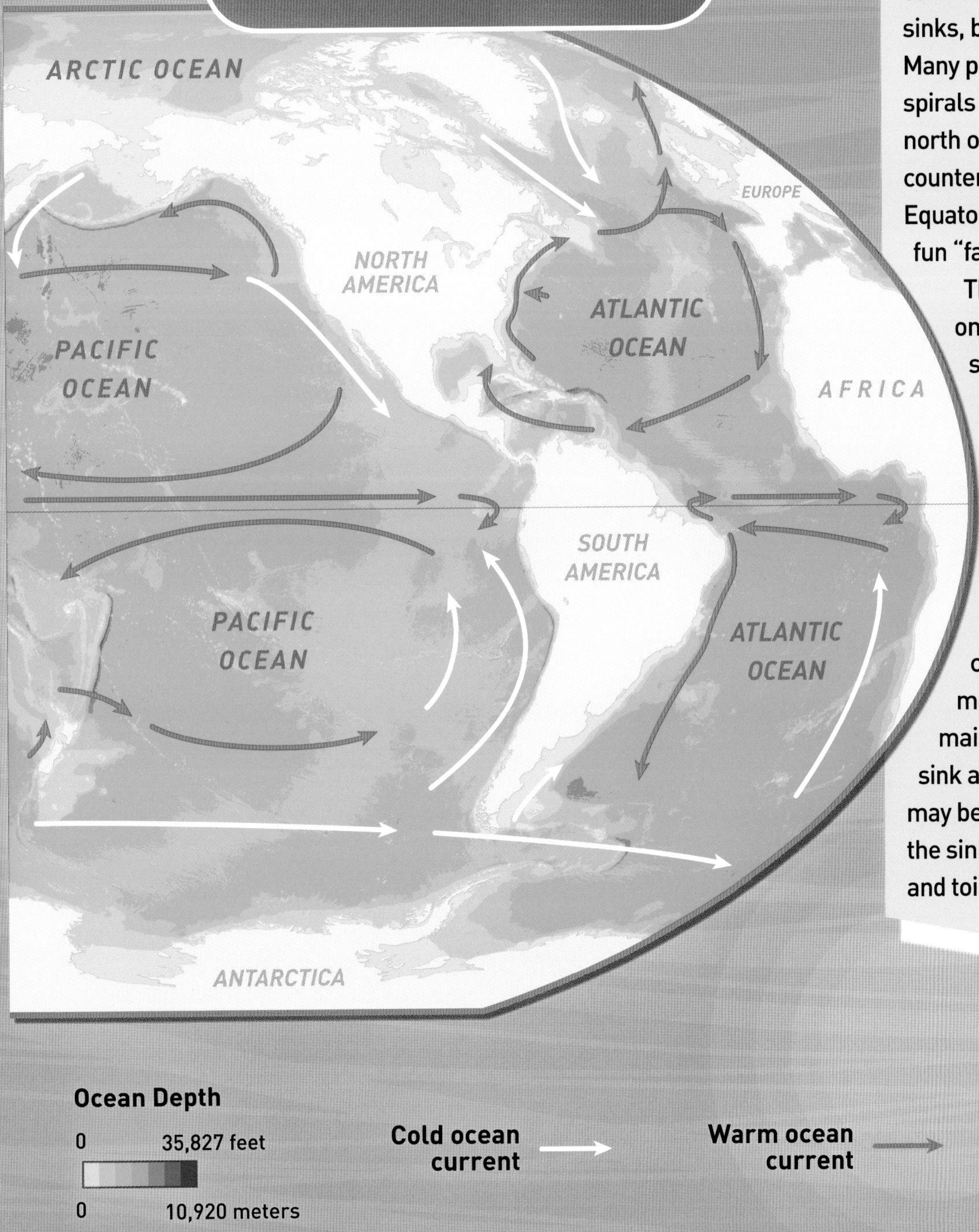

DOWN THE DRAIN

Does the Coriolis effect control how water spirals in sinks, bathtubs, and toilets? Many people think water spirals clockwise down drains north of the Equator and counterclockwise south of the Equator. But it's one of those fun "facts" that isn't true.

The Coriolis effect works only on a large, Earth-size scale. Unless your bathroom sink is the size of a sea, the puddle swirling down the drain isn't big enough to be affected by the Coriolis effect. Its clockwise or counterclockwise motion is determined mainly by the shape of the sink and the way the water may be spinning as it enters the sink. Same goes for tubs and toilets.

ARCTIC OCEAN

EUROPE

NORTH AMERICA

ATLANTIC OCEAN

PACIFIC OCEAN

AFRICA

SOUTH AMERICA

PACIFIC OCEAN

ATLANTIC OCEAN

ANTARCTICA

Ocean Depth

0   35,827 feet

0   10,920 meters

Cold ocean current →

Warm ocean current →

0   1,500 miles

0   1,500 kilometers

GARBAGE PATCHES

Gyres round up large amounts of trash as they swirl around in an ocean. It's estimated that about 8.8 million tons (8 million metric tons) of plastic trash ends up in the ocean each year. Scientists compare that to five grocery bags of plastic trash for every foot (0.3 m) of coastline in the world. A lot of this trash is swept up and gathered in the calmer area that's surrounded by swirling currents. Much of the trash is made up of plastic: Plastic bottles, plastic bags, plastic containers from the supermarket salad bar, and lots of other plastic items that were thrown away instead of being reused or recycled.

At sea, this plastic doesn't decay into natural materials the way a chunk of wood or piece of paper does on land. Instead, the sun's heat and light make the plastic break down into smaller and smaller pieces. Some of these tiny plastic bits are as small as the one-celled marine organisms floating at the surface. These small plastic pieces are called microplastics.

Many plastics release chemicals such as Bisphenol A (BPA for short), when they break down in the ocean. Scientists are studying these chemicals to find out more about how harmful they may be to living things. Plastics also absorb pollutants from the water, such as polychlorinated biphenyls (PCBs for short). PCBs can cause many problems. They harm young ocean animals as they develop and grow. They build up in the bodies of animals that eat them—and the animals that eat those animals, too (including humans). PCBs are also known to cause cancer and other diseases in some animals. Scientists are researching to see how PCBs and BPA affect humans.

PLASTIC PERILS

Garbage causes lots of problems for marine life. Many seabirds, such as albatrosses, mistake plastic trash for food and also feed it to their chicks. Plastic can kill birds by injuring their digestive organs. A bird with a belly full of plastic can also starve to death because there's no room for food. (Scientists estimate that 90 percent of all seabirds are eating plastic!) Other animals, including corals, take in microplastics as they filter food from water.

We can't haul a giant net through it. But we can stop trash from getting into the sea. Recycling also keeps trash from ending up on beaches and in the ocean.

A black-footed albatross mistakes plastic garbage for food on a Hawaiian beach.

TRY THIS!

What do the ocean's "great garbage patches" look like? They aren't floating islands of trash you can see from a jet window as you fly over the ocean. Instead, they are spread across a wide stretch of ocean, with more trash in some areas than others. In the Pacific Ocean, for example, the loops and swirls of gyres and currents create garbage patches in the western Pacific near Japan and in the east between Hawaii and California.

Sprinkle some pepper in a shallow bowl of water and then stir the water slowly, around and around along its edges. You'll see that most of the pepper ends up clumped in the middle of the bowl, much like garbage gathered by a gyre.

THE SARGASSO SEA

You can't build sand castles on the shores of the Sargasso Sea. That's because it has no shores! This sea is an area in the North Atlantic Ocean where a gyre swirls around still, calm water. It's the only sea surrounded by currents instead of land. It covers an area of about two million square miles (5.2 million sq km)—not quite as big as Australia, but bigger than India. It's named after the mats of golden seaweed, called sargassum, that float in it. Sargassum grows little berry-shaped, air-filled sacs that help it float just as inflatable toys help you float in a pool. Layers of sargassum can be as deep as 9.8 feet (3 m).

Inside the Sargasso Sea, the water is warm. It's also very salty because little rain falls here. The sea also loses water due to evaporation. Scientists once thought the Sargasso Sea was a poor habitat for animals, but they later found that it's rich in life. Oceanographer Sylvia Earle describes it as a "floating, golden rain forest." Sea turtle hatchlings and young fish find food and shelter in the Sargasso Sea. Tuna and other large fish hunt in it. There are also animals specially adapted for life in sargassum, some of which aren't found anywhere else.

The **sargassum frogfish** is wonderfully camouflaged! Blotchy coloring and fins that look like bits of seaweed help it hide from predators and prey. The fish also jumps onto floating sargassum to escape predators. Then it crawls away, using its hand-like fins to clamber across the seaweed.

ARCTIC OCEAN

ASIA

NORTH AMERICA

PACIFIC OCEAN

AUSTRALIA

Ocean Depth

0   35,827 feet

0   10,920 meters

A slender **sargassum shrimp's** color helps it blend in as it grazes on animals that grow on seaweed. It hangs out on seaweed "leaves," called blades, because its body resembles a blade. Another kind of shrimp, the cerulean sargassum shrimp, has a rounder, fatter body that makes it look a bit like one of the sargassum's round floats. It clings to seaweed stalks instead.

The **sargassum nudibranch** is a sea slug that looks just like a pinched-off bit of sargassum! It creeps through the seaweed, feeding on prey such as hydroids, which are tiny, jellyfish-like animals.

The **sargassum swimming crab** has a pair of legs that look like paddles, unlike crabs that walk on land. Its colors camouflage it. Adult crabs seize small fish and other prey with their claws.

North Atlantic Drift

Gulf Stream

EUROPE

ASIA

SARGASSO SEA

Canary Current

A **sargassum pipefish's** skinny body looks right at home with fronds of seaweed. Like its "cousin," the seahorse, a pipefish sucks in food with its tubelike mouth.

AFRICA

North Equatorial Current

SOUTH AMERICA

ATLANTIC OCEAN

INDIAN OCEAN

Boundary → ocean current

0   1,500 miles

0   1,500 kilometers

ANTARCTICA

Freshwater eels from Europe, North Africa, and North America swim to the Sargasso Sea to mate and lay eggs. The eggs drift to the ocean's surface. The larvae that hatch will drift with currents as they grow until they arrive back at land, where they'll swim up rivers to live as adults.

THE GLOBAL CONVEYOR BELT

The ocean is in endless motion on its surface. It's also moving beneath the waves and surface currents. These movements of water are called subsurface currents.

Subsurface currents aren't pushed by wind like surface currents. They're caused by differences in the water's density. Cold water is more dense than warm water, so it sinks. Likewise, very salty water is denser than less salty water, so it sinks, too.

This rising and sinking is part of a worldwide system of water movement called the global ocean conveyor belt. The global ocean conveyor belt moves water in a loop around the world. In the process, ocean water is mixed up and turned over from top to bottom.

Let's hop aboard that conveyor belt in the North Atlantic. Here, seawater at the surface freezes and forms sea ice. When seawater freezes, it leaves its salt behind, so now there's cold, super-salty water on the ocean's surface that is very dense, so it sinks. As it sinks, it pushes the cold, deep water south toward the Equator.

This cold seafloor water is called North Atlantic Deep Water, and when it's pushed out of the way, it flows very slowly across the Atlantic seafloor, heading for Antarctica.

When the North Atlantic Deep Water reaches the ocean near Antarctica, it joins forces with the deep, cold water there. This mass of deep, cold water then trudges across the Pacific seafloor. (Some of it loops up into the Indian Ocean.)

When the deep, cold water gets to the North Pacific, something interesting happens: It rises! Why? Because up on the surface, water is being pushed away by winds. So the deep, cold water rises to replace it. Then it warms up and flows as a warm surface current all the way back to the North Atlantic to start the cycle again.

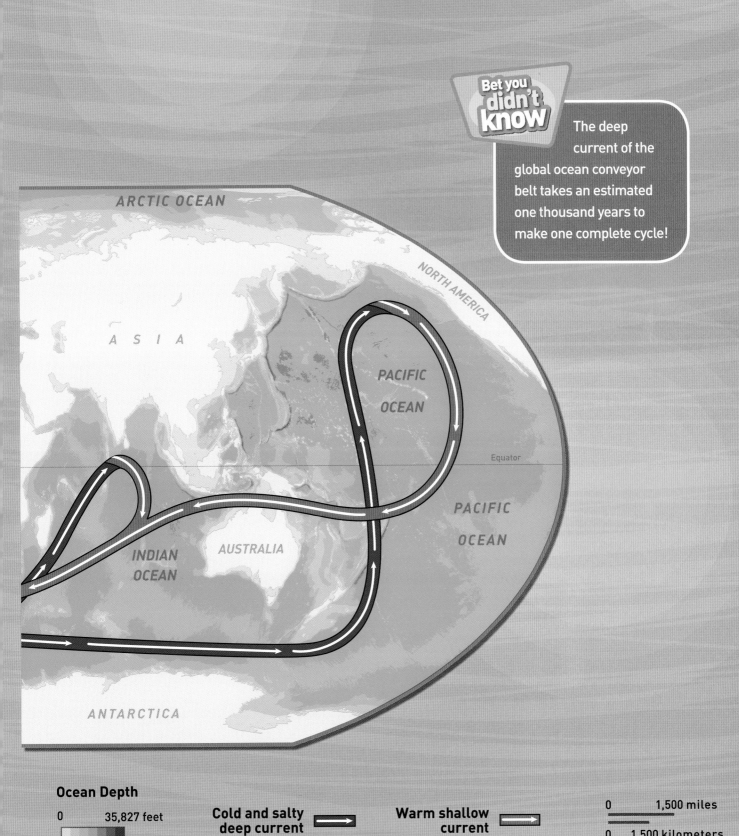

Bet you didn't know

The deep current of the global ocean conveyor belt takes an estimated one thousand years to make one complete cycle!

ARCTIC OCEAN

ASIA

NORTH AMERICA

PACIFIC OCEAN

Equator

PACIFIC OCEAN

INDIAN OCEAN

AUSTRALIA

ANTARCTICA

Ocean Depth

0   35,827 feet

0   10,920 meters

Cold and salty deep current

Warm shallow current

0   1,500 miles

0   1,500 kilometers

LOOK OUT ABOVE:
HERE COMES
DINNER!

Deep currents do more than move water around the globe. They also carry nutrients up to the surface. These nutrients come from the seafloor.

How do nutrients get there? The seafloor is where dead whales, fish droppings, and a lot of dead plankton end up after they sink. Most of this material breaks down as bacteria and other creatures on the seafloor feed on it. This breakdown, called decomposition, turns organisms back into the basic ingredients that formed their cells, such as carbon and nitrogen. Nitrogen is one of the most important nutrients that deep currents carry to the surface—without it, plants and algae will die. (On land, dead plants and animals break down in the same way. The substances that formed them are recycled. They become fertilizer that helps new plants grow.)

Without currents, these nutrients would just sit on the seafloor. But a deep, cold current sweeps the nutrients up to the surface as it rises. This process is called upwelling. The boost of nutrients helps a new "crop" of phytoplankton grow. The phytoplankton, in turn, are eaten by zooplankton. Little fish eat the zooplankton, and big fish eat the little fish.

Upwelling occurs in places where winds push the ocean's surface waters away from the shore. When this water is pushed out of the way, deep water rises up to replace it, carrying nutrients with it.

Bet you didn't know

The nutrients that upwelling brings to the ocean surface help phytoplankton grow—and that means more food for animals such as tiny, shrimplike krill. Krill, in turn, are eaten by many other animals, including whales. Scientists estimate that the combined weight of all the krill in Antarctica is greater than that of any other species—about 418,878,300 tons (380 million metric tons)!

ON THE UP AND UP

Upwelling near certain coasts has made them good fishing areas because the nutrients that are brought up help phytoplankton grow. The phytoplankton, in turn, are eaten by fish. One of the world's most important fishing locations is off the coast of Peru in South America, where upwelling takes place nearly year-round. In other places, upwelling happens only in certain seasons. For example, a big "bloom" of phytoplankton occurs in the northern Atlantic and Pacific in spring, when there is more sunlight.

Upwelling also occurs in the open ocean where different currents meet, and wherever dense water sinks and forces nutrient-filled deep water to rise. That's why, despite severe cold and ice, Antarctica's waters are a rich feeding ground for penguins, seals, and whales.

A "bloom" of algae washes up on a shore in Australia.

Lunar Tides

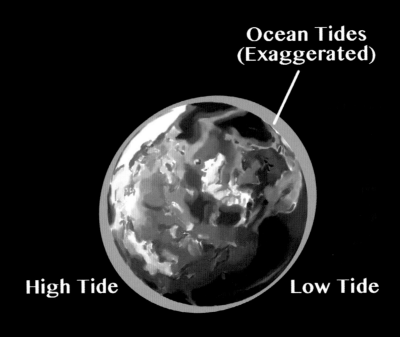

Ocean Tides
(Exaggerated)

Moon

High Tide

Low Tide

Bet you didn't know

A "rip tide" isn't a tide. It's a fast-moving current—or "rip current"—that flows away from a shore as it carries water from waves back out to sea. Rip currents can be very dangerous for swimmers. If you get caught in a rip current, you shouldn't try to swim against it. Instead you should swim sideways out of the current, in a direction that follows the shoreline. Then, when you're out of the rip current, you can swim toward shore.

TIDES

When you stand on a beach and look out at the water, you can't see gyres and other underwater ocean motion. But there is ocean motion you can easily see: the in-and-out flow of tides.

Tides are the regular rise and fall of ocean water that occur every day. On shore, you see the ocean rise when the tide comes in. The water rushes farther up the shore and swallows the sand castle you made earlier in the day. Later, the water doesn't reach as far up on the beach. The tide starts going out, and you may be able to explore parts of the beach that are usually covered by water.

Tides are caused by the moon and the sun, which pull on Earth due to the force of gravity. Gravity is the invisible force that makes all objects, from planets to particles, pull on each other.

The moon is much smaller than the sun but is closer to Earth, so it has the strongest pull on Earth's water. The moon pulls the ocean toward it, making it bulge on that side of Earth. Meanwhile, on Earth's other side, another bulge forms. This bulge is caused by a force, called inertia, that makes objects keep moving in one direction if nothing disturbs them.

High tides occur when a shoreline is under one of the bulges created as Earth spins around and the moon circles Earth, pulling on the water. Low tides occur during the dips between the bulges. That's why many ocean shores experience two high tides and two low tides every day.

The shape of a coast also plays a role in how many tide cycles a place has. The shape alters how water sloshes up and down the shore, so some places have just one high and one low tide a day. Other places may have two tide cycles a day, but of very different sizes.

TIDE'S OUT!

Low tide is a great time to explore the beach. But it's important to know when to expect the tide to come rolling back in again. You don't want to get stuck on a rock or cut off from shore by high tide!

A calendar that shows the times of high tide and low tide is called a tide table.

A place with a twice-a-day tide cycle has two high tides and two low tides every 24 hours and 50 minutes. The high tides are separated by 12 hours and 25 minutes. So are the low tides.

Why the strange number? It's caused by the way Earth spins once, or rotates, on its axis every 24 hours while the moon slowly travels in its monthlong circular journey around Earth.

SUPERSIZE TIDES

Twice a month, tides go wild! Every two weeks, high tide is extra high, and low tide is super low. These special tides are called spring tides. That name has nothing to do with the season—spring tides happen all year. It simply means the tides are "springing forth" more than usual.

Spring tides happen when the moon, sun, and Earth are all in a straight line. Once a month, Earth is in between the sun and moon. Two weeks later, the moon stands between the sun and Earth. In both cases, the moon and sun are working together to pull on Earth's oceans. Their gravitational pull, added together, tugs more strongly and makes the tides move higher and lower than normal.

The opposite also happens twice a month: The high tide isn't as high as usual, and neither is the low tide. This smaller-than-usual tidal range occurs when the moon and the sun are pulling at right angles on Earth.

In this position, the pull of the sun and the pull of the moon partly cancel each other out. Earth's water doesn't bulge as much as a result, so the difference between high and low tide is less. These special tides are called neap tides. ("Neap" is a very old word, but people who study the origin of words aren't sure exactly where this one comes from.)

WILD WIDE TIDES!

Mont-Saint-Michel is an island off the coast of France—sometimes! Its status as an island depends on the tides. At low tide, the water drops away far enough that people can walk across the sand and mud to the island. Spring tides may run out as far as 6.2 to 9.3 miles (10 to 15 km). At high tide, the sea level rises, and the ocean sometimes completely surrounds the island again. A bridge connects the island with the mainland so people can go back and forth.

The sea rushes back in very quickly at high tide. People here say the water pours in "at the speed of a galloping horse."

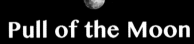

Pull of the Moon

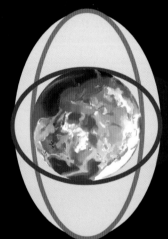

Pull of the Sun

Resultant Tide

Neap Tide

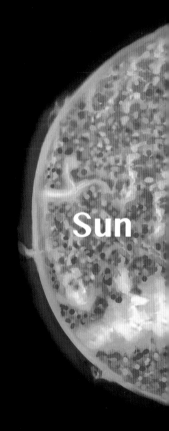

Sun

CHAPTER 4
WILD WEATHER

A huge wave breaks over a lighthouse during a winter storm.

THE WATER CYCLE

The ocean affects your daily weather no matter where you live.

That may seem hard to believe, especially if you live hundreds of miles from any shore. But the ocean covers 71 percent of Earth's surface. And across that vast area, all that water connects with the atmosphere—the layers of air that wrap around our planet. They are both part of the water cycle—the process that brings rain, snow, and even hailstones to your neighborhood.

The water cycle is powered by the sun. Sunshine heats the ocean's surface water and makes some of the liquid water turn into a gas called water vapor. This process is called evaporation. The warm air above the ocean rises, taking the vapor with it.

The air cools as it rises. This cooling allows water vapor to start clumping together to form tiny cloud droplets, and then bigger cloud droplets. This process is called condensation. As more and more water vapor condenses, clouds begin to grow. Winds blow the clouds away from where the water vapor first rose from the ocean. Inside the clouds, cloud droplets combine to form raindrops. The raindrops grow larger and heavier until finally they fall from the sky.

About 90 percent of the water that evaporates from the ocean falls right back into the ocean as rain. The rest falls on land. It piles up as snow and ice on mountaintops, drops into lakes, and patters on the ground. Over time, a lot of this water finds its way back into the ocean. It soaks into the ground and trickles through soil and rock, and then into streams and rivers. Rivers also carry water from melted ice and snow back to sea. Along the way, plants, animals, and people use some of this precious water.

WEATHER VS. CLIMATE

So how's the weather in your climate? Weather and climate are linked, but they're not the same.

Weather is what happens from day to day in a certain place. It consists of the kinds of clouds, the air temperature, the amount of wind, and other features of a day outside. You might have rainy weather one day, and completely different weather the next day.

Climate is what happens weather-wise over a longer period of many years in a particular place. A desert climate, for example, may be very dry and often very hot in summer but cold in the winter. A tropical rain forest climate is rainy and warm year-round. When it comes to climate—it doesn't change from day to day as weather does.

It takes more than a **million cloud droplets** to form a **raindrop.**

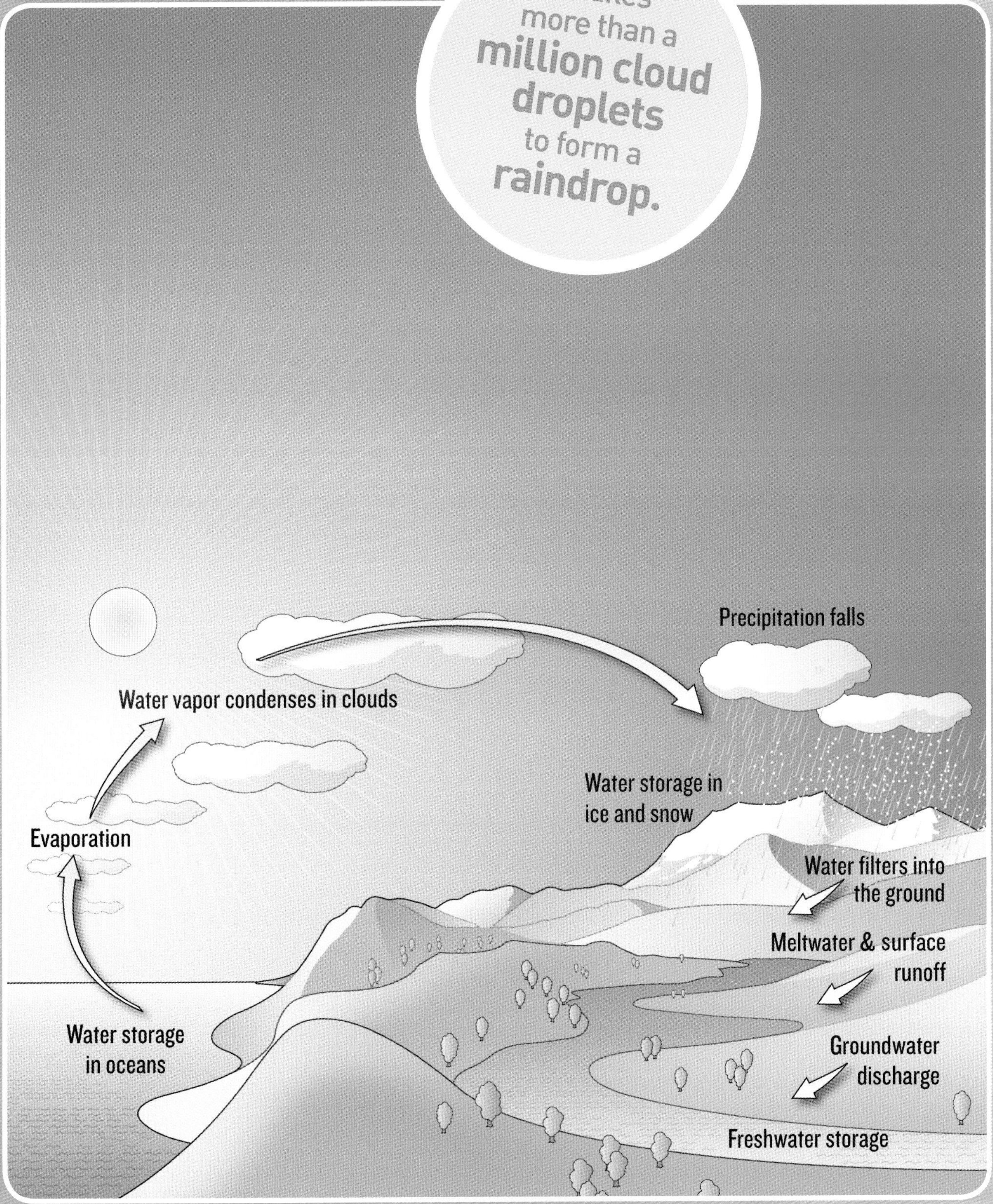

Precipitation falls

Water vapor condenses in clouds

Evaporation

Water storage in ice and snow

Water filters into the ground

Meltwater & surface runoff

Water storage in oceans

Groundwater discharge

Freshwater storage

TAKING THE HEAT

Have you ever walked across a hot sidewalk in bare feet? If so, ouch! You know firsthand (or first foot!) that the ground heats up in the sun. Water heats up, too, though not as quickly as land.

About half of the energy that the sun shines on Earth is soaked up by the ocean's topmost layer of water, which heats up slowly. Ocean water, however, is constantly moving due to waves, currents, and convection. Convection is the rising and sinking of masses of water. So the heat absorbed by the upper layer gets mixed up with deeper water. This means the ocean can soak up and hold a lot more heat than land.

The ocean can also store heat much longer than land, because water loses heat more slowly than land does. This ability to store heat has an important effect on weather and climate. For example, the Pacific Ocean keeps places along the coast of Washington State in the United States warmer in winter than you'd think they would be for a place that far north. The ocean makes the weather warmer because its stored-up heat warms the air above it. Then winds blowing off the ocean onto land carry this warmth over the land nearby. However, in Boston, Massachusetts, U.S.A., the wind usually blows from land to sea, so the Atlantic Ocean's stored-up heat doesn't get a chance to help the shivery city!

Across the ocean, a powerful current called the Gulf Stream warms parts of Europe as it sweeps by because it brings water carrying heat from the Gulf of Mexico.

EUROPE
ASIA
AFRICA
INDIAN OCEAN
ATLANTIC OCEAN

Average sea surface temperature
Low   High

Bet you didn't know

Penguins live along part of Africa's southern coast thanks to a cold current that runs along the southwestern edge of the continent. African penguins hunt fish in the cold water and also jump in to cool off on hot days.

Heat stored in the Pacific Ocean during summer will help keep winter along the northwestern U.S. coast a little warmer in winter.

ARCTIC OCEAN

PACIFIC OCEAN

NORTH AMERICA

ATLANTIC OCEAN

Equator

PACIFIC OCEAN

SOUTH AMERICA

AUSTRALIA

0   1,500 miles

0   1,500 kilometers

ANTARCTICA

The ocean has carved cliffs into Chile's coastal desert shoreline.

DESERT BY THE SEA

Picture a desert, and you probably think of a hot, dry place—not a land next to an ocean. But the driest deserts in the world lie along coastlines. The ocean is even partly responsible for keeping these coastal deserts so dry.

Coastal deserts lie on a continent's western side, where cold ocean currents flow along parts of the coast. This cold water cools winds that blow across it. As a result, the moisture in the air turns into fog, the way your breath turns into a mini-fog cloud on a cold day. The fog blows over the land, but the moisture stays in the air—it doesn't fall as rain.

The Namib Desert in Africa is a coastal desert. So is one of the world's driest places: the Atacama Desert in South America. The Atacama Desert receives very little rain, and some parts of it are said never to have received a single drop since humans began keeping records of the desert's rainfall.

EL NIÑO

Now that you know how the ocean works with the atmosphere to create climate and weather—what do you think might happen if the ocean suddenly behaves weirdly?

One of the ocean's biggest switcheroos is called an El Niño event, and it happens every few years in the Pacific Ocean. An El Niño event is signaled by currents in part of the Pacific Ocean becoming weaker and warmer. Sometimes they also change direction. Such changes affect the weather because large, strong currents tend to follow the same general paths. These paths are so predictable, ships can follow them to cross an ocean faster and save fuel, too.

An El Niño event happens when trade winds, which usually blow east to west at the Equator, weaken or even switch direction. Normally, the trade winds drag ocean water west—away from the coast of South America. Then cold, deep water rises up to replace it. But during an El Niño event, warm water flows in from the western Pacific toward South America's coast. South American fishermen have long known about these odd warm currents. They gave the event its name of "El Niño," which means "little boy" in Spanish, because they noticed the warm currents appeared every few years close to Christmas.

This invasion of warm water causes weather changes around the world. For example, very heavy rains fall on western South America and cause floods, while drier, hotter weather hits Australia and parts of Asia, causing forest fires and droughts. The western United States and Canada have warmer weather and more storms.

Scientists don't yet know everything about how El Niño events work. They have found that El Niño events occur more often now than in the past. Some scientists are working to find out why, and if the increase in El Niño events is linked to changes in Earth's climate due to burning fossil fuels (see pages 182–183).

LA NIÑA

A La Niña event is the opposite of an El Niño. (Its name means "little girl.") During a La Niña, trade winds are extra strong. More upwelling of cold water occurs than usual, which makes water in the eastern Pacific Ocean cooler than normal. It also causes wetter weather in Australia and parts of Asia, a drier winter in the southeastern United States, and colder winters in the northwestern United States.

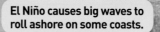
El Niño causes big waves to roll ashore on some coasts.

Bet you didn't know

An El Niño event usually lasts for nine months to a year. A La Niña event usually lasts for one to three years.

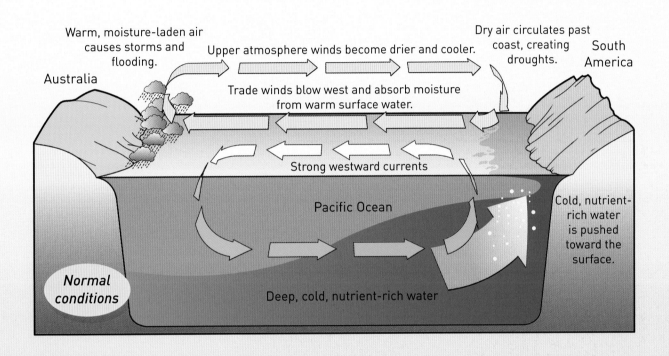

Warm, moisture-laden air causes storms and flooding.

Upper atmosphere winds become drier and cooler.

Dry air circulates past coast, creating droughts.

South America

Australia

Trade winds blow west and absorb moisture from warm surface water.

Strong westward currents

Pacific Ocean

Cold, nutrient-rich water is pushed toward the surface.

Normal conditions

Deep, cold, nutrient-rich water

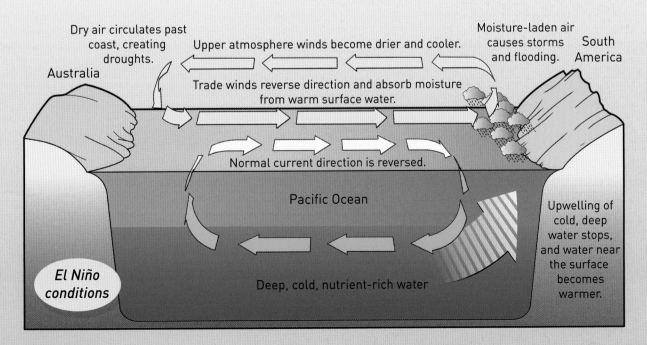

Dry air circulates past coast, creating droughts.

Upper atmosphere winds become drier and cooler.

Moisture-laden air causes storms and flooding.

South America

Australia

Trade winds reverse direction and absorb moisture from warm surface water.

Normal current direction is reversed.

Pacific Ocean

Upwelling of cold, deep water stops, and water near the surface becomes warmer.

El Niño conditions

Deep, cold, nutrient-rich water

MONSOON SEASON

What is summer like where you live? Hot and humid?
Warm and dry? How about hot, cloudy, and wet with rainfall that measures more than 400 inches (1,016 cm) in just a few months?

That's about 10 times more rain than the famously rainy U.S. city of Seattle, Washington, gets in one whole year—and it's what summer is like in much of India! From June to September, India is drenched by warm, wet winds that blow from the Indian Ocean onto the land. These winds are called the summer monsoon.

A monsoon is a change in the direction of the strongest winds in an area from season to season. "Monsoon" comes from an Arabic word, *mausim,* which means "season." In the tropics, monsoons cause wet seasons and dry seasons. In India, the summer monsoon causes a wet season. The winds push currents in the Indian Ocean toward India and send warm, wet air over the land. Rain pours down, and rivers and lakes swell. About 70 percent of Indian's yearly amount of rain falls during the summer monsoon season.

The heavy rain causes problems, such as floods and mudslides, but the water is badly needed after months of hot, dry weather. Farmers depend on the monsoon to bring rain for rice and other crops. Wild animals depend on the rain, too. It waters the fields and forests they live in and produces fruits and leaves for eating. Power plants that use waterpower to produce electricity need rain to refresh the water supply.

Beginning in October, winds and currents turn around and flow in the opposite direction. The currents flow away from India's coast. A spell of drier weather settles in, and sometimes droughts occur.

IT'S RAINING, IT'S POURING

India's monsoons are the most famous, but monsoons occur in other places, too. In North America, for example, a monsoon brings warm, wet weather to parts of the southwestern United States in summer. Australia, the Philippines, western Africa, and parts of Europe experience monsoons, too. On the islands of Borneo and Sumatra in Southeast Asia, orangutans cope with monsoon downpours by using big leaves as umbrellas and rain hats!

an orangutan mom and baby, in Borneo, Indonesia

STORMS
AT SEA

The world's worst storms are born in tropical oceans when warm, moist air rises and forms rain clouds. More air rushes in to replace the rising air, creating winds that spin. A bulge of water forms under the whirling winds. This rainy, windy spiral is called a tropical cyclone. As the winds grow faster and stronger, the depression becomes a tropical storm. Winds racing faster than 74 miles an hour (119 km/h) near the storm's center indicate that it has morphed into a hurricane. The worst hurricanes of all are labeled Category 5. Their winds can reach speeds of more than 155 miles an hour (249 km/h).

When a hurricane slams ashore, it brings huge waves as well as the big bulge of water that formed at sea. This "storm surge" floods the land and tosses boats onto shore like toys. Meanwhile, fierce winds knock down buildings and trees.

A hurricane is not only strong—it's also gigantic. It can measure 186 to 373 miles (300 to 600 km) or more in width and tower as high as 9 miles (15 km). But hitting land is the hurricane's undoing. The storm gets all its energy from the heat contained in the warm, wet air above the ocean. It loses energy as it crosses over land because it's cut off from its energy supply.

Windows are covered with boards before the arrival of another hurricane.

WHAT'S IN A NAME?

Storms are given specific names drawn from official lists kept by the World Meteorological Organization. This international committee keeps separate lists for storms in the Atlantic Ocean, the Indian Ocean, and different regions of the Pacific Ocean. The names are ones familiar to people in the areas where the tropical storms form. For example, "Don" and "Maria" are two names on the 2017 list for storms in the North Atlantic, Gulf of Mexico, and Caribbean Sea. "Shanshan" and "Kai-Tak" are two names provided by China for storms in the western North Pacific and the South China Sea.

Naming storms helps scientists keep track of them when lots of storms are forming in an area. It also helps scientists communicate with people about the storms when they need to warn the public that a very bad storm is coming.

Bet you didn't know

A tropical cyclone is a "hurricane" if it forms in the Atlantic Ocean or the eastern Pacific Ocean. In the northwestern Pacific, however, they're called typhoons. They're called severe tropical cyclones in the southwestern Pacific and parts of the Indian Ocean.

181

CLIMATE CHANGE

Speaking of climate—you've probably heard a lot about a worldwide problem called climate change. Maybe you've also heard it called "global warming." What, exactly, is it? And how is it related to the ocean?

Climate change refers to any big change in Earth's climate that lasts for many years.

Earth has experienced many climates and climate changes—it's been very warm, very cold, and everything in between. In just the past million years, Earth has gone through 100,000-year cycles between warmer periods and colder periods, including ice ages—spans of time when ice sheets covered large areas of land.

These climate changes were caused by natural events—sudden ones, such as huge volcanic eruptions, as well as slow, long-term ones, such as changes in Earth's orbit around the sun.

But when people talk about climate change now, they're usually talking about changes that have occurred over the past two hundred years. What makes this climate change different is that it's happening over a short time span, caused by the burning of fuels such as oil, coal, and natural gas. Burning these fuels produces greenhouse gases.

"Greenhouse gases" include carbon dioxide, water vapor, methane, and nitrous oxide. Earth's atmosphere works a bit like a greenhouse. Sunlight shines through it and warms Earth. Then the greenhouse gases in the atmosphere trap some of that heat instead of letting it all trickle out into space.

Life on Earth as we know it couldn't exist without greenhouse gases. But if they increase swiftly and in large amounts due to human activities, Earth will become much warmer very quickly. (Find out how you can help slow down climate change, on pages 260–261.)

CLIMATE CLUES

Wondering how on Earth we know what past climates were like?

Finding out this information seems impossible. After all, Earth is more than 4.5 billion years old, and its ocean is nearly as old.

Measurements kept by humans are one record of the past. Climate history is also recorded in glaciers, ice sheets, rocks, coral reefs, fossils, and seafloor. Scientists have collected a timeline of climate by drilling into ice sheets and glaciers to pull up long cylinders of ice. These "ice cores" hold trapped bits of history: specks of dust, salt, volcanic ash, and tiny air bubbles. Scientists test the bubbles to measure the amounts of different gases in ancient atmospheres.

Cores from the seafloor show climate history, too, in fossils found there.

A scientist carefully removes cores of ice in Antarctica.

10
25

10
50

The **longest ice cores** taken from ice caps and glaciers measure more than **2 miles** (3 km) long.

183

CHAPTER 5

UNDERWATER EXPLORATION

A diver explores Silfra canyon in Iceland.

BENEATH THE SURFACE

What do you see when you look at the ocean from the shore? You might see seabirds, or ships sailing past. If you were in Fiji in the South Pacific Ocean, you'd see other islands. If you were in the United States on Oregon's coast, you'd see giant rocks. You might even see whales! From many shores, however, all you'll see is water—water, water everywhere as far as the horizon.

For the most part, the ocean's surface looks like an endless expanse of green-blue-gray. But thanks to modern technology, people have been able to sneak a peek at the amazing geography hidden beneath the surface. That geography includes hills, bluffs, mountains, volcanoes, plains, and canyons. The ocean is where you'll find the longest mountain range, the tallest mountain, and the deepest chasm on Earth!

Mapping the seafloor in detail became possible after the early 1900s, when a technology called sonar was invented and developed. "Sonar" comes from letters in the words "sound navigation and ranging." It is a way of using sound to measure distance underwater. A scientist can use a device to send a sound signal into the water. The sound bounces off objects. This echo is then picked up by a receiver. Distances can be figured out by measuring the difference between when a signal is sent and when the echo returns.

an illustration of how a ship uses sonar to collect information about the seafloor

SEEING WITH SOUND

From 1925 to 1927, scientists aboard the German ship *Meteor* used a device called an echo sounder to map the floor of the southern Atlantic Ocean. They recorded more than 67,000 echoes. This was a first in the history of ocean studies. The data were used to make a detailed map.

Today, echo sounders are called precision depth recorders. These machines can tell the difference between echoes bouncing off rock and echoes bouncing off soft, muddy seafloor. As a result, sound can be used to figure out both how deep the seafloor is and what it's made of. Modern research vessels tow sonar systems behind them to measure wide areas of the seafloor all at once.

A deep-sea vent on the Atlantic Ocean seafloor releases clouds of hot water filled with chemicals.

Bet you didn't know

Some animals have their own built-in sonar system, called echolocation. Dolphins, porpoises, and some whales use echolocation to hunt and navigate underwater. Many bats use echolocation to hunt and fly in the dark.

CONTINENTS
ON THE MOVE

The technology that helps us see what's under the sea
today has also helped us figure out Earth's past history—way back to when the continents were clumped together as one huge landmass.

Over billions of years, the continents traveled to where they are today due to a process called continental drift. Continents drift because Earth's outer layer is divided into huge stony slabs called plates. These plates fit together like a jigsaw puzzle. They float on top of a deep layer of dense rock that's partly solid and partly melted. This layer is like a pot of stew simmering on a stove. The hot, molten rock churns constantly and drags the plates along with it.

Another process is at work deep in the ocean. It's called seafloor spreading. Plates on the seafloor move apart as they are pulled by the churning molten rock. A gap called a mid-ocean ridge forms. Melted rock called magma oozes up to fill the gap. The magma cools and becomes new seafloor. This cycle repeats endlessly.

Continental drift and seafloor spreading are both part of a process called plate tectonics. Together, they're constantly rearranging Earth's crust. Right now, Australia, South America, and Antarctica are drifting away from each other. Meanwhile, the Atlantic Ocean is growing wider by about 0.4 to 4 inches (1 to 10 cm) a year. As a result, the Pacific Ocean is slowly shrinking.

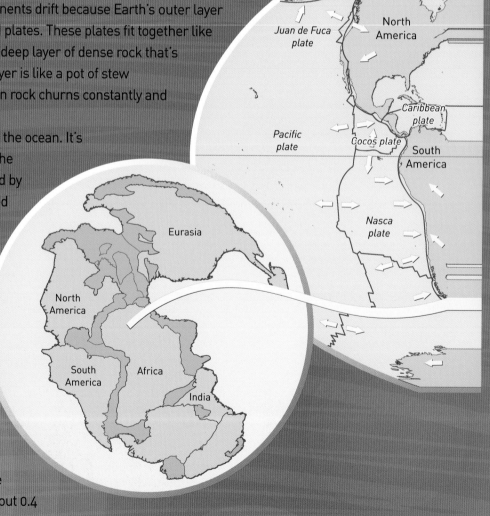

A supercontinent existed about 240 million years ago that we now call **Pangaea.** The ocean that surrounded it is called Panthalassa. "Pangaea" means "all land" and "Panthalassa" means "all sea."

SLIP, SLIDE, SCRUNCH

Earth's surface is made up of about a dozen large plates and a number of smaller ones. In some places, plates slide past each other as they travel in opposite directions. But they don't slide smoothly—they grind against each other. We don't usually feel this grinding. Sometimes, however, the pressure between the plates builds up and is then released very suddenly as the plates slip. This sudden movement causes an earthquake.

In other places, plates slide under and over each other. The plate made of denser rock sinks under the plate that's less dense. This sinking is called subduction. Ocean crust is denser than continental crust, so an ocean plate sinks under continental crust when they meet. The sinking oceanic plate is then melted deep within Earth. Meanwhile, a mountain range forms on the continent above this area of melting. Volcanic mountain ranges such as the Andes in South America formed this way.

North American plate

Eurasian plate

Eurasia

India

Arabian plate

Africa

African plate

Indian plate

Philippine plate

Pacific plate

South American plate

Australian plate

Australia

Scotia plate

Antarctic plate

Antarctica

The San Andreas Fault in California is a long crack in Earth's surface caused by two big plates sliding past each other.

TOWERING TSUNAMIS

The undersea movement of Earth's plates can send a huge wall of water racing toward land. This is called a tsunami.

A tsunami starts off in the ocean as a series of waves caused by an underwater earthquake, volcanic eruption, or landslide. These events suddenly shove a large amount of seawater up or down. The energy from this shove sets waves in motion. The waves travel out from the disturbance in circles, as if a giant rock had fallen into the water and sent out ripples.

At first, the waves are barely noticeable far out in the ocean, even though they may be racing along at more than 500 miles an hour (800 km/h), or about as fast as a jet. But as a tsunami approaches land, its waves slow down sharply because they meet the shallow seafloor. This slowdown causes water to pile up quickly and turn into a huge wave. A tsunami can tower more than 100 feet (30.5 m) high!

Like all waves, a tsunami has a high point called a crest and a low point called a trough. When a tsunami approaches land, its trough often arrives first. It pulls the water near the coast out to sea and exposes a wide area of the seafloor. This is one of the first warning signs—the gigantic wave will probably arrive just a few minutes later. And that wave is often followed by a few more waves. A tsunami causes terrible destruction as it rushes inland, flattening buildings and sweeping away anything in its path.

About 80 percent of tsunamis occur in the Pacific Ocean. An earthquake on one side of the ocean can trigger a tsunami that speeds across the ocean in less then a day and threatens places on the other side. Many countries along the Pacific Rim (see pages 14–15) measure earthquake activity and exchange information in an effort to warn people living near coasts when a tsunami might be coming.

WORLD'S WORST WILD WAVES

Two of the worst tsunamis ever recorded have hit since the year 2000.

On December 26, 2004, an earthquake struck in the Indian Ocean near Indonesia. It caused a tsunami that reached 18 countries, traveling as far as 3,000 miles (4,800 km). More than 230,000 people died, and millions were left homeless.

On March 11, 2011, Japan's biggest earthquake occurred off the coast of its largest island, Honshu. It generated a tsunami that struck Japan's coast shortly after. Water flowed as far as 6 miles (10 km) inland, carrying cars and buildings with it. More than 15,000 people were lost in this disaster.

A tsunami roars into the city of Miyako, Japan, on March 11, 2011.

Bet you didn't know

On March 27, 1964, the most powerful earthquake in U.S. history struck Alaska. It launched a tsunami that caused damage along the coast as far south as California. There, it destroyed most of the town of Crescent City in the northern part of the state.

This diagram shows how energy from an underwater earthquake sends waves moving quickly toward land. The waves grow very tall when they hit the shore.

UNDERWATER MOUNTAINS

Earth's longest mountain range is in the ocean. It's the mid-ocean ridge system, a series of mountains that loop through all the world's oceans. Many scientists compare the ridge system's path around Earth to the pattern of seams on a baseball. Altogether, the ridge system is about 37,000 miles (60,000 km) long. It's many times longer than the longest mountain range on land, the Andes of South America, which is about 4,700 miles (7,600 km) long.

This worldwide mountain range is called "mid-ocean" because in most places, it runs roughly across the middle of an ocean. The Mid-Atlantic Ridge, for example, traces a rough S-shape as it runs through the middle of the Atlantic, which is also roughly S-shaped. But parts of the mid-ocean ridge system aren't smack in an ocean's center. The East Pacific Rise, for example, is off-center where it runs through the southeastern Pacific Ocean. It is closer to South America's western coast than it is to the Pacific's middle.

The mid-ocean ridge system contains thousands of volcanoes and volcanic sections, making it the world's longest volcano chain. About 80 to 90 percent of Earth's volcanic activity occurs along its length. It's all part of the endless process of seafloor spreading.

Most of the mid-ocean ridge system is very deep underwater, but it appears above the waves in some places, such as Iceland.

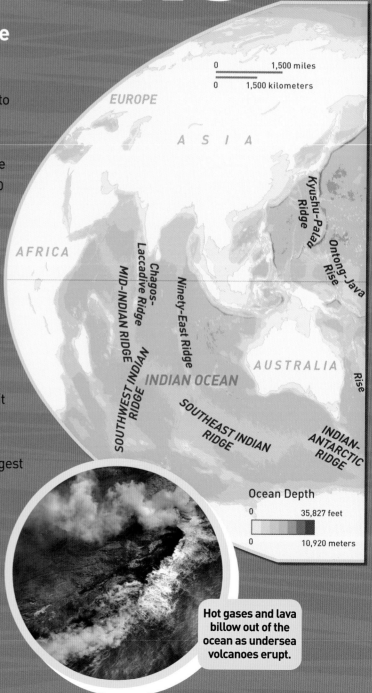

EUROPE

ASIA

AFRICA

Kyushu-Palau Ridge

Ontong-Java Rise

Chagos-Laccadive Ridge

MID-INDIAN RIDGE

Ninety-East Ridge

AUSTRALIA

Rise

SOUTHWEST INDIAN RIDGE

INDIAN OCEAN

SOUTHEAST INDIAN RIDGE

INDIAN-ANTARCTIC RIDGE

0   1,500 miles
0   1,500 kilometers

Ocean Depth

0   35,827 feet

0   10,920 meters

Hot gases and lava billow out of the ocean as undersea volcanoes erupt.

Bet you didn't know

The seafloor spreads at speeds up to 6.3 inches (16 cm) per year in parts of the East Pacific Rise in the southeastern Pacific Ocean. That's one of the fastest rates of spreading in the world. Spreading is balanced out by shrinking in other places.

MAPPING THE OCEAN

The Mid-Atlantic Ridge was discovered in the early 1870s by scientists aboard the wooden sailing ship H.M.S. *Challenger*. They were on a scientific mission to chart the deep seafloor and study the ocean. They didn't have cameras, diving suits, or other tools used by modern scientists. Instead, they measured how deep the seafloor was by dropping weights attached to ropes. Their measurements revealed that the Atlantic's seafloor rose up in the middle.

About 80 years later, mapmaker Marie Tharp and geologist Bruce Heezen began work on a map of the seafloor. In the process, Tharp and her team revealed Earth's mid-ocean ridge system. Tharp also noticed that the Mid-Atlantic Ridge is sliced by a valley, or "rift," as deep and wide as the Grand Canyon. Her work led to the discovery of seafloor spreading and an understanding of plate tectonics (pages 188–189).

ARCTIC OCEAN

PACIFIC OCEAN

NORTH AMERICA

EUROPE

Hawaiian Ridge

Mid-Pacific Mountains

ATLANTIC OCEAN

AFRICA

Equator

Cocos Ridge

EAST PACIFIC RISE

Tuamotu Ridge

Nasca Ridge

SOUTH AMERICA

Sala y Gómez Ridge

CHILE RISE

Rio Grande Rise

MID-ATLANTIC RIDGE

Lord Howe

Louisville Ridge

PACIFIC OCEAN

PACIFIC-ANTARCTIC RIDGE

AMERICA-ANTARCTIC RIDGE

ANTARCTICA

H.M.S. *Challenger* sails near the Kerguelen Islands in the Indian Ocean in the 1870s.

Volcanic cones rise in Alaska's Aleutian Islands.

Bet you didn't know

The island of Nauru in the South Pacific is the world's smallest island nation. It is only about 8 square miles (21 sq km) in size. You could fit about ten Nauru islands in the U.S. capital, Washington, D.C.! Most of the island's 10,000 citizens live on its coastline.

INTRIGUING ISLANDS

An island is an area of land that's surrounded by water. Earth's seven continents are surrounded by water, too, of course, but they are much bigger than islands. The smallest continent, Australia, is nearly four times as big as the largest island, Greenland.

Many of the ocean's islands fall into one of two main groups: continental and oceanic.

Continental islands rise up from land that slopes away from a continent's edge. They're made of the same sort of rock that forms the continent. New Guinea, near Australia, is an example of a continental island. Some continental islands formed as a result of plate tectonics pulling apart the ancient supercontinents. Other islands formed because sea levels rose and cut them off from the mainland, or because weather and water wore away the land connecting them.

Oceanic islands rise up directly from the seafloor. Many of them are the peaks of undersea volcanoes. A chain of volcanoes forms in places where an oceanic plate slides under another plate. The Aleutian Islands, for example, are an oceanic island arc in the North Pacific. Japan is a nation of oceanic islands sitting at the meeting place of four plates—a location that causes it to be rattled by many earthquakes.

Oceanic islands made up of volcanoes also form in places where plates are moving away from each other. Iceland and the Azores are among the islands formed by seafloor spreading, where plates pull apart and magma surges out of the seafloor (pages 188–189). Both Iceland and the Azores are in the North Atlantic Ocean and experience many earthquakes and volcanic eruptions.

HOT SPOTS

Some oceanic islands pop up over a "hot spot" in the seafloor. A hot spot is a deep pocket of magma that is not part of a mid-ocean ridge but erupts over long spans of time. An island forms as lava heaps up. Over millions of years, a chain of islands forms as the oceanic plate travels slowly over the hot spot.

The Hawaiian Islands, for example, formed over a hot spot. These islands sit on the Pacific plate, which moves in a north-westerly direction. Today, the hot spot fuels volcanoes on the Big Island of Hawaii. It's also building an undersea volcano called Loihi nearby. Someday, Loihi will rise above the water and become the next island in the Hawaiian chain.

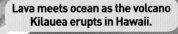

Lava meets ocean as the volcano Kilauea erupts in Hawaii.

THE BIRTH OF AN ISLAND

In November 1963, off the southern coast of Iceland, the pressure of superhot magma burst through a weak spot on the seafloor. It exploded out of the Atlantic Ocean in a pillar of steam, smoke, ash, and rocks. The fiery fountain rose as high as 4 miles (6 km) into the sky.

Lava built up as the volcano kept erupting. Soon, it was clear that a new island was being born. In just a few days, it was already 147 feet (45 m) tall. About six months later, it had grown to 560 feet (171 m) tall and a mile (1.6 km) wide. The new island was named Surtsey after Surtr, a "fire giant" in ancient stories.

But even as Surtsey spewed lava and steam, new life began to appear on its dark landscape. Birds landed on the island, and in the spring of 1964, seeds washed up on the coast. Insects arrived, too. The next year, delicate white flowers grew along the shore.

Scientists realized they had a rare opportunity to see how life would unfold on a brand-new island. The island, which is part of Iceland, was declared a nature reserve in 1965. People needed special permits to visit, and nobody was allowed to bring seeds, plants, or animals. Scientists wanted to find out how the island would change naturally, without humans adding organisms to it on purpose or by accident.

Today, there is less of Surtsey to protect. The ocean is slowly taking back the island, and scientists think it may be underwater by 2100!

EXPLODING ISLAND!

Krakatau (sometimes called Krakatoa) was a volcanic island in Indonesia. You read that correctly: "was." In August 1883, Krakatau erupted violently. Cracks opened in its sides. Seawater flowed into the volcano, where it turned into steam so quickly that the island exploded. The explosion was so loud, it was heard as far as 2,980 miles (4,800 km) away in Australia!

Nobody lived on the island. But the explosion caused tsunamis, which struck islands and shores nearby. Thousands of people were killed. Ash, which rocketed up to 50 miles (80 km) high, blanketed the sky. Just a third of the island remained.

In 1930, a new volcanic island emerged from the sea where Krakatau once stood. It has continued to grow and occasionally erupt since that time.

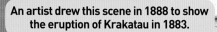
An artist drew this scene in 1888 to show the eruption of Krakatau in 1883.

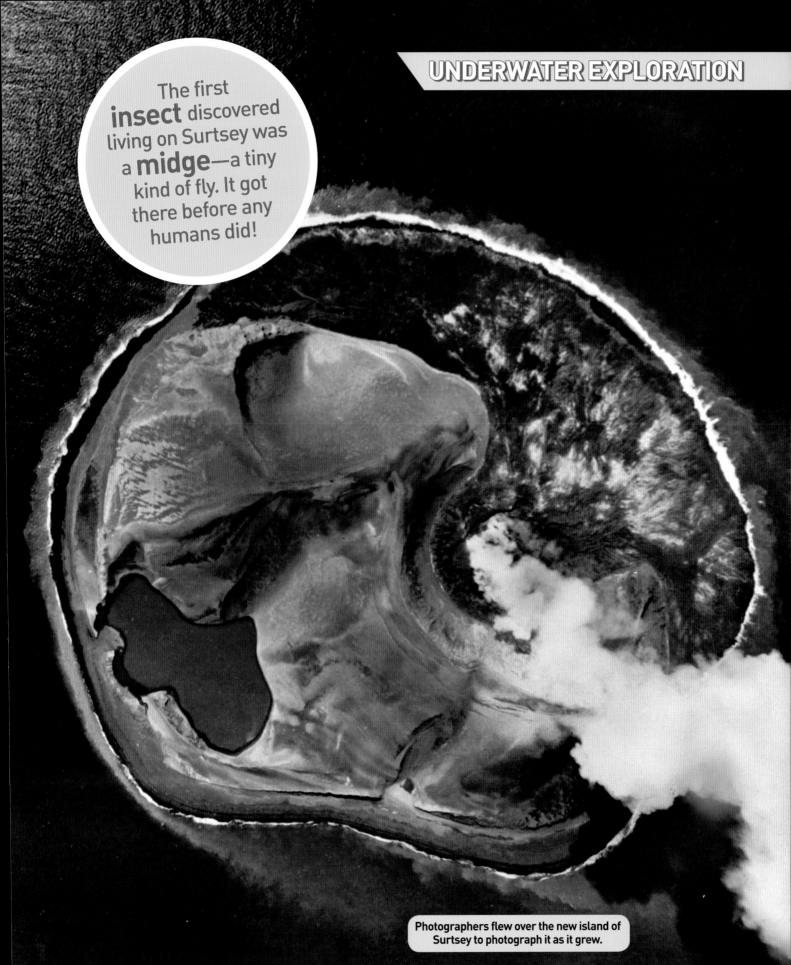

The first **insect** discovered living on Surtsey was a **midge**—a tiny kind of fly. It got there before any humans did!

Photographers flew over the new island of Surtsey to photograph it as it grew.

Atolls in the Maldives form rings in the Indian Ocean.

The Tuamotu Islands in the southwestern Pacific Ocean form the longest chain of coral atolls in the world. They span more than 1,200 miles (1,931 km). The Tuamotus are part of French Polynesia.

CORAL ISLANDS

Explosions and eruptions are dramatic ways to make an island. But oceanic islands can also build up quietly, over long spans of time, on the remains of ancient undersea volcanoes. These islands start out as structures built by small, soft-bodied animals called stony corals.

A stony coral is a polyp—an animal with a tubular body that's stuck to a surface on one end and has tentacles for feeding on the other. It secretes limestone to make a stony, protective cup around its soft body. As more polyps build cups that are stuck to each other, they combine to form a structure called a coral reef. Over time, old polyps die, but new ones continue to build new cups on top of the old reef.

A coral reef may grow so big that it nearly reaches the ocean's surface. Sand, rock, and soil carried by waves may get caught on it and pile up over time. Seeds washed or blown onto the island take root and grow. The Bahamas and the Florida Keys are made up of coral islands.

Coral reefs and coral islands sometimes surround a shallow pool of water called a lagoon. At one time, the lagoon was the site of a volcanic island, and the reefs grew on its slopes. The volcano, however, eventually stopped erupting. Over millions of years, the volcano slowly eroded and sank beneath the waves. The ring of reefs left behind is called an atoll. Most atolls exist as groups rather than as lonely rings in the middle of nowhere. The Maldives in the Indian Ocean, for example, is made up of 26 atolls.

PILED-UP ISLES

A barrier island is a skinny island that lies along a coastline. Many barrier islands are pile-ups of sand deposited by waves, such as the chain of islands that stretch for hundreds of miles along the coasts of Texas and Mexico.

Some barrier islands, however, were created by massive, slow-moving rivers of ice called glaciers. As the glaciers plowed across land, they scraped up rock and soil. When they melted, they left behind heaps of material, called moraines, and also caused floods. New York's Long Island contains moraines left by a glacier about 21,000 years ago.

Long Island, New York, was formed by the advance and retreat of glaciers.

AMAZING ISLAND ANIMALS

Giant turtles, lizards, and crabs, oh my! Ocean islands are home to many animals not found on continents. These animals may be larger or smaller than similar species on the mainland. They may look completely different because they've adapted to their habitats.

Unfortunately, the arrival of humans on islands has caused many special island animals to become extinct. Sometimes humans simply hunted the animals until there were none left. Animals that arrive with humans also endanger island wildlife and may also bring diseases.

Fortunately, in many places, people are working to protect island wildlife and restore their habitats. Here are a few of the amazing animals living the island life!

Madagascar is a large island in the Indian Ocean that split off the continent of Africa about 165 million years ago. Most of its wildlife is found nowhere else. This silky sifaka is one of about 100 species of lemurs, which are mammals unique to Madagascar. It lives in rain forests and can jump as far as 30 feet (9.3 m) from one tree to another!

The **coconut crab** lives on tropical islands in the Indian Ocean and parts of the Pacific. This giant "cousin" of hermit crabs can be up to 3 feet (1 m) long. It tears open coconuts it finds on beaches with its claws. It also eats other foods, such as berries and any small prey it can catch. It can even climb trees!

Hawaiian honeycreepers are a group of birds found only in the Hawaiian Islands. Many species of these honeycreepers are found on just one of the islands. One species, the 'akiapola'au, lives only on the Big Island of Hawaii. It taps on branches with its long bill to detect insects hiding inside and then uses its bill to fish them out. Most of Hawaii's birds are endangered species.

The endangered **kiwi** of New Zealand is about the size of a chicken but has useless wings that are only about an inch (3 cm) long. However, it has strong legs and claws for running fast and digging burrows. A kiwi comes out of its burrow at night to hunt for worms, sniffing for them with a pair of nostrils at the end of its beak.

The world's largest lizard, the **Komodo dragon**, lives on a few islands in southeastern Indonesia. A really big dragon can be up to 10 feet (3 m) long and weigh up to 300 pounds (136 kg). It preys on everything from small lizards to big water buffalo. Some scientists, however, wonder if this giant lizard is actually a miniature version of even bigger lizards that once existed in Australia.

The Galápagos Islands in the Pacific Ocean are famous for their one-of-a-kind animals. Among them is the world's largest tortoise, the Galápagos tortoise. Males of this species can be up to 6 feet (1.83 m) long and weigh up to 573 pounds (260 kg). Tortoises from different islands have evolved differently shaped shells. Other unique Galápagos animals include a seagoing lizard called the marine iguana and a diving, fish-eating bird called the flightless cormorant—the only cormorant in the world that can't fly.

GETTING THERE

How do animals get to islands in the first place? That depends partly on the island. Animals may be living on a piece of land that, over time, gets cut off from the mainland by movements of Earth's crust or a rise in the sea level. Animals, especially reptiles, can wash up on shore after floating on clumps of plants torn off by a storm. Some species swim there. Birds and insects, of course, can fly to islands. Spiders and other small animals can blow in on winds.

The **tuatara** is a lizardlike reptile that lives on islands around New Zealand. It's the only living species of its kind. It's often called a living fossil because it's hardly changed at all from its ancestors, which lived millions of years ago. It's famous for having a "third eye" on top of its head!

UNDERSEA MOUNTAINS AND VOLCANOES

On January 8, 2005, the U.S. Navy submarine U.S.S. *San Francisco* was zooming at top speed in the Pacific Ocean. Then disaster struck: The submarine crashed into an undersea mountain that wasn't shown on the chart the crew was using for navigation. One sailor died, and many of the other 136 crew members suffered injuries.

This mountain was a seamount—an undersea volcano. Seamounts have jagged peaks that never grew high enough to rise above the ocean's surface as islands. Many seamounts are extinct volcanoes—ones that don't erupt anymore. Another kind of extinct undersea volcano is a guyot, which has a flat top. A guyot is what remains of a volcanic island that sinks underwater and loses its top to wave action.

The ocean may contain about 100,000 seamounts, but many of them—like the one hit by the submarine—haven't yet been charted. The existence of seamounts has been known since the 1800s, but it wasn't until the 1930s that they were first explored and named. More seamounts have been discovered since the invention of technology that makes undersea exploration possible. Still, scientists estimate that 80 to 90 percent of the seafloor remains a mystery.

Thousands of newly discovered seamounts appear on a map of the seafloor that was created in 2014, boosting the known number from about 5,000 to about 20,000.

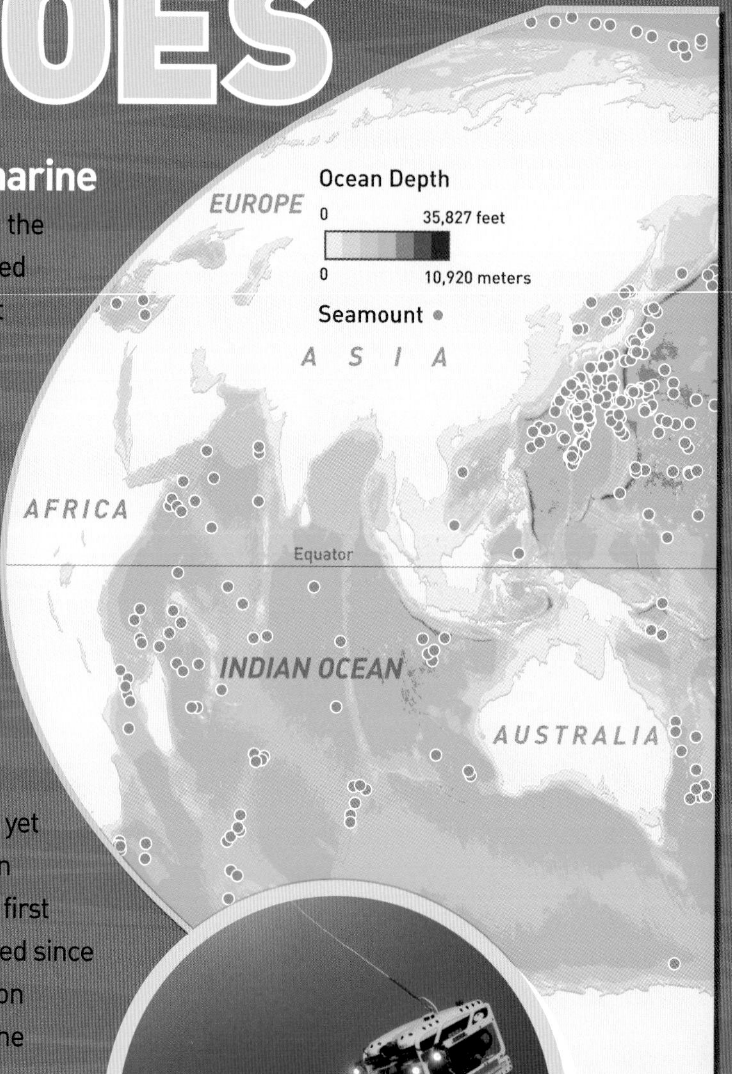

Ocean Depth

| 0 | | 35,827 feet |
| 0 | | 10,920 meters |

Seamount •

EUROPE

ASIA

AFRICA

Equator

INDIAN OCEAN

AUSTRALIA

A diver uses a special camera to explore a seamount in Indonesia.

A coral reef on an Indonesian seamount is filled with colorful life.

ARCTIC OCEAN

NORTH AMERICA

EUROPE

ATLANTIC OCEAN

AFRICA

PACIFIC OCEAN

SOUTH AMERICA

0   1,500 miles

0   1,500 kilometers

ANTARCTICA

SEAMOUNT SEA LIFE

Seamounts are home to an amazing variety of wildlife. They provide corals and sponges with hard surfaces they can fasten on to. They also change the speed and direction of currents flowing around them, which causes the water to swirl up nutrients from the seafloor. The nutrients feed animals that live on the seamount's slope, as well as many other hungry animals that visit.

Seamounts are also important rest stops for marine animals that travel, or migrate, long distances from season to season. Humpback whales, tuna, and other creatures visit seamounts to find food. Scalloped hammerhead sharks gather at certain seamounts to find mates. Fish called orange roughies cluster at seamounts to lay eggs. So far, scientists have studied only a few hundred of the ocean's thousands of seamounts. They've discovered that some seamounts have species that may be found nowhere else, just as many islands do.

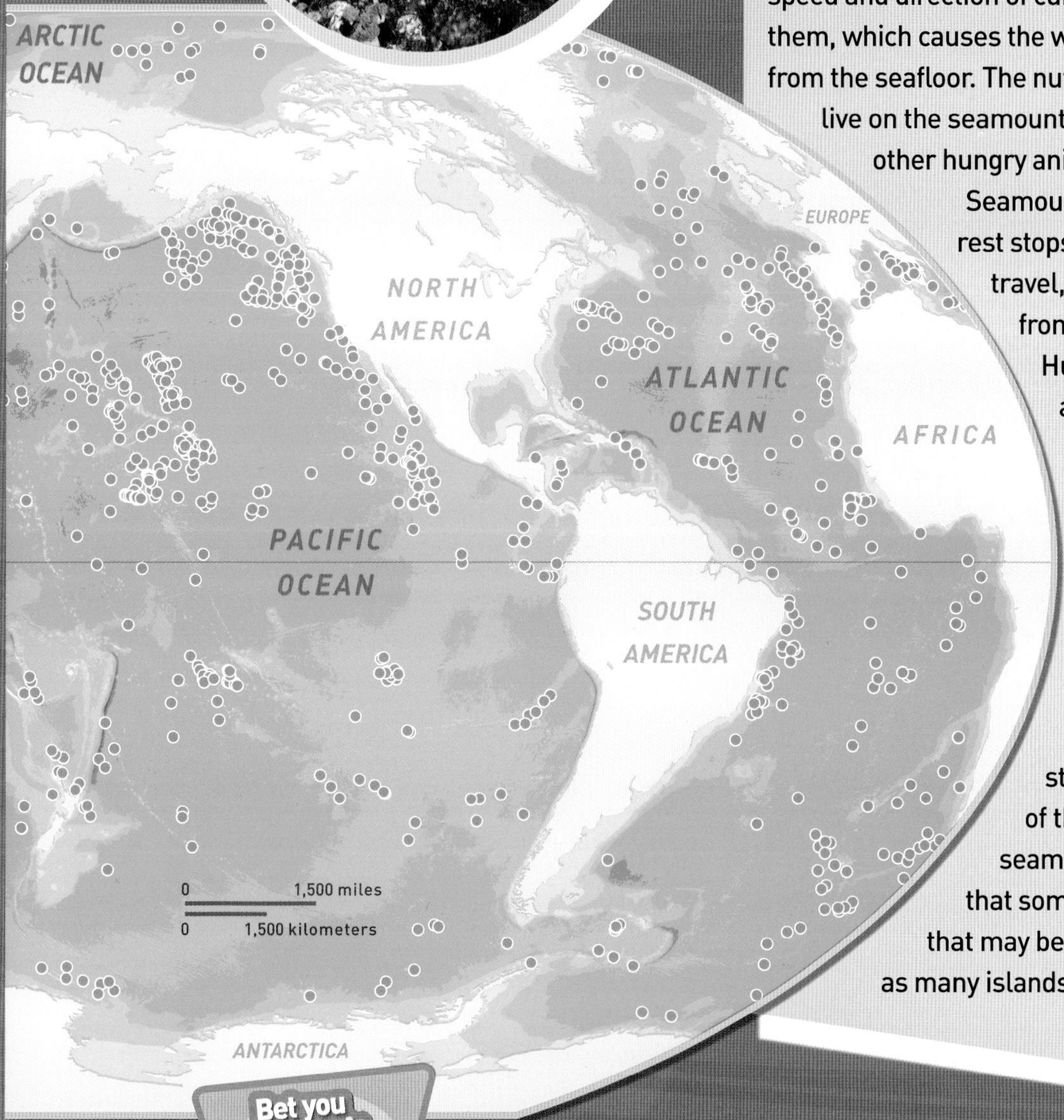

Bet you didn't know

Researchers who explore seamounts often find species new to science. In 2006, for example, a weird sponge was collected from a seamount off California's coast. It was later identified as a new species of "killer sponge" covered in tiny hooks that snag prey.

TRENCHES: EARTH'S DEEPEST CANYONS

An ocean trench is a canyon that forms in a subduction zone in the ocean, where one tectonic plate sinks under another tectonic plate. Melted rock produced by this sinking rises. It forms a chain of volcanoes that lies alongside the trench. Earthquakes rumble along their length. (If an ocean plate sinks under a continental one, it produces a volcanic mountain range on land.)

Trenches are Earth's deepest canyons. The Mariana Trench, for example, is a gash in the seafloor of the Pacific that is more than 1,580 miles (2,540 km) long—nearly six times as long as the Grand Canyon. It contains the deepest place on Earth: Challenger Deep, which is 35,827 feet (10,920 m) beneath the ocean's surface—nearly seven times as deep as the Grand Canyon.

The Pacific Ocean contains most of the world's trenches, but deep trenches slice the seafloor in other oceans, too. The Indian Ocean, for example, boasts the Java Trench, which drops to a depth of 23,376 feet (7,125 m). The Atlantic Ocean plunges 28,232 feet (8,605 m) in the Puerto Rico Trench.

Trenches are not only deep but also pitch dark and extremely cold. The weight of all the water above causes pressure that is more than a thousand times greater than the air pressure you feel on Earth's surface. Yet animals manage to survive in this harsh environment. Some are big enough to be caught on camera, but most of them can be seen only with a microscope.

a snailfish from the Arctic Ocean

CREATURES OF THE TRENCH

Intense pressure underwater can crush devices sent down to explore the deep sea. But engineers have designed unmanned vehicles that can endure this pressure. These vehicles have sent back pictures of animals that live in ocean trenches at different depths.

In 2008, for example, scientists found snailfish living in the Japan Trench in the Pacific Ocean at a depth of 4.8 miles (7.7 km). In 2014, deep-sea devices filmed another kind of snailfish swimming even deeper, more than 5 miles (8.2 km) down in the Mariana Trench. Other creatures filmed miles down in trenches include eels, rat-tail fish, and hefty shrimplike animals nearly one foot (0.3 m) long that scientists refer to as "supergiant amphipods."

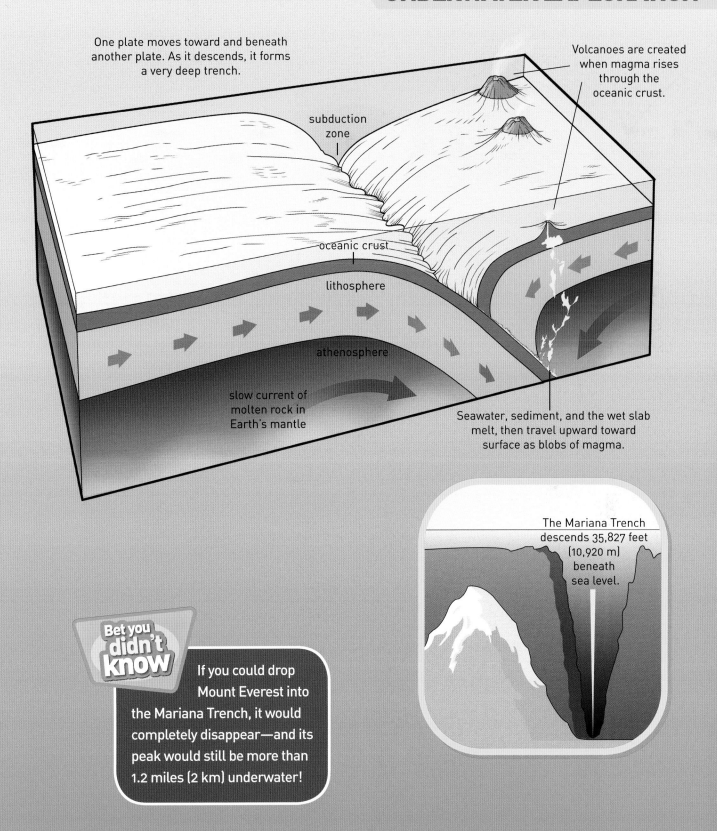

One plate moves toward and beneath another plate. As it descends, it forms a very deep trench.

Volcanoes are created when magma rises through the oceanic crust.

subduction zone

oceanic crust

lithosphere

athenosphere

slow current of molten rock in Earth's mantle

Seawater, sediment, and the wet slab melt, then travel upward toward surface as blobs of magma.

The Mariana Trench descends 35,827 feet (10,920 m) beneath sea level.

Bet you didn't know
If you could drop Mount Everest into the Mariana Trench, it would completely disappear—and its peak would still be more than 1.2 miles (2 km) underwater!

THE ABYSSAL PLAINS

Abyssal plains are wide, flat spaces that lie between the continents and the ocean's mid-ocean ridges. They are found at depths ranging from 13,123 feet to 19,680 feet (4,000 to 6,000 m).

Seamounts rise in some parts of abyssal plains, but for the most part these plains are the smoothest, flattest places on Earth—even though they lie on top of rough, rocky seafloor! What makes them smooth is a layer of sediment that covers them. Sediment is all the material that drifts down from above and settles on the seafloor.

Sediment includes material formed from rocks washed in from land by rivers, dragged in by chunks of ice, and blown onto the ocean's surface by winds. Grains of sand and particles of clay, for example, flow into the ocean with river water. Sand grains are bigger than clay particles, so they settle closer to coastlines. Clay particles flow farther out to sea and are also blown far from shore. Sediment also contains minerals that were once dissolved in the seawater but have dropped, or precipitated, out of it.

Sediment is also made up of particles from once-living things, such as the "marine snow" of microscopic skeletons and shells of one-celled organisms (see pages 48–49). Sediment in the deep sea contains more material from living things than sediment in shallower coastal waters, because it receives less of the minerals washed off the land. If nonliving materials make up more than 30 percent of sediment, the sediment is called "ooze."

LAYER UPON LAYER

Sediment piles up faster near continents than in the deep sea. In these areas, sediment can settle at a rate of 0.04 inches (1 mm) per year. That adds up to 3.3 feet (1 m) every thousand years.

Far out on the abyssal plains, however, it can take a thousand years for 0.04 inches (1 mm) of sediment to build up.

Sediment isn't distributed equally on the abyssal plains. It is very thin near the mid-ocean ridges and thicker farther away. This is because new seafloor is constantly created along the ridges. The age of seafloor increases the farther away from the ridge it is, and it has accumulated lots of sediment over time.

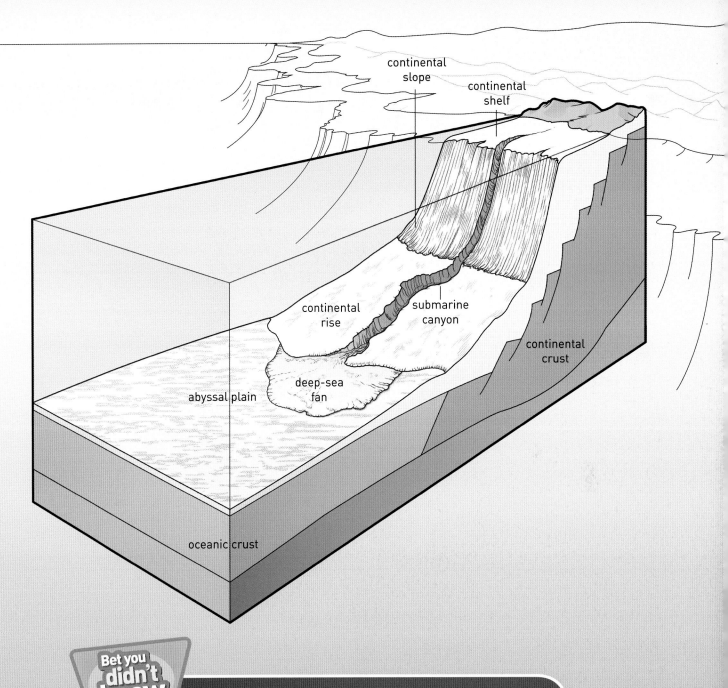

continental
slope

continental
shelf

continental
rise

submarine
canyon

continental
crust

deep-sea
fan

abyssal plain

oceanic crust

Bet you didn't know

About 30 percent of the ocean's floor is covered by the abyssal plains. They are most common in the Atlantic Ocean, which has many big rivers pouring into it, adding sediment. The average thickness of sediment in the Atlantic Ocean is about 3,280 feet (1,000 m)—about twice as thick as sediment in the Pacific Ocean.

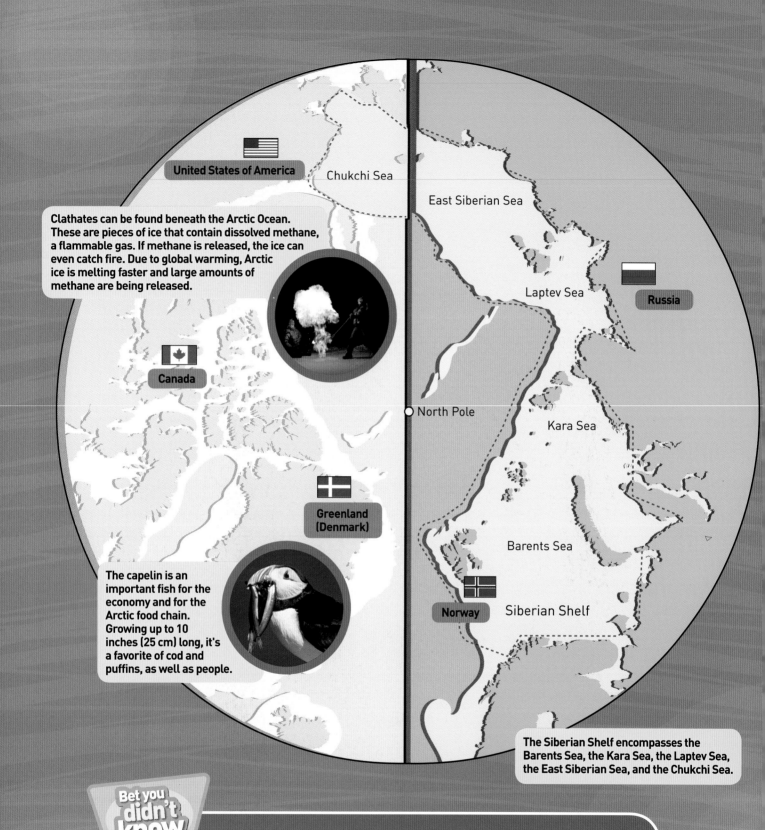

United States of America

Chukchi Sea

East Siberian Sea

Clathates can be found beneath the Arctic Ocean. These are pieces of ice that contain dissolved methane, a flammable gas. If methane is released, the ice can even catch fire. Due to global warming, Arctic ice is melting faster and large amounts of methane are being released.

Laptev Sea

Russia

Canada

North Pole

Kara Sea

Greenland (Denmark)

The capelin is an important fish for the economy and for the Arctic food chain. Growing up to 10 inches (25 cm) long, it's a favorite of cod and puffins, as well as people.

Barents Sea

Norway   Siberian Shelf

The Siberian Shelf encompasses the Barents Sea, the Kara Sea, the Laptev Sea, the East Siberian Sea, and the Chukchi Sea.

Bet you didn't know

The widest continental shelf is the Siberian Shelf in the Arctic Ocean. It is part of the continent of Asia and is up to 802 miles (1,290 km) wide. That's more than a thousand times wider than the shelf along parts of the coast of California in the United States, which may be less than 0.6 miles (1 km) wide.

SLIPPERY SLOPE: WHERE SEA MEETS LAND

We tend to think of a beach as where the land meets the ocean. But the actual meeting place is offshore and underwater. That's because a continent doesn't end where it gets wet! The real edges of a continent are formed by land that dips out of sight into the sea. This land is called a continental margin.

A continental margin is usually made up of three parts:

- The continental shelf slopes gently away from the coast to a depth of about 656 feet (200 m). Continental shelves average about 40 miles (65 km) wide, but there's lots of variety. Around the United States, for example, the shelf ranges from 12 to 250 miles (19 to 402 km) wide. The East Coast's shelf is mostly broad and shallow; the West Coast's shelf is narrow and steep. Shelves hardly exist at all in places like Chile because there is a deep trench close to shore.

- Beyond the shelf is the continental slope, which drops steeply as it swoops toward the abyssal plains. The slope is typically about 87 miles (140 km) wide. It reaches to a depth of about 10,500 feet (3,200 m). Canyons carve through some shelves and slopes. In some places, the continental slope plunges into a trench. In others, it's covered by a deep layer of sediment.

- At the base of the continental slope is a heap of sediment called the continental rise. The rise is made up mainly of sediment that washes off or slides down the slope. It can be up to 9 miles (15 km) deep in places. It covers up the zone where continental crust gives way to oceanic crust.

SHELF LIFE

Lots of sunlight, plenty of nutrients, and shallow water make continental shelves a great place for living things! All the ocean's plants grow here. You'll also find seaweed forests and coral reefs. Animals include sea snails, sea urchins, crabs, lobsters, clams, and sponges, as well as swimmers such as cod, tuna, snapper, and mackerel. Mammals such as sea otters and harbor seals hunt here, and gray whales and other large marine animals swim over the shelf as they migrate.

Continental shelves make up about 8 percent of the land that's covered by the ocean, yet they have provided about 90 percent of the fish and shellfish humans catch for food. Today, oil companies drill for oil on shelves and slopes (see pages 248–249).

CHAPTER 6

ALONG THE COAST

A bat star is revealed at low tide in Montaña de Oro State Park in California.

THE SEASHORE

The seashore is an ever changing place. (You know this for certain if you've ever built a sand castle, only to have it swallowed up by the sea.) The tide rises and falls, rearranging sand and stones and even tossing logs around like sticks. Storms scoop out whole chunks of shoreline and plop them somewhere else. Even stony cliffs are shaped by the action of waves.

Entire coastlines change over long spans of time, too. About 18,000 years ago, for example, vast areas of North America, Europe, and northern Asia were covered by glaciers. The sea level was about 400 feet (122 m) lower than it is today because so much water was frozen in sheets of ice. As a result, continental shelves that are underwater today were dry land back then. Scientists have found ancient mammoth and mastodon teeth far from shore, which shows that these extinct elephant species roamed there 11,000 years ago.

If you could straighten out all of Earth's ocean coastlines and link them together, you could wrap them around Earth at the Equator many times. The country of Canada alone has about 125,579 miles (202,100 km) of coastline—the most of any nation. Canada is the world's second largest country and bumps up against three oceans: the Atlantic in the east, the Pacific in the west, and the Arctic in the north. It also has thousands of ocean islands, including some that are pretty big, such as Newfoundland. Newfoundland is in the Atlantic Ocean off Canada's east coast and is bigger than the nation of Iceland.

THE MOST COAST

Alaska is the biggest state in the United States. It also has a lot of coastline: it measures about 6,642 miles (10,690 km) long. Or is it actually 33,904 miles (54,563 km) long? The answer depends on how you measure it and what kind of maps you use.

Some maps, such as a world map, show the outlines of land but not a lot of detail. Other maps show much more detail, including every wiggle and bend on a shoreline. The more close-up the view, the more detail the map shows. Plus, there are different ways of deciding where shoreline ends and "inland" places begin. And do you figure out the shoreline at high tide or low tide? All of these decisions will affect the measurement of a coastline.

New Hampshire has the **shortest coastline** of any U.S. state bordered by an ocean. It measures only about 18 miles (29 km) long.

IT'S A SHORE THING

Swoosh, shhh. Swoosh, shhh. The rise and fall of waves on a beach has a steady rhythm that many people find relaxing. But waves are a challenge for organisms that live in and on a shore. They've had to adapt to life in a habitat that changes from minute to minute—and depending on exactly where they live on shore, that habitat may also change drastically for hours between high tide and low tide (see pages 220–221). These organisms must cope with changes in light, temperature, and salinity, as well as to being suddenly exposed to predators.

The part of a beach that lies in between the high-tide mark and the low-tide mark is called the intertidal zone. The intertidal zone is divided into several narrower zones:

The **low intertidal zone** is almost always underwater. It's only exposed when the tide's very low. You'll usually find seaweed, sea anemones, sea stars, and crabs here.

The **mid intertidal zone** is usually underwater but is exposed during low tide. Organisms here must cope with the risk of drying out or being eaten by birds and other predators during low tide. Clams, worms, and other creatures living in sand hunker down to wait for water to return. Crabs hide under seaweed and rocks. During high tide, however, organisms must deal with waves! Mussels hang on to rocks by strong threads. Seaweed clings with rootlike parts called holdfasts.

The **upper intertidal zone** is covered with water during high tide. Organisms here are adapted to cope with their habitat being exposed to the air. Tiny snails hide in their shells. Barnacles, which glue themselves tightly to rocks, firmly shut their shells. Many creatures hide under soggy seaweed.

The **splash zone** is at the outer limits of the high tide. It gets a little water when high tide splashes it, and it may get drenched during storms, but most of the time it's dry here. Small barnacles, periwinkle snails, and limpets are among the few animals that can live in the splash zone.

STRANDED

If you walk along a beach, you may find a long, wavering line of debris in the upper intertidal zone. This debris is called the strandline. It's made up of stuff washed up by waves or high tides, such as shells, feathers, wood ranging from sticks to logs, dead seaweed, and (unfortunately) litter. It's also called the wrack line ("wrack" is the name of a kind of seaweed, and it also refers to dried-up seaweed). The strandline is both a habitat and supermarket for animals! Push a chunk of it aside, and a swarm of little crustaceans called sand hoppers will bounce around. Shorebirds and crabs pick through it, looking for food.

The **purple sea urchin** lives in the intertidal zone. It chews a **hole** into a **stone** with its five tiny, tough teeth so it has a place to hide from predators.

highest high tide

high tide zone

mid tide zone

low tide zone

lowest low tide

black lichens

rock louse

periwinkle

hermit crab

spray zone

limpets

encrusting algae (ralfsia)

barnacles

clown nudibranch

rockweed

corralina seaweed

fiddler crab

chitons

aggregating anemones

sea star

sea lettuce

mussels

red crab

green anemones

eel grass

purple sea urchin

brittle sea star

215

Scientists estimate that, added up, the world's ocean beaches hold about seven quintillion, five hundred quadrillion grains of sand. If you want to write that amount in numbers, it's 7,500,000,000,000,000,000 grains!

SAND-SATIONAL

Have you ever built a sand castle or dug a deep pit at the seashore? These are just some of the fun things you can do on a beach. A beach is a shore that's covered with sediment (material that settles to the bottom of water). This sediment is moved from place to place by waves, currents, and tides.

On a sandy beach, the sediment is mainly—well, sand! Sand is made up of minerals, such as quartz, feldspar, and sparkly flecks of mica. It can also be made of shells and coral.

A flat sand beach may look lifeless except for gulls and other birds, but it's not! The sand itself is packed with living things. Some of them, such as clams and mole crabs, are big enough to see— though they will burrow deeper into the sand to stay out of sight. Others are microscopic worms and other creatures that live on and in between individual grains of sand. A handful of wet sand may be home to about 10,000 of these tiny animals!

SANDY LAND

Mineral sand forms when granite and other rocks are broken down by a process called weathering. Waves weather rock by smashing into cliffs. Water also weathers rock by freezing and thawing in cracks. Sand grains may come from cliffs near the beach. Rocks that are weathered far from the shore also produce sand, which rivers carry down to the sea.

Sand grains that are smooth and round have been polished over time as they tumbled in waves. You might find jagged sand grains on a beach that's near a river that has delivered bits of rock only recently formed by weathering.

Sand beaches get their color from the main ingredients in their sand. Volcanic islands, for example, may have black-sand beaches made of volcanic ash and bits of basalt, a black volcanic rock. Many tropical islands have white-sand beaches made of fine particles of coral, shell, and exoskeletons of marine animals. A mineral called olivine lends a greenish color to some beaches, while garnets add a rosy hue to others.

The islands of Bermuda in the North Atlantic are famous for pink-sand beaches.

217

RUGGED, ROCKY BEACHES

Most people picture a flat, sandy shore when they think of a beach, but many beaches are rugged and rocky. Instead of sand, a rocky beach may be covered with larger particles, such as rough gravel or small, flat pebbles called shingles. It may even be covered by large, round rocks called cobbles. If you visit a shingle or cobble beach, you can hear a loud clattering as the surf runs down the shore because the stones rattle as they tumble in the water.

You're most likely to see gravel, pebbles, and rocks on steep beaches that are pounded by high, strong waves. These waves have enough energy to carry larger particles higher on the beach. The sand tends to trickle out as the water washes back into the ocean.

Other rocky beaches are rocky because they're covered with big stones and boulders and even chunks of the bedrock lying under the beach. ("Bedrock" is solid rock underground.) Many volcanic coastlines have jagged heaps of black rock from lava that flowed there millions of years ago. In Ireland, lava that flowed about 60 million years ago formed pillars as it cooled and created a strange landscape called the Giant's Causeway.

Life isn't always easy on a rocky beach. But clams and other burrowing animals can survive on a gravel beach where they can tunnel into sand and mud. Seaweed clings to rocks. Worms live in tubes of sand and mucus stuck on the undersides of cobbles. Beaches with stones, boulders, or outcrops of rock provide lots of tide pools, as well as living space for barnacles, sea stars, and other clinging animals.

STUCK IN PLACE

A limpet is a type of sea snail. Many limpets are adapted for a life spent clinging to rocks. Each has a muscular foot that clamps onto a rock. Its body also makes a fluid that glues it in place. Its shell is shaped like a dome, so when a wave slams down on it, the water strikes the top and then flows off to the sides without sucking the limpet off the rock.

The limpet also uses the edge of its shell to grind the rock and make a groove that fits its shell perfectly. This space is its home. The limpet creeps away from its home to graze on algae. Look for pale, round limpet "scars" on rocks the next time you're on a rocky beach. You can find limpets on many rocky shores worldwide.

Acorn barnacles pack themselves so tightly onto rocks that 9 square feet (1 sq m)—an area about the size of three typical game boards—may contain up to **70,000** of them!

The giant green anemone is a common sight in **tide pools** of western North America. It catches fish and other prey with its stinging tentacles. An anemone can live for **80 years** or more.

LIVING THE TIDE POOL LIFE

Tide pools are little ponds of life on a rocky shore. They are pockets of water left behind among the rocks at low tide. Tide pools range from tiny puddles holding about as much water as a beach pail to small ponds the size of a kiddie wading pool.

A tide pool is a great place to explore. It provides an opportunity to see close-up many animals that live in the subtidal zone—the area past the low-tide mark that's usually always underwater (see pages 214–215). Hermit crabs scuttle across the bottom looking for food. Sea anemones spread their tentacles wide, looking like flowers glued to the rocks. Mussels and barnacles on the rocks open their shells to filter food from the water. Prickly sea urchins and snails graze on algae cloaking the rocks, which may also be spangled with sea stars. You may even see little octopuses hiding under rocks!

A tide pool makes a great oasis for sea creatures at low tide, but it comes with some special challenges. On a hot day, for example, water evaporates from a tide pool. As a result, the water left in the tide pool becomes extra salty. It also gets very warm, and the oxygen level drops. Tide pool organisms must be able to survive these sorts of changes.

ADAPTABLE SCULPINS

The sculpin is a little fish that lives in tide pools along the western coast of North America. Its skin is usually olive green and blotched with brown markings that camouflage it. It is adapted for life in water with lots of changes in temperature, salinity, and oxygen content, which makes a tide pool the perfect home for a sculpin. This fish can even breathe air for a few hours if necessary! If a wave washes the fish out of its tide pool, it will use its sense of smell to find its way back!

221

SEASHORE HOME

The **blue-ringed octopus** is small—its body is about the size of a golf ball, and its arms are about 2.8 inches (7 cm) long. At rest, this little octopus is yellow or tan in color. Blue circles appear on its body when it's scared or angry—pay attention because its bite is deadly to humans as well as prey! The blue-ringed octopus can be found in tide pools and shallow water along coasts in parts of Australia, Japan, and Indonesia.

Animals of the seashore have many ways of surviving in their ever changing habitat. As you know from reading about tide pools (pages 220–221), many animals spring into action to filter food from seawater when the tide comes in.

Other animals search up and down the beach for food. Gulls pick through wrack looking for small animals to eat. Small birds called ruddy turnstones use their beaks to toss stones aside as they look for mole crabs and other food. Other shorebirds, such as sandpipers, scurry along the edge of the surf and probe the sand with their bills to dig out meals. Kelp flies snack on rotting seaweed. Here are just a few of the many amazing animals you can find on shores.

The **sooty oystercatcher** lives on rocky shores in Australia. It feeds at the water's edge during low tide, keeping a lookout for oysters, mussels, and other shellfish. When the oystercatcher spies prey, it uses its sharp, strong bill to pry open the shell and eat the animal inside. It can also use its bill as a hammer to open shells by smashing them.

The **mole crab** gets its name from its ability to burrow quickly into sand. This grape-size animal digs itself in backward, with its head facing the ocean. Then it uses its feathery antennae to filter out bits of food from seawater washing over it. Different kinds of mole crabs are found on sandy shores around the world.

Rocky seashores are home to **chitons**, which are in the mollusk group along with snails and clams. A chiton's shell is divided into eight plates. It creeps along on a large, muscular foot, which it also uses to clamp itself tightly to rocks so it won't wash away in the waves as it grazes on algae. The biggest species is the giant Pacific chiton, which is up to 1 foot (0.3 m) long.

The **geoduck** ("gooey duck") is the world's biggest burrowing clam. It digs itself into muddy sand of beaches along the West Coast of North America, from Alaska to Baja California. The clam's odd name comes from a Native American word that means "dig deep." Geoducks live buried up to 3 feet (1 m) deep and stretch their siphons to the surface to filter-feed. A geoduck can weigh up to 14 pounds (6.4 kg) and live up to 150 years.

Boo! It's a **ghost crab**! Ghost crabs are so perfectly camouflaged, they're nearly invisible on the sandy beaches where they live. They can also vanish quickly because they live in burrows in the sand. These burrows may be up to 4 feet (1.2 m) long. Ghost crabs are found as far north as Rhode Island in the United States and as far south as the coast of Brazil in South America.

Bat stars graze on seagrass, but they don't eat the grass itself! They feed on the thin film of **algae, bacteria,** and other **organisms** that cover the grass.

A Florida manatee calf snacks on seagrass in warm, shallow water.

SEAGRASS MEADOWS

Most of the "plants" you see growing in the ocean are actually supersize algae called seaweed. But seagrasses really are plants, complete with roots and stems. They are the only flowering plants that live completely in the ocean.

Seagrasses take root in muddy seabeds close to shore in places where the water is mostly calm and clear, such as bays and lagoons. They're found in many places around the world, especially in warm waters, but some species also grow in cool water. A species called common eelgrass even grows in the Arctic Ocean. It can survive being under ice for several months each year.

A seagrass bed is an important habitat for many kinds of organisms. Algae grows on blades of seagrass, and bacteria, sponges, and other organisms live on them, too. Snails, sea slugs, sea urchins, and other animals visit to eat these organisms—and these predators, in turn, are preyed upon by sea stars, crabs, fish, octopuses, and other creatures. Large animals that eat seagrass include green sea turtles, some species of ducks and geese, and ocean mammals such as dugongs and manatees. When seagrass dies, it's consumed by bacteria, worms, crabs, and other animals.

Many animals use seagrass beds for shelter. The stems protect them from rough waves and also provide places to hide from predators. Seagrass beds are often called "nurseries" because so many fish, shellfish, and other animals grow up in them. Just one acre (0.4 ha) of seagrass may be home to up to 40,000 fish and 50 million invertebrates, such as snails.

GREEN GROWING GRASS

Seagrasses spread by growing special stems, called rhizomes, under the seafloor. Roots and shoots sprout at various points along the rhizome to form new clumps of seagrass. Seagrasses also produce seeds.

To make seeds, flowers must receive a dose of a substance called pollen, usually from another plant of its own species. On land, bees and other animals often carry pollen from flower to flower. The wind also spreads pollen. Seagrass pollen travels to seagrass flowers by drifting in the water. Seagrass seeds travel this way, too.

KELP FORESTS

Kelp is a type of seaweed that forms forests in cool, shallow waters near coasts where currents and upwelling deliver lots of nutrients. Kelp forests are found on long stretches of the western coastlines of North and South America and in a few other places, such as along islands near Australia. Like other seaweeds, kelp needs sunlight, so it usually grows in water no deeper than about 82 feet (25 m), though if the water's really clear, kelp forests can grow in deeper areas.

The biggest "tree" found in many kelp forests is the giant kelp, the world's largest species of seaweed. This brown seaweed can grow up to 148 feet (45 m) long. It also grows fast, especially in springtime, when it may lengthen by as much as 2 feet (0.6 m) in one day!

A strand of kelp clings to the rocky seafloor with rootlike parts called holdfasts. Its "trunk" is a stemlike stalk called a stipe. Leaflike blades grow from the stipe. Long-stemmed kinds of kelp have air-filled bulbs at the bases of their blades, which help the stipe and blades float. Most of the time, kelp sways in the water like trees in the wind. But strong storm waves can tear up a kelp forest and fling the kelp onto the shore.

Like seagrass meadows, kelp forests provide food and shelter for many other species. Animals such as seahorses, bristle worms, sea stars, crabs, and anemones live in kelp forests. Sea snails nibble on kelp blades and stipes, while sea slugs gobble up the slime that covers the kelp. Other animals feed on the blades that fall off the kelp and collect on the seafloor. Many fish visit kelp forests to hunt for food and also to hide from predators. Kelp forests are also important "nurseries" for the young of species—such as spiny lobsters and rockfish. Seabirds and seals feed and shelter in kelp forests, too.

URCHINS AND OTTERS

Sea otters visit kelp forests to find sea urchins, one of their favorite foods. Sea urchins feed on kelp. In a healthy kelp forest, predators such as sea otters keep populations of sea urchins in check.

Sea otters live in shallow waters along coasts in the northern Pacific Ocean. More than 100 years ago, they nearly became extinct after being heavily hunted for their thick, soft fur. Sea otters were first protected by law in 1911, when only about 2,000 otters remained. Today, there are about 125,000.

Without sea otters and other predators to eat them, sea urchin populations grow by leaps and bounds. They gobble up kelp blades and chomp on their holdfasts, which causes kelp to lose its grip on the seafloor and float away. Urchins also devour new kelp sprouts. In this way, urchins can destroy an entire kelp forest. In some places, divers remove herds of sea urchins to help kelp forests grow.

Bet you didn't know

The blue-rayed limpet lives in kelp forests along the coasts of northern Europe. It feeds on kelp blades. In fall, the limpet creeps down to the holdfast, just before the kelp sheds its old blades, and starts feeding there instead.

A harbor seal swims through a kelp forest looking for food.

The Italian city of **Venice** is famous for its streets of water. The city's buildings occupy **118 islands** in the large coastal Venetian Lagoon.

LOVELY LAGOONS

A lagoon is a shallow body of water that is separated from the ocean by coral reefs, barrier islands, or hills of sand called sandbars.

Coral reefs form lagoons that look like pools in the ocean. These reefs grew on the slopes of volcanic islands that sank into the ocean over millions of years. They're known as atolls (see pages 198–199), and the pools of seawater in them are called atoll, or coral, lagoons.

Coral lagoons are often bright turquoise blue instead of dark blue like the ocean. The bright blue color is partly due to the lagoon being shallow. It's also due to limestone leaching out of the coral reef and into the water. The limestone particles scatter blue light, like air molecules do to create blue sky.

Lagoons that lie between a coastline and barrier islands or sandbars are called coastal lagoons. They're created when the ocean scoops up and carries away sediment. A coastal lagoon, however, isn't totally cut off from the ocean. Currents and winds carry water through any open ends of a lagoon. Channels called inlets may also slice through islands and let seawater flow into and out of a lagoon. A coastal lagoon that is also fed by rivers flowing off the land may have "brackish" water—a mixture of salty and fresh water.

The water inside a coastal lagoon is calmer than the open ocean, so these lagoons are often used as harbors for boats. Animals also make use of them for the shelter they provide. Gray whales, for example, migrate to coastal lagoons on the Baja California Peninsula of Mexico in winter to give birth to their calves. Two of the peninsula's coastal lagoons are protected as a whale sanctuary. Sea lions, seals, green sea turtles, and many other animals also use these lagoons.

BELIZE IT OR NOT!

An atoll called Lighthouse Reef sits in the Caribbean Sea off the coast of Belize. It surrounds a lagoon that's about 23 miles (38 km) long and 5 miles (8 km) wide. Inside the lagoon is a natural wonder: the Great Blue Hole. The hole is a deep pit that formed about 18,000 years ago when a cave beneath the lagoon's limestone floor collapsed. It is about 410 feet (125 m) deep and more than 1,000 feet (305 m) across.

Divers love to plunge into the Great Blue Hole. Inside, they can see coral-reef creatures such as sponges, angelfish, and barracudas. Sharks swim in the hole, too!

MIGHTY MANGROVES

MILES OF MANGROVES

The world's largest mangrove forest is the Sundarbans, which sprawls across India and Bangladesh. It grows where three mighty rivers pour into the Bay of Bengal, which is part of the Indian Ocean. It covers about 3,860 square miles (10,000 sq km)—an area more than twice the size of the U.S. state of Rhode Island.

Animals found in the Sundarbans include tigers, monkeys, pythons, crocodiles, river dolphins, and about 300 species of birds. Fish, shrimp, and other marine animals live among the trees' roots. The forest provides many people with a living, such as collecting wild honey and fishing.

About 35 percent of the world's mangrove forests have been cut down to make way for shrimp farms and other uses. Pollution has harmed others. Fortunately, large parts of the Sundarbans are protected as a park and wildlife preserve.

Most trees can't grow in thick, waterlogged mud—especially mud that's flooded with salt water when the tide rolls in. But this habitat is perfect for mangrove trees.

Mangrove shrubs and trees grow in tropical and subtropical places. They form forests on shorelines that are protected from strong waves. They grow aboveground roots that prop them up in mud and water. Some mangroves even grow roots from their branches!

The tangled roots block the flow of water and make sediment drop out of it. In this way, a mangrove forest stops sediment carried in by rivers from rushing into the ocean. It also builds new land along the shore and helps prevent the shore from being washed away, or eroded, by storm waves.

Mangroves have adapted to life in this harsh habitat. Some species, for example, deal with the problem of low oxygen levels in muddy soil by growing special roots that stick up from the mud to absorb oxygen from the air. Other adaptations help mangroves cope with salt water: Many mangroves have roots that filter salt out of the water taken up by the plant, while other species "sweat" salt out of glands in their leaves.

Mangrove forests provide food and shelter for a wide variety of animals. Birds nest in their branches. Barnacles, sponges, anemones, crabs, and other animals cling to the roots, and fish hide among them. Insects, snakes, lizards, and frogs creep on trunks and twigs. People harvest fruit, wood, and seafood in the forests.

A tiger prowls amid mangroves in India.

The **tallest** species of **mangrove trees** grow in parts of Ecuador. They can stand **200 feet** (60 m) tall.

Large mangrove forests grow in Los Haitises National Park in the Dominican Republic in the Caribbean Sea.

EXCELLENT ESTUARIES

An estuary in a coastal area is a body of water partly surrounded by land in which freshwater meets and mixes with salty seawater. This mixture of fresh and salty water is called "brackish" water. Many estuaries are located where rivers and streams flow into oceans.

Estuaries often teem with life because they are nutrient-rich habitats. An estuary's nutrients are delivered to it by rivers and streams draining off the land, as well as by deep currents swirling in from the sea.

All these nutrients feed a lot of plants as well as tiny organisms, such as algae and bacteria, which are eaten by bigger organisms. Young fish find food and shelter in estuaries. Clams, shrimp, and other shellfish are plentiful. Many birds hunt and nest in estuaries, and others stop to feed and rest while migrating.

Some estuaries are known by the kinds of plants that live in them. A mangrove forest, for example, is a kind of estuary. A salt marsh is an estuary filled with grasses and other plants that can survive in brackish water. Salt marshes take the place of mangrove forests on coastlines where it's too cold for mangroves to grow.

Herons and other wading birds perch in trees in Maryland's Chesapeake Bay.

A PEEK AT THE CHESAPEAKE

The largest estuary in the United States is the Chesapeake Bay. It is about 200 miles (320 km) long and stretches from the northeastern corner of Maryland to the coast of Virginia. Freshwater from six states and Washington, D.C., drains into it. The bay's salt marshes and other wetlands filter sediments from the water. They also filter out pollutants. In addition, the bay acts as a shield between the land and the ocean, which is especially important during storms and floods.

The Chesapeake Bay's wildlife includes blue crabs, horseshoe crabs, oysters, and more than 350 kinds of fish. Leatherbacks and other sea turtles sometimes swim in its waters. Hundreds of bird species live in the bay or visit it while migrating. Every winter, about a million ducks, geese, and swans spend time here.

The world's largest reptile is the estuarine crocodile (also called the saltwater crocodile). Males typically grow to be 17 feet (5 m) long. These crocodiles live in estuaries and other habitats in parts of Australia, India, and Southeast Asia.

Ocean water carries white sand to the beaches of Hill Inlet on Whitsunday Island in Australia.

CAVES, CLIFFS, AND STACKS

Estuaries and lagoons have buffers to protect them from ocean currents and waves. But many coastlines don't—and some of them provide amazing examples of the ocean's power and its ability to shape the land.

Water slowly wears down, or weathers, rock. Waves weather rocks by pounding against them. Sand, pebbles, and rocks in the water work like sandpaper as the waves fling them against the shore. Chemicals in seawater dissolve certain types of rock, such as limestone. Waves also work like giant hammers that pound air into cracks in rock, which can cause it to split. Weaker rock weathers first. Then the water carries the weathered rock bits away. Stronger rock is left behind. This process is called erosion.

Erosion can happen very quickly—waves can totally reshape a beach in the course of a single storm! Erosion also happens over very long spans of time. Over time, erosion creates towering cliffs and yawning caves in some places. It can also carve spectacular sculptures called sea arches.

A sea arch forms when waves batter a headland (a part of the shore that sticks out into the ocean). The battering carves a cave in the headland. The cave grows deeper until it tunnels right through the headland, forming an arch. Eventually, the arch collapses, leaving columns of rock called sea stacks.

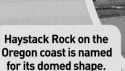

Haystack Rock on the Oregon coast is named for its domed shape.

HEY, STACK!

Haystack Rock is a sea stack on the coast of the U.S. state of Oregon. It's made of volcanic rock left over from a volcanic eruption about 15 million years ago that sent lava flowing for miles across the land. The giant stack stands 235 feet (72 m) tall. Skinny sea stacks called the Needles hover nearby.

Haystack Rock is protected by law as a bird sanctuary. Seabirds such as tufted puffins and gulls build nests on it—and bald eagles visit to prey on their chicks. It's also been declared a "marine garden" for the tide pools at its base. Haystack is visited by as many as 200,000 tourists every year.

Bet you didn't know

The White Cliffs of Dover are a wall of chalky cliffs on England's southeastern coast. They're made of the remains of phytoplankton called coccolithophores, which piled up on the seafloor more than 70 million years ago, when this part of the world was underwater.

Water and wind carved El Arco, a sea arch that sits right where the Pacific Ocean meets the Gulf of California.

CHAPTER 7

WHEN PEOPLE AND OCEANS MEET

A boy rides the waves while on a beach vacation.

LIVING
BY THE SEA

There are more than 7.2 billion people on Earth—and about 44 percent of them live within 93 miles (150 km) of the ocean. That's more than three billion people!

Humans have a long history of living near the ocean. People have settled on shorelines of bays, seas, and estuaries since ancient times. In fact, researchers have found prehistoric tools on the coast of the Red Sea in Africa that date back about 125,000 years. They have also found oyster shells that prehistoric people threw away, which showed that early humans quickly learned how to find food in the sea.

Coastal areas were also logical places to live as humans began building settlements and trading with each other. They were good jumping-off places for travelers to set sail for other lands and transport goods to them. The beauty, fresh air, and cool water found at beaches attracted people, too. In ancient Rome, wealthy people even traveled to seaside places for vacations, just as many people do in modern times.

Of course, the things that attract people to live by the sea can also be harmed by so many humans living there. Building homes and businesses replaces natural habitats, such as wetlands and mangrove forests. Litter builds up on beaches, and sewage enters waterways. Some solutions to these problems include restoring and protecting habitat, planning new construction carefully, and strict laws about how waste is handled.

SEA LEVEL SHIFTS

Climate change is causing sea levels to rise. The rise is caused mainly by two factors: The ocean is absorbing heat from the atmosphere, which makes it expand, or take up more space. Warmer temperatures are also melting ice sheets in Antarctica and other places. The melting water flows into the ocean and adds to sea-level rise. Scientists predict that the sea level may rise between 2.6 and 6.6 feet (0.8 and 2 m) by 2100.

Rising sea levels pose a threat to people living along coasts and on low-lying islands. It's estimated that more than 150 million people worldwide live within 3 feet (1 m) of the high-tide level—and 250 million live within 16 feet (5 m) of it.

Freshwater sources on land, as well as habitats, will also be affected by salty water seeping into them.

The image here shows the world as it is now, with only one difference: All the ice on land has melted and drained into the sea, raising it 216 feet (65.8 m) and creating new shorelines for our continents and inland seas.

Old fishing villages dot the shores of the Ionian Islands in Greece.

CORDOVA, AK
P.W.S.

A fishing boat hauls in
a net filled with herring
in Sitka Sound, Alaska.

About
one billion
people get most
of the **protein**
they need
from fish.

GONE FISHING

Humans have always been clever when it comes to getting a meal! Prehistoric people had to figure out what was edible and what wasn't.

At some point, they figured out that fish and other sea creatures could be eaten. Early fishers caught fish with spears, traps, handheld nets, and fishing rods with hooks. In some parts of the world, these ancient fishing methods are still in use today. This kind of fishing is called subsistence fishing if fishers are catching fish just for their family or village. In some places, people use traditional methods to catch fish to sell in markets, too.

Today, most ocean fish sold in stores and restaurants are caught by modern fishing methods that catch huge numbers of fish at once. This kind of fishing is called commercial fishing.

Commercial fishing vessels often use huge nets, depending on what species they're catching. These nets may be long "drift nets," which hang like curtains in the sea. Drift nets can be many miles long, and they're banned or restricted by laws in many parts of the ocean. Another kind of net, called a purse seine, can catch whole schools of fish at once because it closes around the fish like a giant trash bag being pulled shut. Otter trawls are nets dragged along the seafloor to catch fish that dwell near or on it.

These fishing methods cause many problems, such as "bycatch"—the capture of animals that the fishers aren't hunting. This includes whales, dolphins, sea turtles, and other air-breathing animals that drown in nets. As for unwanted fish, their bodies are thrown away, which is both wasteful and damaging to fish populations. Otter trawls also destroy the seafloor, raking it up like bulldozers flattening a forest.

FISH FROM THE FARM

Some farmed fish are raised in pens along the coast. Others, such as Pacific pink salmon, are "ranched." This means they're raised in pens at a fish hatchery until they reach a certain size. Then they're set free to swim down rivers to the ocean, where they grow up in the wild. Later, many of them are caught by fishers.

Aquaculture sounds like a great way to produce protein-rich food for a growing human population, but it poses some problems. One concern is that farmed fish can spread diseases to wild fish. Diseases can spread quickly among animals kept in large numbers in small spaces. Farmed fish that escape not only spread disease but also compete with wild fish for food.

A salmon farm in Highlands, Scotland

EXPLORING THE OCEAN

The earliest known explorers to set sail through the vast ocean were ancestors of the Polynesians, a name for people who live on the thousands of islands scattered across the Pacific Ocean. As far back as 50,000 years ago, these ancestors probably sailed on rafts made of logs, staying within sight of land.

About 3,500 years ago, Polynesian sailors headed out to sea in double-hulled canoes powered by sails and paddles. They navigated using the stars, wind direction, and currents. In this way, they hopped from island to island across the Pacific, finally settling in the Hawaiian Islands about 1,700 years ago.

Many early ocean explorations focused mainly on the water's surface and the land sticking out of it. Today's journeys of discovery often take us right down to the seafloor! To explore these dark, cold, high-pressure depths, scientists mainly use two important machines: remotely operated vehicles and submersibles.

A remotely operated vehicle, or ROV, is a robot equipped to work underwater. An undersea ROV has arms that can lift, grab, slurp, and scoop, as well as sensors and cameras for recording information. It can even bring live animals up to the surface. The ROV is tethered to a ship. Scientists aboard the ship control the ROV and send it commands through a cable. The ROV likewise sends information back through the cable. Some ROVs can dive as deep as 2.5 miles (4 km).

A submersible is a small underwater vehicle that the people inside can control. Its strong walls don't collapse under the intense pressure of the deep sea. Cameras, sensors, robot arms, and other devices allow the crew to collect samples and record information.

DEEP-DIVE RECORD!

On March 26, 2012, explorer and film director James Cameron plummeted to Earth's deepest spot in the Mariana Trench (pages 14–15). He traveled there in a submersible called *DEEPSEA CHALLENGER*.

It took two hours and 36 minutes for *DEEPSEA CHALLENGER* to reach the bottom. For the next few hours, Cameron explored the area, which he described as looking as barren as the moon's surface. He filmed the exploration and made a movie about it called *Deepsea Challenge 3D*.

Cameron's dive marked the first time a person dove alone to the bottom of Challenger Deep.

DEEPSEA CHALLENGER

Bet you didn't know

A dropcam is a camera inside a clear ball attached to a heavy weight. It's dropped off a ship to film underwater. Later, it separates from the weight and rises back to the surface, where scientists retrieve it.

INTO THE DEEP

It isn't every day that you discover new creatures living in a bizarre habitat! But that's just what happened in 1977, when scientists in the deep-sea submersible *Alvin* saw animals swarming in an area of the Pacific seafloor that they thought would be lifeless. It was a hydrothermal vent—a brand-new-to-science ecosystem. An ecosystem is a community of living things interacting with each other and the nonliving parts of their habitat.

A hydrothermal vent—as you'll recall from pages 48–49—forms on seafloor ridges in places where water seeps into cracks. Inside the cracks, the water touches roasting-hot rock and magma and heats up to a scalding 752°F (400°C). That's above the boiling point on Earth's surface, but at this depth, the pressure keeps the water from turning into steam. Instead, it shoots out of the seafloor just like geysers on land.

Minerals dissolved in the water make it look like billowing black or white smoke. (That's why hydrothermal vents are also called "black smokers" and "white smokers.") The minerals drop out of the clouds and settle around the vent. Over time, they build up to form weird-looking chimneys and smokestacks.

Cold seeps are places in the seafloor where water filled with chemicals oozes up and out of the sediment covering it. These chemicals include methane, the main ingredient in the natural gas used for heating homes.

Both vents and cold seeps are home to animals found nowhere else. Here are just a few of these amazing creatures.

Bet you didn't know

Life on land depends on plants carrying out photosynthesis (pages 42–43) to turn sunlight into food. But there's no sunlight deep in the ocean. Instead, life around hydrothermal vents and cold seeps depends on bacteria using the energy in chemicals to make food. This process is called chemosynthesis.

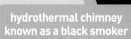

hydrothermal chimney
known as a black smoker

A **giant tube worm** doesn't have a mouth or stomach. It feeds by absorbing chemicals from the water with a red, feathery organ sticking out of the top of its tube. Inside its body, billions of bacteria turn the chemicals into food. This food nourishes the worm, which can grow to be 6.6 feet (2 m) long.

The **deepsea vent octopus** is almost colorless, unlike most other octopuses. It doesn't need color to hide from predators or prey in its dark world. It uses four of its arms to find food by touch while pushing itself along with the rest of its arms.

Vent shrimp in the Caribbean Sea pack together so closely that just 1.2 square yards (1 sq m) may contain 2,000 of them! Scientists notice that crowded shrimp feed mainly on bacteria living in their mouths and gills. In less crowded conditions, they become predators that eat snails and other creatures—including each other.

Giant white vent clams grow up to 10.2 inches (26 cm) long. They filter food from the water as clams on shorelines do. But they also get nutrients from bacteria living inside them. Deep-sea crabs and other animals feed on young clams.

Methane ice worms live on clumps of frozen methane at cold seeps. They eat bacteria growing on the ice. They use the leglike structures along their sides to dig burrows in the ice as they search for bacteria. Clams, tube worms, mussels, and other animals also live at cold seeps.

A container 20 feet (6.1 m) long can hold about 48,000 bananas. The ship *Emma Maersk* can transport about 11,000 of these containers at a time, so it could carry 528 million bananas—enough to circle Earth more than twice at the Equator!

NO SMOKING

SHORE TO SHORE BY SHIP

Cheese, chocolate, cars, computers, phones, toothbrushes, teddy bears—these are just some of the many things that cross the ocean on ships. Ships transport more than 90 percent of the products and materials traded between countries. And these ships are huge! The Danish vessel *Emma Maersk*, for example, can hold as much cargo as a freight train 43 miles (69.2 km) long.

Many cargo ships are designed to carry particular types of cargo. Bulk carriers are made for carrying loads of coal, grain, and other cargo that isn't packed in boxes. Tankers are made to carry fluids, such as oil. Cars travel on car-carrier ships that can carry as many as 8,500 vehicles. As for those computers and teddy bears, they're shipped in giant container boxes. Containers come in specific sizes so they can be neatly stacked on each other. They're loaded onto ships using giant cranes. After being unloaded, containers are attached to trucks or plopped onto train cars and hauled away.

Ships also carry unwanted cargo: "invasive species," which are organisms that show up in a habitat where they don't normally live. These organisms stow away in water carried in the bellies of the big ships. This water is ballast—weight that's added to a ship to make it ride lower in the water, which helps keep it from being tossed around by waves.

The invaders sometimes reproduce wildly in their new habitat and compete with living things already in the habitat or prey on them. New international agreements call for killing organisms in ballast water before discharging it.

LOST AT SEA

On January 10, 1992, a storm struck a ship sailing across the Pacific Ocean and sent some containers into the water. At least one container broke, spilling 28,800 plastic ducks and other toys into the ocean.

But these toys didn't go to waste when they were lost at sea because they floated. They became useful tools for oceanographer Curtis Ebbesmeyer, who gathered information on where they washed up on beaches around the Pacific. This information was matched up with computer programs of Pacific currents. The lost objects helped scientists ask new questions about how the ocean's gyres work (for more on gyres see pages 156–157).

Some toys circled the Pacific several times. One plastic duck floated through the Arctic and was found in Maine in July 2003. A plastic frog traveled all the way to Scotland and was found in August 2003.

Curtis Ebbesmeyer holds a collection of floating objects that have helped him track ocean currents.

247

FUELING OUR PLANET

Every day, the world's human population uses an average of about 93 million barrels of oil, natural gas, and other liquid fuels. Meanwhile, the oil industry produces about 94 million barrels of these fuels a day. More than a third of that comes from sites in the ocean.

Oil and natural gas deposits are what's left of plants, animals, and other organisms that lived many millions of years ago. When they died, their remains were buried by sand and mud and squashed by layers of rock. Intense pressure combined with heat inside Earth caused chemical changes in the material and turned them into oil and natural gas. These products are called "fossil fuels" because they are very, very old, like the fossil bones of dinosaurs and other prehistoric animals.

Humans discovered and used oil fields on land and close to shore first. But over the past hundred years, companies have moved farther from shore, drilling for oil on continental slopes and shelves (pages 208–209).

Rigs called oil platforms are used for drilling oil offshore. An offshore oil field is like a port city, with sleeping quarters, gyms, and movie theaters for workers and ships coming and going to deliver supplies and take away any oil that isn't sent out through pipelines. Working on a platform is a dangerous job: Oil burns, and explosions can happen. Drilling for oil also comes with dangers to the environment in the form of oil spills that pollute the ocean.

A tiny oiled crab rests in the hand of a worker cleaning up after the *Deepwater Horizon* spill.

WHEN A WELL EXPLODES

On April 20, 2010, an oil platform in the Gulf of Mexico called *Deepwater Horizon* exploded into flames. The explosion was caused by natural gas rising through a pipe that connected the platform with an oil well more than 5,000 feet (1,524 m) below in the seafloor.

Oil gushed out of the well for nearly three months. By July 15, when a cap was finally clamped onto the well, more than 200 million gallons (757 million L) had spilled. Thousands of sea turtles, birds, and other animals died.

Today, the Gulf continues its slow recovery. Dolphins, for example, are still dying at higher rates than normal. But there are some hopeful signs, such as back-to-normal numbers of snails, insects, and spiders in some coastal salt marshes. Scientists will continue to study how oil spills harm food webs, from microbes to dolphins.

An **oil barrel** contains 42 gallons (159 L) of crude oil—enough to completely fill a typical **bathtub.**

This is one of many oil rigs that stand in the North Sea in northern Europe.

Clean-up crews work to remove oil from a Gulf Shore beach in Alabama after the *Deepwater Horizon* spill.

REHABBING HABITATS

The best way to save a habitat is not to harm it in the first place! Luckily, sometimes we can help save a damaged habitat. This process is called habitat restoration.

How do you restore a habitat? That depends on the habitat and the kind of damage that's been done. Restoration may start with a big cleanup. This is how people began cleaning up the oil that spread across the waters of the Gulf of Mexico (page 248) and washed up on many beaches in the area in 2010.

Boats towed devices called skimmers across the water. Oil stuck to the skimmers. The skimmers were then wiped clean and the oil placed in barges to be taken away. On beaches, workers with shovels removed oil and balls of tar on the sand. Sand along many miles of beaches was put through a giant sifter that caught blobs of tar and shells coated with oil. The machine washed the sand, too.

These solutions, however, couldn't be used in wetlands. Nearly half the shoreline polluted by oil consisted of wetlands. Trying to clean up a wetland, such as a marsh, can often cause more damage because the plants get trampled by people and squashed by machines. Blasting a marsh with water forces oil deeper into the ground and also breaks the soil apart, which causes erosion. Gentle methods, such as raking by hand, helped without harming. But the best treatment for many marshes was to leave them alone and let them recover slowly and naturally.

Even with help, it will take a long time for beaches and wetlands to fully recover. Oil buried in sand, for example, will take a long time to break down. In the meantime, chemicals from the oil can get into the food web, where it sickens and kills wildlife. Efforts to restore the Gulf will continue for many more years.

Algae that's removed from coral reefs with the help of the Supersucker is sent to farms to be used as fertilizer for crops!

REEF RELIEF

A healthy coral reef is a rainbow of life. An unhealthy reef clearly shows it's dying: It's filled with the bleached "bones" of coral and dark blobs of decaying organisms. But coral reefs in different places have been successfully restored. Sometimes, simply banning fishing has helped reefs recover, but other reefs have needed more help.

In bays of the Hawaiian Island of Oahu, for example, non-native algae had invaded the water and taken over the reefs. So a machine called a "Supersucker" was brought in to slurp algae off the coral. In addition, Hawaiian species of algae-eating sea urchins are being raised and released so that they can gobble up any scraps of algae left behind and stop it from growing back. In 2015, scientists reported that the algae was at its lowest level in 20 years.

SAVING
SEA LIFE

When you hear bad news about the ocean's health, it can make you feel as if you've been knocked down by a powerful wave. Your heart might sink, for example, when you learn that 75 percent of Earth's coral reefs are threatened by everything from overfishing to climate change. So it's important to remember that many people around the world are working to save the ocean and its wildlife. Their work is part of wildlife conservation—the ongoing effort to use resources wisely so that we protect ecosystems and living things and their habitats. Here are a few conservation success stories!

Atlantic puffins are plump seabirds found in the North Atlantic. They were once abundant along the coast of Maine in the United States. But people collected puffin eggs and shot the adult birds, both for food and for feathers, which were used to stuff pillows and decorate hats. By 1901, only one pair of puffins remained in the United States. In 1973, a project began to bring back puffins. Scientists collected chicks from a puffin colony in Canada and brought them to islands in Maine. Years later, these chicks returned to nest. Today, more than a thousand pairs of puffins nest on several Maine islands, and Project Puffin has inspired other seabird projects worldwide.

Atlantic cod live in the North Atlantic Ocean and parts of the Arctic Ocean. They used to be plentiful, but their numbers started dropping steeply after cod fishers started using large boats and big nets in the 1950s. By the 1990s, the cod supply was running out. Today, cod numbers are still down in many places, but fishers in the North Sea in Europe have something to cheer about: The North Sea cod population is slowly growing. This recovery is due to fishing rules put into place in 2006. These rules strictly control how many cod fishers could catch. Fishers also had to avoid fishing in places where young cod were growing up. These rules give fish time to grow up and reproduce.

The **dugong** lives in warm, shallow waters around islands and along coasts in the Indian Ocean and parts of the western Pacific Ocean. It's become rare because of threats such as overhunting, damage to the seagrass meadows where it feeds, and drowning in nets set for fish. But people are working to help dugongs. For example, in the Indian Ocean, dugongs have been protected around the Andaman Islands by laws since 1992. In 2011, researchers started work on a project to identify the most important feeding places for dugongs. Protecting these habitats would help dugongs and other species, too.

Gray whales in the eastern Pacific Ocean once teetered on the edge of extinction. They were heavily hunted by whalers in the mid-1800s. Many whales were killed in the warm-water lagoons of Baja California in North America, where they gathered to give birth and breed. By the 1930s, there were fewer than 2,000 gray whales left. In 1936, hunting of gray whales was banned. Today, there may be from 19,000 to as many as 25,000 gray whales in the eastern Pacific.

Stoplight parrotfish and other species of fish live on coral reefs in Bermuda, which lies in the western North Atlantic Ocean. Beginning in the 1940s, fishers used big, cagelike traps called fish pots to catch coral reef fish. By the 1980s, huge numbers of fish were being trapped as the island's human population grew. The pots were also catching stoplight parrotfish and other species that helped keep the coral reef healthy by eating algae. Fish pots were banned in 1990, and the fish population began to grow. Today, many reefs are again filled with colorful species.

253

SAVING THE SEAS:
PROTECTING
MARINE AREAS

In 1872, Yellowstone National Park in the United States was created. It was the world's first national park. It was also the world's first major wildlife sanctuary, or "safe place," where hunting and trapping animals wasn't allowed. Today, about 14 percent of Earth's land areas are protected in some way—and someday, maybe more of the ocean will be, too.

Places set aside for wildlife conservation in the ocean are called Marine Protected Areas (MPAs for short). Nations create MPAs in the waters they control. For example, a nation with an ocean coastline has control over the ocean up to 200 nautical miles (370 km) from its shore. Its government sets the rules about how this area is used and who can fish, mine, or drill there.

Some MPAs are sanctuaries where no fishing, mining, drilling, or other activities are allowed. Other MPAs allow fishing but have rules limiting both how much can fishers can catch and bycatch (fish caught accidentally—see pages 240–241). Researchers have found that MPAs with a complete ban on fishing and other activities are the most successful.

A well-managed MPA is great for the animals living inside it. And it also benefits people. An MPA lets habitats recover from damage. It provides a safe place for fish to lay eggs and their young to grow up. As a result, there are more fish in the area outside the MPA because the fish spread out from this safe nursery.

Gray sharks and red snappers patrol Kingman Reef in a protected area of the Pacific Ocean.

SUPERSIZE THAT MPA!

One of the world's biggest marine protected areas is the Pacific Remote Islands Marine National Monument. It's in the middle of the Pacific Ocean, covers an area about three times the size of California, and wraps around a group of islands and atolls. The MPA is home to sea turtles, whales, giant clams, sharks, and coral-reef fish. Millions of seabirds nest nearby.

In 2015, the United Kingdom announced plans to create another protected MPA. The Pitcairn Islands Marine Reserve is 322,138 sq miles (834,334 sq km). It will protect corals, reef fish, marine mammals, and seabirds, as well as Earth's deepest coral reef.

A southern right whale and her calf swim in the waters of the De Hoop Marine Protected Area of South Africa.

Bet you didn't know

New Zealand is an island nation in the southwestern Pacific Ocean. In 1988, it created an ocean sanctuary to protect the endangered Hector's dolphin, a small species (5 feet [1.5 m] long) found only in shallow coastal waters around New Zealand.

ENRIC SALA
ON PRISTINE SEAS

Enric Sala is a marine ecologist— a scientist who studies the relationships between ocean organisms and their habitats. He fell in love with the ocean as a boy growing up on the Mediterranean coast of Spain, where he swam and dived in the sea. Today, he's an Explorer-in-Residence at National Geographic. In this role, Dr. Sala explores the ocean with teams of scientists to find, study, restore, and protect places in the ocean that are still truly wild. This effort is called the Pristine Seas project, which got its start in 2008.

"Pristine" means "pure, unspoiled." To Dr. Sala, it means a place that has a natural ecosystem similar to what it had before humans began using it. "That typically means that no species have gone extinct, and that the large predators at the top of the food chain are abundant," he explains.

To find pristine places, Dr. Sala dives in parts of the ocean where few people have ever gone—even to places where the fish have never seen a person before! "We look for the most remote and least inhabited places, places that have received the lowest human impacts," Dr. Sala says.

PLENTY OF PREDATORS

On one of his early visits to a pristine reef, Dr. Sala noticed there were lots of large predators, such as sharks and red snappers—way more than he usually saw on dives. His research team studied how these predators controlled the numbers of smaller fish on the reef. They found that healthy coral reefs had lots of large predators. But these animals were fewer in number on unhealthy reefs that were covered in algae. What was going on?

To find out, Dr. Sala's team and other researchers worldwide had to do a lot of exploring. "We learned about it mostly by comparing pristine reefs with degraded reefs where the predators had been fished, and studying what predators eat and how much they eat," he explains. "Then we drew a web of who-eats-who, and ran mathematical models to explore what would happen to a reef if predators were removed."

Can places like an unhealthy reef be restored? Yes, says Dr. Sala, if they're fully protected from fishing and other direct human impacts. "In Cabo Pulmo, Mexico, marine life has rebounded by five times in only 10 years after it was protected from fishing," he points out, "and the large groupers and sharks are back."

WILD WONDERS

Getting protection for these amazing places is what the Pristine Seas project is all about. "The goal of Pristine Seas is to help to save the 20 wildest places in the ocean, in large marine reserves—national parks in the sea," declares Dr. Sala.

To achieve this goal, Dr. Sala meets with government leaders in many countries. He shares films and photos of the wonders beneath the waves. He works to persuade officials to set up Marine Protected Areas. "First, I want them to develop an emotional connection with the sea," Dr. Sala says. "If we cannot take them on our expeditions, we bring images to them. It's easier to inspire them to protect a place if they can see it and fall in love with it first."

But Dr. Sala also uses data to make his point. "We use our scientific studies to show them how important and unique those places are," he says. "Finally, we also show them that preserving a place is economically more beneficial than destroying it."

How does that work? One of the answers is "big fish"! "If you don't kill the fish, they take a longer time to die, and they grow larger," explains Dr. Sala. "Divers are attracted to places with lots of fish, so many marine reserves now make a lot of money from tourism—much more than previously from fishing."

But that doesn't mean people living near the protected areas have to stop eating fish. "Inside marine reserves, fish grow and reproduce so much, that many of them—and their babies—spill over the boundaries of the reserves. That helps to replenish the populations of fish around the reserves, and also helps the fishermen."

SWIMMING WITH SHARKS

Seeing the harm that's been done to the ocean can be discouraging. Dr. Sala notes that he's seen plastic trash on beaches on the most remote islands in the Pacific because it's carried there by currents. Still, pristine places are symbols of hope. And exploring them has provided Dr. Sala with amazing experiences to share with others.

He's had a giant manta ray ask to be scratched. He's seen reefs covered with brightly colored giant clams. He's been inspected by fish that've never seen people before. "Twinspot snappers in the Line Islands not only came close," he reports, "but they bit my ponytail and as much gear as they could get a hold of."

One of his best known stories is about swimming underwater with a school of 200 hammerhead sharks swimming over him. What's *that* like? "Exhilarating!" says Dr. Sala. "And at the same time, a real privilege. It's like walking among a pride of lions in Africa—only that I would not be comfortable walking next to lions!" The sharks, he says, were simply curious about him.

Experiences like these help Dr. Sala share the wonder of the ocean when he talks to people about Pristine Seas. Saving pristine places is important for many reasons—Dr. Sala describes them as "beautiful and sacred, the last places that we have not destroyed because of our greed." They are also "the instruction manual of the ocean," he explains, "the places where we can learn what the ocean works like without fishing."

A TALK WITH OCEANOGRAPHER GRACE SABA

WHAT DO OCEANOGRAPHERS DO?

Oceanographers work in many different settings. Some oceanographers do research mainly in a laboratory. Other oceanographers spend lots of time doing "field research," such as going out to sea to collect water samples or diving to study a reef. Oceanographers also use computers to create computer models of the ocean—that's a computer program that re-creates how the ocean works.

TELL US MORE ABOUT WHAT YOU DO.

I'm an assistant professor in the Department of Marine and Coastal Sciences at Rutgers University in New Jersey. My field research takes me all over the globe. I study plankton and their role in food webs to find out how ecosystems respond to changes in climate over time. I teach oceanography and work with students who are training to be the next generation of marine scientists. My students conduct hands-on experiments to find out how organisms respond to changing environments, and use underwater robots called gliders to observe how the ocean works.

WHAT INSPIRED YOU TO BECOME AN OCEANOGRAPHER?

I grew up on a farm in Kansas, which is about as far as you can get from any ocean! But I spent all my free time outside by the creek behind our farmhouse. Mostly, I enjoyed finding crawdads and keeping tabs on tadpoles as they changed into frogs. My mom gave me Jacques Cousteau's book *The Ocean World* when I was eight years old, and I was fascinated with the complexity of the mysterious ocean and its inhabitants. I knew then that I wanted to be a marine biologist.

WHAT'S YOUR FAVORITE MARINE ORGANISM?

Antarctic krill are fascinating organisms. They are one of the most important animals in coastal Antarctic ecosystems. They support penguins and other sea birds, fish, seals, and whales. In order to survive the cold Antarctic winters, young life stages of krill need to feed under the ice on ice algae. It is because of this dependence on sea ice that scientists are concerned about the krill population as more ice melts in parts of Antarctica due to global temperatures rising.

WHY DID YOU CHOOSE TO STUDY PLANKTON?

I respect plankton because they have the toughest job—they make up the base of the food web in the ocean. They support all other marine life, including fish, sharks, and whales. Plankton do this not only by being a food source for many animals, but also by pooping, which sinks through the water and is fed on by animals that live in the deep ocean and on the seafloor.

WHAT DO YOU FIND MOST FASCINATING ABOUT THE OCEAN?

The links between the land, ocean, and atmosphere. These connections can range from large-scale (global) ones to small-scale (local) ones. A global example is an El Niño event. But even small-scale events can have large impacts on the coastal ocean. A localized rainfall in a heavily farmed coastal area can dump excess nutrients into the ocean, changing the type of phytoplankton that grow, and ultimately affect the entire food chain.

krill in Antarctica

WHAT IS THE MOST AWESOME EXPERIENCE YOU'VE HAD AS AN OCEANOGRAPHER?

A dive in the submersible *Alvin*. During one eight-hour dive from the surface to the seafloor, I was able to see several different habitats and observe organisms I had never seen before. I dove through a dense jellyfish bloom near the surface, basked in the flashing lights of bioluminescent animals in the twilight zone, and saw an abundance of life in the dark near black smoker chimneys on the ocean floor.

WHAT TIPS CAN YOU OFFER FOR KIDS WHO ARE EXPLORING A SHORELINE?

The most abundant organisms that live in the ocean include viruses, bacteria, and microscopic plants and animals that cannot be seen by the naked eye. In fact, one drop of seawater contains millions of organisms. So use a magnifying glass or a microscope, if you can, to examine a few drops of seawater. Other organisms like to hide. The key to finding them is to dig deep in the sand for animals like sand crabs and look in cracks or under rocks in tide pools for sea stars, anemones, barnacles, fish, worms, and many shelled creatures. You will be surprised to see what comes to life before your eyes.

WHAT WOULD YOU LIKE PEOPLE TO KNOW ABOUT THE OCEAN TO HELP THEM UNDERSTAND WHY IT'S SO IMPORTANT TO LIFE AND HOW THE PLANET WORKS?

The ocean helps regulate our climate and makes our planet livable. As if that isn't enough, phytoplankton, the microscopic plants in the sea, produce more than half of the oxygen we breathe. Fish and shellfish provide food for billions of people worldwide.

WHAT ADVICE WOULD YOU GIVE KIDS WHO WANT TO STUDY THE OCEAN?

The best way to start studying the ocean is to get in there. Observe organisms on the shoreline or put on a mask and snorkel and explore a little deeper.

HOW YOU CAN HELP

All the problems facing the ocean can flatten you like a wave that catches you by surprise. But there are many things you can do to help the ocean and make the world a better and cleaner place.

sea lion

CURB GLOBAL CLIMATE CHANGE

According to scientists, burning fossil fuels, such as oil and gasoline, releases heat-trapping gases into the atmosphere. The result is global climate change—a change in Earth's climate. This phenomenon threatens the ocean and its life—and humans—in many ways.

It may seem as if this is too big a problem for an ordinary person to tackle, but every bit of effort helps: You can help reduce the burning of fossil fuels by turning off lights when you leave a room, replacing traditional lightbulbs with fluorescent bulbs, putting on a sweater instead of turning up the heat, drying clothes on a clothesline instead of in the dryer, and getting to school by walking, biking, riding a bus, or joining a carpool. This effort is called "reducing your carbon footprint."

REDUCE, REUSE, RECYCLE

red crab

Recycling an aluminum can, drinking from a reusable container, and using cloth dish towels to clean a counter don't sound like activities that can help the ocean. But these everyday choices are small actions that add up to make a big impact. Take that aluminum can, for example: It can be melted down and used to make new cans with just a fraction of the energy it takes to dig up and refine a new batch of aluminum. Saving energy means less fossil fuel is burned and fewer greenhouse gases are sent into the sky and sea. Drinking from a reusable water bottle saves energy, too, because you use it thousands of times instead of throwing away thousands of plastic bottles. It also keeps plastic trash out of the ocean. Using cloth towels instead of paper towels, which is made from trees, saves energy and trees—so you're helping conserve forests as well as the ocean!

JOIN AN ORGANIZATION OR PROJECT

Check with a local nature center or science museum to see if it has a club or project focusing on the ocean, a community project to clean up a beach, or a citizen-science project that needs volunteers. There are also projects you can find online that seek data from near and far from "citizen scientists"—people who are interested in learning about science and observing the natural world. Many of these projects welcome participation by kids. For example, the National Oceanic and Atmospheric Administration (NOAA) works with the Southeast Atlantic Marine Debris Initiative to run the Marine Debris Program. This program tracks the types of trash on beaches and where the trash is found using a phone app. Find out more at *marinedebris.noaa .gov/partnerships/marine-debris-tracker*.

PICK UP THE TRASH

Help keep your neighborhood, parks, and beaches clean. Put on a pair of gloves to pick up trash. You can also help cut down on litter at its source by buying fewer products that use a lot of packaging. For example, you can buy fruit that's sold loose in bins instead of in plastic packaging.

USE FEWER PLASTIC PRODUCTS

Plastics that end up as ocean debris entangle, drown, and kill tens of thousands of marine animals each year. Thousands of albatross chicks die because their parents feed them plastic objects, mistaking them for food. When you use a reusable cloth bag for shopping instead of a plastic bag from the store, for example, you're helping to reduce the amount of energy and raw materials used to make plastic bags. In addition, plastic bags often end up in the ocean when they're blown off the street or out of garbage cans into storm drains, which drain into waterways. Leatherback sea turtles, which feed on jellyfish, mistake the bags for their prey and eat them—a mistake that sickens and slowly kills them.

OCEAN-SMART PET CARE!

Consider avoiding pet foods that use seafood products. Don't flush cat litter, even the flushable kind, down the toilet—it contains germs that can harm marine animals. So do dog droppings—germs can wash into the ocean from rainwater running off streets. So don't forget to scoop that poop!

EAT SUSTAINABLY

If you eat fish and other marine organisms, make sure that your food is produced sustainably. Projects such as FishWatch (*www.fishwatch.gov*) and Seafood Watch (*www.seafoodwatch.org*) keep track of fisheries, species, and sustainability issues so you can check to see what seafood is okay to eat. You can also look for "ecolabels" on food in stores.

ENJOY THE BEACH RESPONSIBLY

Pack it in, pack it out! Clean up your stuff after you've enjoyed a day at the beach. Don't remove animals, plants, rocks, and the like from tide pools or anywhere else. If you turn over a rock on the beach to see what's under it, put it back the way you found it so the little animals living there don't dry out.

humpback whale

DON'T BUY MARINE ANIMALS AS SOUVENIRS

At home, don't buy items such as coral jewelry or shark products. If you are traveling with your family, don't buy souvenirs such as tortoiseshell hair accessories, shells, dried seahorses, or anything else made from marine animals.

USE FEWER CHEMICALS

Water on land drains into the sea and takes chemicals with it. Encourage your family to use as little fertilizer as possible in your yard. Grow plants that are native to your area and can thrive. Use nontoxic cleaning products at home. Remember, whatever goes down the drain ends up in waterways! Nothing should go down a drain— unless it, er, comes out of your body first.

GLOSSARY

Abyssal plain—wide, flat area of seafloor that lies between a mid-ocean ridge and a continent

Abyssal zone—dark ocean layer that starts at about 13,100 feet (4,000 m) underwater and extends to about 19,700 feet (6,000 m)

Aquaculture—the raising and harvesting of water-based plants and animals, especially for food

Atoll—a ring of coral reefs and islands

Barrier island—a narrow island that lies along a coastline

Bay—a rounded indentation in the shore of a sea, partly surrounded by land, that is usually smaller than a gulf

Bioluminescence—light produced by a living thing

Bivalve—a mollusk with a hinged shell. Clams, scallops, oysters, and mussels are all bivalves.

Boundary current—a current that makes up one of a gyre's borders

Brackish—a mixture of fresh and salty water

Bycatch—the capture of animals that fishers aren't hunting

Camouflage—an organism's ability to disguise its appearance, often by using its coloring or body shape to blend in with its surroundings. An example is a fish that looks like a stone.

Macaroni penguin

Cephalopod—a mollusk with jaws and limbs, such as an octopus

Cetacean—a mammal that lacks hind legs, has flippers for front legs, and has a tail flattened sideways for swimming. Whales, dolphins, and porpoises are cetaceans.

Chiton—a mollusk with eight hard plates on its back

Climate—the kind of weather conditions that are normal for an area over the span of many years

Climate change—a big change in Earth's climate that lasts for a very long time. For example, Earth experienced an ice age that began about 80,000 years ago and lasted until about 18,000 years ago.

Commercial fishing—fishing to obtain fish to sell in large amounts

Continent—a large landmass made of rock that is less dense than the rock that forms the ocean's floor. Earth has seven continents: Africa, Antarctica, Asia, Australia, Europe, North America, and South America.

Continental drift—the slow, steady movement of plates of continental crust across Earth due to currents in molten (melted) rock below the surface

Continental island—an island that is part of the land that slopes away from a continent's edge and is made of the same continental rock

Continental margin—the edges of a continent that lie beneath the ocean

Continental rise—a pile of sediment that lies at the base of the continental slope

Continental shelf—a gentle slope that drops away from a continent's coast to a depth of about 650 feet (200 m)

Continental slope—a steep slope that drops away from the edge of a continental shelf

Coriolis effect—the way in which winds seem to veer right in the Northern Hemisphere and left in the Southern Hemisphere because of Earth's rotation. The Coriolis effect also causes water currents to travel in curved paths and loops through the ocean.

Crustacean—an animal with a hard exterior skeleton and jointed legs. Shrimp, lobsters, and crabs are crustaceans.

Current—the movement of water from one place to another

Cyanobacteria—bacteria also known as "blue-green algae"

Dead zone—a body of water where organisms that require oxygen cannot survive

Density—a measure of how tightly packed a substance's particles are. For example, a brick is heavier than a piece of polystyrene of the same size because it is much more dense. In the same way, a sample of salt water is more dense than a same-size sample of freshwater.

Diatom—a kind of microalgae that uses silica in seawater to make a glasslike, boxy shell.

Echinoderm—an animal with a skeleton made of hard, fused plates covered by tough skin and with a body that takes the shape of a circle surrounded by rays. Sea stars and sea cucumbers are echinoderms.

Ecosystem—a community of living things interacting with each other and the nonliving parts of their habitat

Endangered—relating to an animal or plant found in such small numbers that it is at risk of becoming extinct, or no longer existing

Environment—the natural features of a place, such as its weather, the kind of land it has, and the type of plants that grow in it

Estuary—a coastal area partly surrounded by land where freshwater meets and mixes with salty seawater. Many estuaries are where rivers and streams flow into oceans.

Eutrophication—an overgrowth of algae caused by an overload of nutrients

Extinction—the state of no longer existing, or being alive. When all the members of a species die out, they are said to go extinct.

Floe—an individual piece of pack ice

Gastropod—a mollusk with a single shell, such as a snail. Some gastropods, such as slugs, have tiny internal shells or no shells at all.

Gill net—a long, drifting net that catches fish by their gills. Also called drift nets.

Glacier—a river of densely packed ice and snow that flows slowly across land. Icebergs are formed by a process called calving in which ice breaks off a glacier and floats on the ocean.

Global Conveyor Belt—the movement of water in a giant loop through the world ocean

Gravity—the invisible force that makes all objects, from planets to particles, pull on each other

Greenhouse gas—a gas in the atmosphere that traps heat. Carbon dioxide, water vapor, methane, and nitrous oxide are examples of greenhouse gases.

Gulf—a large area in a sea partly surrounded by land

Guyot—a flat-topped seamount

Gyre—a large loop made up of many currents

Habitat—a place in nature where an organism lives

bottlenose dolphin

throughout the year, or for shorter periods

Hadalpelagic zone—the deepest depths of the ocean, below 19,700 feet (6,000 m)

Hydrothermal vent—an opening on the seafloor that releases very hot water filled with minerals

Ice sheet—a massive blanket of land ice more than 20,000 square miles (50,000 sq km) in size. Ice sheets cover most of Antarctica and Greenland.

Invasive species—species that are introduced accidentally or on purpose from their native habitat to a new location. Also called "introduced species" or "exotic species." Invasive species typically have a bad effect on native plants and animals.

Invertebrate—an organism without a backbone. Invertebrates include insects, corals, crustaceans, and mollusks.

Lagoon—a shallow body of water separated from the ocean by coral reefs, barrier islands, or hills of sand called sandbars

Larva (plural: larvae)—an immature form of an invertebrate animal, such as a crab

Microalgae—one-celled algae related to many-celled algae called seaweed

Midnight zone—the dark ocean layer that starts at about 3,250 feet (1,000 m) beneath the surface and plunges to about 13,100 feet (4,000 m)

Migration—the seasonal movement from one location to another. The migration may be prompted by various environmental cues, including weather and availability of food. Sea turtles, whales, and seabirds are examples of marine animals that migrate.

Mollusks—soft-bodied, legless animals that often have shells, such as snails and clams

Multi-year ice—ice that doesn't thaw out completely in summer and lasts for many years

Neap tide—a tide with a smaller-than-average range between high and low that occurs twice a month, when the moon, sun, and Earth form a right-angle triangle with each other

Oceanic island—an island that rises up directly from the seafloor. Many oceanic islands are the peaks of undersea volcanoes

Otter trawl—a fishing net that is dragged along the seafloor

Pack ice—sea ice that floats on the ocean and isn't connected to land

Photic zone—the upper ocean layer that ends at a depth of about 650 feet (200 m) deep. Sunlight penetrates this zone.

Photophores—light-producing organisms found on an animal

Photosynthesis—the process of using energy from sunlight to make food out of water and air. Plants and algae both make food by photosynthesis.

Phytoplankton—microscopic algae and other organisms floating on and near the ocean's surface that make food from light by photosynthesis.

Pinnipeds—animals with four flippers for legs. Seals, sea lions, and walruses are pinnipeds.

Plate tectonics—a theory that explains the movement of continents and the spreading of the seafloor. According to this theory, Earth's surface is made up of large rocky plates of crust that move due to the constant churning of molten rock beneath the surface.

Polyp—an animal with a tubular body that is attached to a surface at one end and open at the other for feeding, as well as getting rid of waste materials

Predator—an animal that hunts other animals for food. Its behavior is "predatory."

Prey—an animal that is hunted and eaten by other animals

Purse seine—a fishing net shaped like a pouch that is pulled shut around a school of fish

Salinity—a measurement of the amount of salt in water

Sea—a large area of the ocean located at its edge that is partly surrounded by land.

Seafloor spreading—the movement of plates on the seafloor caused by currents in the molten (melted) rock beneath it. The plates move away from each other, which causes a gap to form. Molten rock oozes out of the gap and creates ridges and new seafloor.

Sea level—the average level of the ocean's surface

Seamount—an extinct underwater volcano that does not stick up above the ocean's surface

Sediment—loose material that settles to the bottom of an ocean, lake, pond, or other body of water. Sand and soil

spotted jellyfish

are examples of sediments.

Sonar—a way of using sounds and echoes to measure distance underwater

Spring tide—a tide with an extra-wide range between high and low that occurs twice a month, when the moon, sun, and Earth form a straight line

Strait—a narrow waterway that connects two larger bodies of water

Strandline—a line of dead seaweed, shells, feathers, and other material washed ashore and left behind by the tide

Subduction—a process in which a plate made of dense rock sinks under a plate made of less dense rock when the two plates meet

Subsistence fishing—fishing to feed a family or village

Subsurface current—a current in the ocean's deeper zones that is caused by differences in water density due to differences in temperature and salinity

Surface current—a current of water that is driven mainly by strong winds that blow steadily across the ocean

Swim bladder—a gas-filled organ that helps a fish rise, sink, or stay in one place in the water

Thermocline—a sharp drop in temperature that marks a boundary between the ocean's surface waters and deeper, colder water

Tide—the regular daily rise and fall of ocean water due to the gravitational pull of the moon and sun

Tide pool—a pool of water found among rocks at low tide

Trawl net—a fishing net that is dragged behind a ship

Trench—a canyon formed where an ocean plate slides under, or subducts, a continental plate

Tsunami—a giant wave caused by an earthquake or other large force in the ocean, such as a massive undersea landslide

Twilight zone—the very dim ocean layer that starts at about 650 feet (200 m) beneath the surface and reaches a depth of about 3,250 feet (1,000 m)

Upwelling—the movement of deep, cold, nutrient-rich water from the seafloor to the ocean's surface

Vertebrate—an organism with a backbone. Vertebrates include mammals, fish, reptiles, amphibians, and birds.

Zooplankton—small living things, such as crab larvae and one-celled organisms, that float on and near the ocean's surface and feed on phytoplankton and other zooplankton

FIND OUT MORE

GREAT WEBSITES, MOVIES, AND PLACES TO VISIT

WEBSITES

- Look for marine wildlife on National Geographic's "Animals" website: kids.nationalgeographic.com/animals.
- Dive into much of National Geographic's info on oceans by following links on this page: ocean.nationalgeographic.com/ocean.
- National Geographic Kids has an ocean website: kids.nationalgeographic.com/explore/ocean-portal.
- Take the controls of a submersible on NOVA's "My Submarine Ocean Explorer" website: coexploration.org/oe/kws/start.html.
- Explore many marine topics when you visit the Smithsonian Institution's ocean website "Ocean Portal—Find Your Blue": ocean.si.edu.
- A world of ocean news and information awaits you at the website of the National Oceanic and Atmospheric Administration (NOAA): oceanexplorer.noaa.gov.
- Find out more about marine sanctuaries and things you can do to help the ocean here: sanctuaries.noaa.gov/education.
- NOAA offers many marine photo albums you can enjoy online, such as one about coral reefs (photolib.noaa.gov/reef) and another about all kinds of marine wildlife (photolib.noaa.gov/animals/index.html).
- Learn more about issues related to climate change on this Environmental Protection Agency (EPA) website for students: epa.gov/climatestudents.
- Information and activities about climate change can be found on this National Aeronautics and Space Administration (NASA) website: climatekids.nasa.gov.

MOVIES

- *Planet Ocean* (2012): This documentary presents information about people, oceans, and issues such as climate change.

BBC
- *The Blue Planet* (2008): This four-part series about the ocean explores marine life from plankton to whales.
- *The Great Barrier Reef* (2013): Explore Australia's huge coral reef system in this documentary.
- *Oceans: Exploring the Secrets of Our Undersea World* (2008): Cameras go underwater to explore everything from sharks to shipwrecks in this series.
- *Ocean Voyagers* (2008): This documentary focuses on humpback whales, their behavior, and their migration.
- *Shark* (2015): This four-part series focuses on sharks and the scientists who study them.

DisneyNature
- *Oceans* (2010): Marine animals star in this multipart series about the seas.

National Geographic
- *Amazing Planet—Ocean Realm* (2007): This episode in National Geographic's Amazing Planet series takes viewers beneath the waves.
- *Drain the Ocean* (2010): This movie uses computer animation to bring undersea geography to life.

Nature
- *Ocean Giants* (2012): Go eye-to-eye with whales and dolphins in this three-part series.

Netflix
- *Mission Blue* (2014): Sylvia Earle stars in this documentary about her campaign to create marine sanctuaries worldwide.

NOVA
- *Earth from Space* (2013): Get a satellite's-eye view of your planet and see how the ocean's currents travel around it.

PLACES TO VISIT

U.S.A.
- ABQ BioPark Aquarium, Albuquerque, New Mexico
- Alaska SeaLife Center, Seward, Alaska
- Aquarium of the Pacific, Long Beach, California
- Birch Aquarium, Scripps Institution of Oceanography, San Diego, California
- The Estuarium, Dauphin Island Sea Lab, Dauphin Island, Alabama
- Florida Aquarium, Tampa, Florida
- Georgia Aquarium, Atlanta, Georgia
- Hatfield Marine Science Center, Newport, Oregon
- Maui Ocean Center, Wailuku, Hawaii
- Milstein Family Hall of Ocean Life, American Museum of Natural History, New York, New York
- Monterey Bay National Marine Sanctuary, central coast of California
- Mote Marine Aquarium and Laboratory, Sarasota, Florida
- Mystic Aquarium and Institute for Exploration, Mystic, Connecticut
- National Aquarium, Baltimore, Maryland
- New England Aquarium, Boston, Massachusetts
- New York Aquarium, Brooklyn, New York
- North Carolina Aquariums, located in Pine Knoll Shores and Fort Fisher as well as on Roanoke Island, North Carolina
- Ocean Experience, Putnam Museum & Science Center, Davenport, Iowa
- Oregon Coast Aquarium, Newport, Oregon
- Sant Ocean Hall, Smithsonian Institution's National Museum of Natural History, Washington, D.C.
- Seattle Aquarium, Seattle, Washington
- Shedd Aquarium, Chicago, Illinois
- Shores & Aquarium, Columbus Zoo, Columbus, Ohio
- Steinhart Aquarium, California Academy of Sciences, San Francisco, California
- Virginia Aquarium and Marine Science Center, Virginia Beach, Virginia
- Waikiki Aquarium, Honolulu, Hawaii
- Woods Hole Science Aquarium, Woods Hole, Massachusetts

CANADA
- Fisheries Museum of the Atlantic, Lunenburg, Nova Scotia, Canada
- Fundy Discovery Aquarium, Huntsman Marine Science Center, St. Andrews, New Brunswick, Canada
- Vancouver Aquarium, Vancouver, British Columbia, Canada
- Water Gallery, Canadian Museum of Nature, Ottawa, Ontario, Canada

MEXICO
- Veracruz Aquarium, Veracruz, Mexico

SOUTH AMERICA
- Aquarium de Valencia, Valencia, Venezuela
- Aquarium, Temaikèn, Buenos Aires, Argentina
- Rodadero Sea Aquarium and Museum, Santa Marta, Colombia

EUROPE
- Aquarium of Alghero, Sardinia, Italy
- Aquarium of Cattolica, Emilia-Romagna, Italy
- Aquarium of Genoa, Liguria, Italy
- Aquarium, London Zoo, London, England, United Kingdom
- Aquatopia, Antwerp, Belgium
- Haus des Meeres, Vienna, Austria
- Kotka Maretarium, Kotka, Finland
- Le Musée de la Mer, Biarritz, France
- Marine Invertebrates gallery, Natural History Museum, London, England, United Kingdom
- Maritime Museum and Aquarium, Gothenburg, Sweden
- National Marine Aquarium, Plymouth, England, United Kingdom
- NAUSICAÁ, Centre National de la Mer, Boulogne-sur-Mer, France
- L'Oceanogràfic, Valencia, Spain
- Oceanopolis, Brest, France
- Ozeaneum, Stralsund, Germany
- National Maritime Museum, London, England, United Kingdom
- North Sea Oceanarium, Hirtshals, Jutland, Denmark
- SeaQuarium, Rhyl, Wales, United Kingdom
- Underwater Observatory Marine Park, Eilat, Israel

ASIA
- Churaumi Aquarium, Okinawa, Japan
- National Museum of Marine Biology and Aquarium, Pingtung, Taiwan
- Osaka Aquarium, Osaka, Japan
- Port of Nagoya Public Aquarium, Nagoya, Japan
- S.E.A. Aquarium, Sentosa Island, Singapore
- Shanghai Ocean Aquarium, Shanghai, China

AFRICA
- National Marine Aquarium, Swakopmund, Namibia
- Two Oceans Aquarium, Waterfront, South Africa
- uShaka Marine World, Durban, South Africa

AUSTRALIA
- The Aquarium of Western Australia, Hillarys Boat Harbour, Western Australia
- Reef HQ Aquarium, Townsville, Queensland

INDEX

PHOTO CREDITS

COVER: Front, (jellyfish), bluehand/Shutterstock; (blue parrot fish), Khramtsova Tatyana/Shutterstock; (coral), mehmettorlak/ iStockphoto; (Blacktip Reef Shark), Ian Scott/Shutterstock; (Hawksbill Sea Turtle), Rich Carey/Shutterstock; (Clownfish), Kletr/Shutterstock; (sea-horse), Chen Ws/Shutterstock; (diver), Dudarev Mikhail/Shutterstock; (ROV), Norbert Wu/Minden Pictures; (sparkles), Lonely/Shutterstock; (wave pattern), Nataleana/Shutterstock; Back: (sea shell), Fotana/Shutterstock; (lionfish), Mathieu FoulquiÈ/Biosphoto; (tropical fish), ehtesham/ Shutterstock; (blue sea star), Pete Oxford/Minden Pictures; Spine (blue tang fish), Tim Laman/National Geographic Creative; front flap (blue tang fish), Tim Laman/National Geographic Creative; back flap (UP), courtesy of Christina Wilsdon; back flap (LO), courtesy of Rick Keil; **CHAPTER 1:** 1, Kapitan Khlebnikov/ Dreamstime.com; 2 (shark), Jim Agronick/Shutterstock; 2 (jellyfish), bluehand/Shutterstock; 3 (octopus), Reinhard Dirscherl/ ullstein bild via Getty Images; 3 (clownfish), Kletr/Shutterstock; 3 (blue tang fish), Khramtsova Tatyana/Shutterstock; 3 (coral), mehmettorlak/iStockphoto; 4 (UP LE), Michael Stubblefield/Getty Images; 4 (UP RT), Danita Delimont/Gallo Images/Getty Images; 4 (CTR), Ian Scott/Shutterstock; 4 (LE LE), Rich Carey/Shutterstock; 4 (LO RT), Dana Stephenson/Getty Images; 5 (UP LE), EpicStockMedia/Shutterstock; 5 (UP RT), Steve Allen Travel Photography/Alamy Stock Photo; 5 (CTR), Paul Nicklen/National Geographic Creative; 5 (LO), Brian J. Skerry/National Geographic Creative; 6 (UP), courtesy of Christina Wilsdon; 6 (LO), Diana Ponikvar/Getty Images; 7 (UP), courtesy of Rick Keil; 7 (CTR), Ethan Daniels/Shutterstock; 7 (LO), Stephen Frink/Digital Vision; 8 (LE), Brian J. Skerry/National Geographic Creative; 8 (RT), David Doubilet/National Geographic Creative; 9 (UP), Enric Sala/National Geographic Creative 9 (CTR), Brian J. Skerry/National Geographic Creative; 9 (LO), Paul Nicklen/National Geographic Creative; 10-11, Luis Quinta/Nature Picture Library; 12, MarcAndreLeTourneux/ Shutterstock; 13, NASA; 14, Mark Thiessen/National Geographic Creative; 16 (UP), Perfect Lazybones/Shutterstock; 16 (LO), Pniesen/Dreamstime.com; 17 (UP), Shilo Watts/Getty Images; 17 (LO LE), robertharding/Alamy Stock Photo; 17 (LO RT), Viktor Gmyria/Dreamstime.com; 18 (UP), Tim Zurowski/All Canada Photos/Getty Images; 18 (LO), Susanne Neal/Dreamstime.com; 19 (UP), nouseforname/Shutterstock; 19 (CTR), Suzi Logan/ Shutterstock; 19 (LO), simon margetson travel/Alamy Stock Photo; 20, Stephen Emerson/Alamy Stock Photo; 21, ChameleonsEye/ Shutterstock; 22 (UP), elleon/Getty Images; 22 (LO), Atelier Sommerland/Shutterstock; 23 (UP), Denis Burdin/Shutterstock; 23 (LO LE), Georg Gerster/Science Source; 23 (LO RT), Boris Stroujko/Shutterstock; 24 (UP), WaterFrame/Alamy Stock Photo; 24 (LO), Fred Bavendam/Minden Pictures; 25 (UP), Brian J. Skerry/National Geographic Creative; 25 (CTR), David Shale/ Nature Picture Library; 25 (LO), Roland Seitre/Minden Pictures; 26, NASA/GSFC/METI/ERSDAC/JAROS, and U.S./Japan ASTER Science Team; 28 (UP), stockphoto-graf/Shutterstock; 28 (LO), Birgitte Wilms/Minden Pictures; 29 (UP), haveseen/Shutterstock; 29 (CTR), javarman/Shutterstock; 29 (LO LE), Eric Isselee/ Shutterstock; 29 (LO RT), Anton Balazh/Shutterstock; 30 (UP), Georgette Douwma/Nature Picture Library; 30 (LO), Andrea Izzotti/Shutterstock; 31 (UP), Ingo Arndt/Minden Pictures; 31 (LO LE), sserg_dibrova/iStockphoto/Getty Images; 31 (LO RT), Andrea Izzotti/Shutterstock; 33, jele/Shutterstock; 34-35, Emory Kristof/ National Geographic Creative; 34 (LO), Paul Nicklen/National Geographic Creative; 35 (UP RT), Kent Kobersteen/National Geographic Creative; 35 (CTR), Stafford, Edward/National Geographic Creative; 35 (LO), Design Pics Inc/Alamy; 36-37, Paul Nicklen/National Geographic Creative; 36 (LO), Renato Granieri/ Alamy; 37 (UP RT), Kevin A Raskoff; 37 (CTR), Flip Nicklin/National Geographic Creative; 37 (LO), Paul Nicklen/National Geographic Creative; 38, April Turner/iStockphoto/Getty Images; 39, Carl Purcell/Photo Researchers RM/Getty Images; 41, Stuart Armstrong; 42, Georgette Douwma/The Image Bank/Getty Images; 43, Jan Wlodarczyk/age fotostock RM/Getty Images; 44, Spencer Sutton/Science Source; 45, Jeff Rotman/Nature Picture Library; 45 (INSET), Kerryn Parkinson/NORFANZ/Caters News/ ZUMAPRESS.com/Newscom; 46, David Wrobel/Visuals Unlimited/ Corbis; 47, Peter David/The Image Bank/Getty Images; 48, Davis Meltzer/National Geographic Creative; 49, courtesy of Kevin Raskoff, California State University, Monterey Bay, the Hidden Ocean Arctic 2005 Exploration, NOAA-OER; 49 (INSET), NOAA/ MBARI; 50 (UP), David Shale/NPL/Minden Pictures; 50 (LO), Norbert Wu/Minden Pictures; 51 (UP LE), Steven S Eilenberg; 51 (UP RT), Norbert Wu/Minden Pictures; 51 (LO LE), David Liittschwager/National Geographic Creative; 51 (LO RT), David Shale/Nature Picture Library; **CHAPTER 2:** 52-53, Mark Conlin/ Oxford Scientific RM/Getty Images; 54 (UP), Conservation International/Caters News Agency; 54 (LO), AP Photo/Rex Features; 55 (UP), Paul Zahl/National Geographic Creative; 55 (CTR), LauraD/Shutterstock; 55 (LO LE), Paul Zahl/National Geographic Creative; 55 (LO RT), LauraD/Shutterstock; 56, Stuart Armstrong; 57 (phytoplankton), George F. Mobley/National Geographic Creative; 57 (stingray), Stephen Frink/Digital Vision; 57 (tiger shark), Greg Amptman/Dreamstime.com; 57 (green sea turtle), Cigdem Sean Cooper/Dreamstime.com; 57 (sea star), Vilainecrevette/Shutterstock; 57 (hermit crab), Lynsey Allan/ Shutterstock; 57 (jellyfish), iStock.com/vilainecrevette; 57 (fire shrimp), Iliuta Goean/Shutterstock; 57 (antarctic krill), Ingo Arndt/ Minden Pictures; 57 (mussels), Bill Curtsinger/National Geographic Creative; 58 (LE), Norbert Wu/Minden Pictures; 58 (RT), courtesy of Dr. John R. Dolan, Laboratoire d'Oceanographique de Villefranche/NOAA; 59, Jubal Harshaw/ Shutterstock; 60, Kongsak/Shutterstock; 61, Jeff Mondragon/ Alamy; 62, Alex Mustard/Nature Picture Library; 63, Sirachai Arunrugstichai/Moment Open/Getty Images; 64, Jak Wonderly/ NGP; 65, Jak Wonderly/NGP; 66, David Doubilet/National Geographic Creative; 67, Enric Sala/National Geographic Creative; 68, Thomas P. Peschak/National Geographic Creative; 69, David Doubilet/National Geographic Creative; 70, Tim Laman/National Geographic Creative; 71, Chris Newbert/Minden Pictures; 72 (UP LE), Dave Fleetham/Design Pics/Getty Images; 72 (UP RT), Ethan Daniels/Shutterstock; 72 (LO LE), Georgette Douwma/Nature Picture Library; 72 (LO RT), Norbert Wu/Minden Pictures; 73 (UP LE), Darlyne A. Murawski/National Geographic Creative; 73 (UP RT), Peter Leahy/ShutterPoint Photography; 73 (CTR), Pete Oxford/Minden Pictures 73 (LO LE), Kim Briers/Shutterstock; 73 (LO RT), Richard Whitcombe/Shutterstock; 74, Svetlana Lukienko/ Shutterstock; 75, Sirachai Arunrugstichai/Moment RF/Getty Images; 76 (UP), Doug Perrine/Nature Picture Library; 76 (CTR), imageBROKER/Alamy; 76 (LO), Michael Stubblefield/iStockphoto/ Getty Images; 77 (UP LE), courtesy of the Monterey Bay Aquarium Research Institute (c) 2004 MBARI; 77 (UP RT), John N.A. Hooper QM; 77 (CTR LE), age fotostock/Alamy; 77 (CTR RT), NOAA Okeanos Explorer Program, Gulf of Mexico 2012 Expedition; 77 (LO), Vilainecrevette/Shutterstock; 78, Vudhikrai/Shutterstock; 79, Boris Pamikov/Shutterstock; 80, The Natural History Museum/ Alamy; 81, Alex Mustard/Nature Picture Library; 82, Reinhard Dirscherl/ullstein bild via Getty Images; 83, Stocktrek Images, Inc/ Alamy; 84, Carrie Vonderhaar/Ocean Futures Society/National Geographic Creative; 85, Carrie Vonderhaar/Ocean Futures Society/National Geographic Creative; 87, Barry B. Brown/ DanitaDelimont.com/Getty Images; 88, Jeff Hunter/ Photographer's Choice/Getty Images; 89, Georgette Douwma/ Nature Picture Library; 90, Pete Oxford/Minden Pictures; 91, RGB Ventures/SuperStock/Alamy; 92, David Shale/Nature Picture Library; 93, David Shale/Nature Picture Library; 94 (UP), David Doubilet/National Geographic Creative; 94 (LO), plovets/ iStockphoto/Getty Images; 95 (UP LE), David Burdick/NOAA; 95 (UP RT), NOAA/NOS/NMS/FGBNMS; National Marine Sanctuaries Media Library; 95 (LO), Pete Oxford/Minden Pictures; 96, Fred Bavendam/Minden Pictures; 97, Paul Nicklen/National Geographic Creative; 98, Becca Saunders/Auscape II/Minden Pictures; 99, Fred Bavendam/Minden Pictures; 100, Brian J. Skerry/National Geographic Creative; 101, Ron Offermans/Buiten-beeld/Minden Pictures; 102 (UP), Brian J. Skerry/National Geographic Creative; 102 (LO), Tim Laman/National Geographic Creative; 103 (UP RT), Brian J. Skerry/National Geographic Creative; 103 (UP LE), Matthew Propert/NGP; 103 (LO), Brian J. Skerry/National Geographic Creative; 104-105, Carlton Ward/ National Geographic Creative; 104 (UP), Kjeld Friis/Shutterstock; 104 (LO), Paul Nicklen/National Geographic Creative; 105 (UP LE), Doug Perrine/Nature Picture Library; 105 (UP RT), Joel Sartore, National Geographic Photo Ark/National Geographic Creative; 105 (LO), Ralph Pace; 106, Reinhard Dirscherl/ullstein bild/Getty Images; 107, Martin Strmiska/Alamy; 108, David Fleetham/Alamy; 109, Frank & Joyce Burek/National Geographic Creative; 110, Tim Laman/National Geographic Creative; 111, Georgette Douwma/ Nature Picture Library; 112 (UP), Gwen Lowe/SeaPics.com; 112 (CTR), Jelger Herder/Buiten-beeld/Minden Pictures; 112 (LO), Norbert Wu/Minden Pictures; 113 (UP LE), Paul Kay/Oxford Scientific RM/Getty Images; 113 (UP RT), Brian J. Skerry/National Geographic Creative; 113 (CTR), Doug Perrine/Nature Picture Library; 113 (LO), Joel Sartore, National Geographic Photo Ark/ National Geographic Creative; 114, Sergey Uryadnikov/ Shutterstock; 115, C & M Fallows/Oceanwideimages.com; 117, Jason Edwards/National Geographic Creative; 118, Wahrmut Sobainsky/NiS/Minden Pictures; 119, Biosphoto/Christopher Swann; 120 (LE), Tui De Roy/Minden Pictures; 120 (RT), Masa Ushioda/Alamy; 121 (UP), Brian J. Skerry/National Geographic Creative; 121 (CTR LE), Wil Meinderts/Buiten-beeld/Minden Pictures; 121 (CTR RT), Rich Carey/Shutterstock; 121 (LO LE), D. Parer & E. Parer-Cook/Minden Pictures; 121 (LO RT), Doug Perrine/Nature Picture Library; 123, Brian J. Skerry/National Geographic Creative; 124, Brian J. Skerry/National Geographic Creative; 126 (UP), Hiroya Minakuchi/Minden Pictures/National Geographic Creative; 126 (LO), Nansen Weber/National Geographic Creative; 127 (UP), Anthony Pierce/Corbis; 127 (LO LE), Flip Nicklin/Minden Pictures; 127 (LO RT), Luis Quinta/Nature Picture Library; 128, Hiroya Minakuchi/Minden Pictures; 129, Flip Nicklin/Minden Pictures/photo obtained under NMFS permit 987; 130, age fotostock RM/Getty Images; 131, Karoline Cullen/ Shutterstock; 132, Barry B. Brown/wildhorizons.com; 133, Stephen Frink/Getty Images; 134 (LE), Frans Lanting/National Geographic Creative; 134 (RT), Alex Mustard/Nature Picture Library; 135 (UP), Brian J. Skerry/National Geographic Creative; 135 (CTR LE), Matthew Maran/Nature Picture Library; 135 (CTR RT), Douglas Klug/Moment RF/Getty Images; 135 (LO), Yukihiro Fukuda/Nature Picture Library; 136, Paul Nicklen/National Geographic Creative; 138, Paul Nicklen/National Geographic Creative; 139, Doug Allan/ NPL/Minden Pictures; 140, Daniel J Cox/Oxford Scientific RM/ Getty Images; 141, Wayne R Bilenduke/Stone Sub/Getty Images; 142, Milo Burcham/SuperStock; 143, Michael Gore/FLPA/Minden Pictures; 144 (UP), Jeff Mauritzen/NGP; 144 (LO), Michael Quinton/ Minden Pictures; 145 (UP), FLPA/Steve Young/Minden Pictures; 145 (CTR LE), Steffen Foerster/Shutterstock; 145 (CTR RT), Matthias Breiter/National Geographic Creative; 145 (LO LE), Chris Johns/National Geographic Creative; 145 (LO RT), FLPA/John Watkins/Minden Pictures; 146, Kiah Walker/USFWS Volunteer; 147, Roberta Olenick/All Canada Photos/Getty Images; 148 (UP), Keith Szafranski/iStockphoto; 149 (CTR), Shannon Hibberd/ National Geographic Creative; 148 (LO), Anastasiya Maryankova/ iStockphoto; 149 (UP LE), kwest/Shutterstock; 149 (UP RT), Tui De Roy/Minden Pictures; 149 (LO LE), Leksele/Shutterstock; 149 (LO RT), Luc Hoogenstein/Buiten-beeld/Minden Pictures; 150, Paul Nicklen/National Geographic Creative; **CHAPTER 3:** 152-153, mattpaul/RooM RF/Getty Images; 155, Alex Pix/Shutterstock; 158, Mint Image/Frans Lanting/Getty Images; 159, Ethan Daniels/ Alamy; 160 (UP), Fred Bavendam/Minden Pictures; 160 (LO), David Shale/Nature Picture Library; 161 (UP LE), Norbert Wu/Minden Pictures 161 (UP RT), Robert Sisson/National Geographic Creative; 161 (LO LE), Wil Meinderts/Buiten-beeld/Minden Pictures; 161 (LO RT), Robert Sisson/National Geographic Creative; 165, Suzanne Long/Alamy Stock Photo; 166, Spencer Sutton/Science Source; 167, Peter Carroll/First Light/Corbis; 168 (LE), Hemis/Alamy; 168 (RT), Vincenzo Innocente/Getty Images; 169, Spencer Sutton/ Science Source; **CHAPTER 4:** 170-171, Roger Coulam/Alamy Stock Photo; 172, Patrick Foto/Shutterstock; 173, Stuart Armstrong; 175 (UP), Dan Sherwood/Design Pics/Corbis; 175 (LO), AlbertoLoyo/ iStockphoto/Getty Images; 176, Mark Conlin/Oxford Scientific RM/ Getty Images; 177, Stuart Armstrong; 178, Thomas Marent/Minden Pictures; 179, Martin Puddy/Getty Images; 180, Arthur Tilley/Getty Images; 181, Provided by the SeaWiFS Project, NASA/Goddard Space Flight Center, and ORBIMAGE; 183, Albert Moldvay/National Geographic Creative; **CHAPTER 5:** 184-185, Alex Mustard/Nature Picture Library; 186, Fearnstock/Alamy; 187, Ralph White/Corbis Documentary/Getty Images; 189, Kevin Schafer/Minden Pictures; 190, Jiji Press/AFP/Getty Images; 191, José Antonio Peòas/Science Source; 192, Chris Clor/Blend Images//Corbis; 193, North Wind Picture Archives/Alamy; 194, De Agostini Picture Library/Getty Images; 195, SuperStock/Alamy; 196, Universal History Archive/ UIG via Getty images; 197, Omikron/Getty Images; 198, Reinhard Dirscherl/Alamy; 199, NASA; 200 (UP), Kevin Schafer/Minden Pictures; 200 (LO LE), Wil Meinderts/Buiten-beeld/Minden Pictures; 200 (LO RT), Douglas Peebles Photography/Alamy; 201 (UP LE), Eric Isselee/Shutterstock; 201 (UP RT), Pablo Hidalgo/ Dreamstime.com; 201 (CTR), Anna Kucherova/Shutterstock; 201 (LO), Tui De Roy/Minden Pictures; 202, Brian J. Skerry/National Geographic Creative; 203, Brian J. Skerry/National Geographic Creative; 204, David Shale/DeepSeaPhotography.com; 205, Stuart Armstrong; 206, Estuary to Abyss 2004 Expedition. NOAA Office of Ocean Exploration; 207 (UP), Ralph White/Corbis Documentary/ Getty Images; 207 (LO LE), Peter David/Taxi/Getty Images; 207 (LO RT), Charles D Winters/Photo Researchers RM/Getty Images; 208, Stuart Armstrong; **CHAPTER 6:** 210-211, Sean Crane/Minden Pictures; 212, NASA image courtesy Jeff Schmaltz, LANCE MODIS Rapid Response Team at NASA GSFC; 213, PeopleImages.com/ Digital Vision/Getty Images; 215, Stuart Armstrong; 216, Subbotina Anna/Shutterstock; 217, Danita Delimont/Alamy; 218, Organics image library/Alamy; 219, Eric Nathan/Alamy; 220, Stephen Simpson/Getty Images; 221, Darlyne A. Murawski/National Geographic Creative; 222 (UP), dpa picture alliance/Alamy; 222 (LO), Science Faction/Getty Images; 223 (UP LE), Yusran/iStock. com; 223 (UP RT), George Grall/National Geographic Creative; 223 (CTR), Doug Wilson/Alamy; 223 (LO), EcoPrint/Shutterstock; 224, Stephen Frink Collection/Alamy; 225, WaterFrame/Alamy; 226, David Courtenay/Getty Images; 227, Mcburnie, Kyle/National Geographic Creative; 228, Steve Allen Travel Photography/Alamy; 229, Greg Johnston/Getty Images; 230, Steve Winter/National Geographic Creative; 231, Kevin Schafer/Minden Pictures; 232, Jay Fleming/Corbis; 233, Greg Probs/Corbis; 234, Michael DeFreitas/ Getty Images; 235, Kerrick James/Corbis; **CHAPTER 7:** 236-237, BlueOrange Studio/Shutterstock; 238, Veenenbos, Kees/National Geographic Creative; 239, morpheas/Getty Images; 240, Design Pics Inc/Alamy; 241, iStockphoto/Getty Images; 243, Kaloterakis, Nick/National Geographic Creative; 244, Image courtesy of New Zealand American Submarine Ring of Fire 2007 Exploration, NOAA Vents Program, the Institute of Geological & Nuclear Sciences and NOAA-OE; 245 (UP LE), DeepSeaPhotography.com; 245 (UP RT), Image courtesy of NOAA Okeanos Explorer Program, Galapagos Rift Expedition 2011; 245 (CTR LE), Woods Hole Oceanographic Institution Archives; 245 (CTR RT), courtesy of NOAA Okeanos Explorer Program, MCR Expedition 2011; 245 (LO), NOAA Okeanos Explorer Program, Gulf of Mexico 2012 Expedition 246, Dan Barnes/E+/Getty Images; 247, Rich Frishman; 248, Carrie Vonderhaar/Ocean Futures Society/National Geographic Creative; 249, Martin Smith/FLPA/Minden Pictures; 250, Jim McKinley/Alamy; 251, Hawaii Department of Land and Natural Resources; 252, AP Photo/Robert F. Bukaty; 253 (UP), Brian J. Skerry/National Geographic Creative; 253 (CTR LE), Flip Nicklin/ Minden Pictures; 253 (CTR RT), Andrea Izzotti/Shutterstock; 253 (LO), Wild Horizons/UIG via Getty Images; 254, Brian J. Skerry/ National Geographic Creative; 255, Thomas P. Peschak/National Geographic Creative; 256, Manu San Felix/National Geographic Creative; 257, Enric Sala/National Geographic Creative; 258, courtesy of Grace Saba; 259, George F. Mobley/National Geographic Creative; 260 (UP), Michael Zysman/Shutterstock; 260 (LO), aodaodaodaod/Shutterstock; 261, idreamphoto/ Shutterstock; 262, Leksele/Shutterstock; 263, Rick Rhay/ iStockphoto; 264, Jak Wonderly/NGP; 272, Martin Ruegner/age fotostock RM/Getty Images

CREDITS

The publisher would like to thank everyone who worked to make this book come together: Priyanka Lamichhane and Shira Evans, senior editors; Angela Modany, associate editor; Lori Epstein, photo director; Mike McNey, map production; Sean Philpotts, production director; Anne LeongSon, production assistant; Grace Hill, managing editor; Joan Gossett, editorial production manager; Susan Bishansky, project manager; Jennifer Agresta, fact checker; and Stuart Armstrong, illustrator.

Since 1888, the National Geographic Society has funded more than 12,000 research, exploration, and preservation projects around the world. The Society receives funds from National Geographic Partners, LLC, funded in part by your purchase. A portion of the proceeds from this book supports this vital work. To learn more, visit www.natgeo.com/info.

For more information, visit nationalgeographic.com, call 1-800-647-5463, or write to the following address:

National Geographic Partners
1145 17th Street N.W.
Washington, D.C. 20036-4688 U.S.A.

Visit us online at nationalgeographic.com/books

For librarians and teachers: ngchildrensbooks.org

More for kids from National Geographic:
kids.nationalgeographic.com

For information about special discounts for bulk purchases, please contact National Geographic Books Special Sales: ngspecsales@ngs.org

For rights or permissions inquiries, please contact National Geographic Books Subsidiary Rights: ngbookrights@ngs.org

Jülide Dengel, Art Director/Designer
Greg Jackson, Designer

Trade hardcover ISBN: 978-1-4263-2550-2
Reinforced library edition ISBN: 978-1-4263-2551-9

Printed in Hong Kong
16/THK/1

orca